And the Fans Go Wild...

"Even after my many successful years in business and politics, I was still able to gain a great deal of inspiration and helpful advice from Nikki Stone and her incredible contributors. Nikki's work demonstrates why I was so thrilled to develop such a strong relationship with the Olympic movement."

Mitt Romney, Business Executive, Presidential Candidate, Massachusetts Governor, and President of the Salt Lake Olympic Committee

"These inspirational stories and lessons will challenge readers to overcome their personal obstacles to success and encourage them to achieve their potential. *When Turtles Fly* is a great read and one that I would recommend to old and young alike."

Dick Marriott, Chairman, Host Hotels and Resorts

"Nikki Stone knows how to deliver motivation! With unique inspiration, compelling and moving stories, instructive hands-on advice, memorable philosophies, and powerful contributors all wrapped up in a package that helps support an extremely important charitable cause, who could ask for more. *When Turtles Fly* will be a book you reference again and again for both your personal and professional life. I give it a perfect 10!"

Peter Vidmar, Olympic Gymnastics Champion, National Speakers Association Hall of Fame, and Chairman, USA Gymnastics

"Nikki Stone took on a monumental task of interviewing a number of the great minds in our time. Her efforts are a short cut for you to launch your personal and professional aspirations into outer space. This book is packed with great stories, powerful information and take home tools. Thank you Nikki!"

Vince Poscente, NY Times Bestselling Author of *The Age of Speed*

"It's obvious why Nikki Stone has climbed to the top of her game, both in the air and on the stage. Nikki is a dynamic personality with a powerful message. She will challenge you to reach levels you didn't know were attainable and provide the support you need to stay at these new heights. Don't miss the opportunity to learn from a woman who has personally experienced overcoming incredible odds to reach unbelievable goals."

Steve Gardner, CEO, FIVE STAR Speakers & Trainers

"Nikki Stone learned many valuable lessons on her journey toward Olympic Gold. In *When Turtles Fly*, not only does she share these lessons, but she also shares stories and wisdom from an amazing array of successful sports and business people. Some of them are world famous, and some you may never have heard of, but each story is equally compelling. If you can't find many valuable lessons in this book, then you just aren't searching very hard."

Dan Jansen, Olympic Gold Medalist and Motivational Speaker

"What a great book! This is a keeper for everyone's personal library. I am pre-ordering 30 of them for gifts to give to students for graduation, couples getting married, and any holiday or occasion that calls for a thoughtful and meaningful gift."

Frank Candy, President of the American Speakers Bureau Corp

"I have worked with Nikki for years and our clients and coworkers love her inspiration. She offers profound, easy-to-apply tools for taking life's scariest risks, overcoming the most challenging obstacles and finding the confidence to make sure that you stand out in a crowd."

Jean Nelligan, Sr. Marketing Manager, Meeting Management, John Hancock

"*When Turtles Fly* strikes many chords. As you read each and every narrative of the gifted people Nikki references, you're given insightful advice as to their success. Life changing lessons are learned each and every day, sometimes, when you least expect them. You'll be filled with new found aspirations, even *before* you put this book down."

Phil Mahre, Olympic Gold Medalist

"Nikki does a great job at connecting to the reader on so many different levels with a variety of contributors from all walks of life. There is something intriguing in this book for everyone and you'll gain a wealth of knowledge for your path to success from the inspirational stories and relatable and creative self-help activities."

Bonnie Blair, 5-time Olympic Gold Medalist and Motivational Speaker

"Though Nikki Stone's story screams of extraordinary achievements, her hands-on tools in *When Turtles Fly* will help take anyone to Olympic-sized success. You have to ask yourself if you are complacent in your current station in life or whether you want to reach your full potential. Nikki and her contributors will truly inspire you and the specific tools will make sure you find your ultimate success. Her book is a marvelous addition to anyone's must read portfolio."

Terry Shorrock, Panasonic Shows & Events Director

When Turtles Fly
The Secrets of Successful People Who Know How to Stick Their Necks Out

By Nikki Stone

NEW YORK

When Turtles Fly
Secrets of Successful People Who Know How To Stick Their Necks Out

Cover Design by: Rachel Lopez
Rachel@r2cdesign

ISBN 978-1-60037-675-7

Library of Congress Control Number: 2009931499

Published by

MORGAN JAMES PUBLISHING
1225 Franklin Ave., STE 325
Garden City, NY 11530-1693
Toll Free 800-485-4943
www.MorganJamesPublishing.com

In an effort to support local communities, raise awareness and funds, Morgan James Publishing donates one percent of all book sales for the life of each book to Habitat for Humanity. Get involved today, visit **www.HelpHabitatForHumanity.org**.

Table of Contents

Acknowledgments

I can sincerely say that this book would not have been written without the support, contribution and consideration of a great many people. I have always thought the acknowledgments section was one of the most important parts of a book because it recognizes all these people. As in aerial skiing, a book requires a major player—the author—as well as a whole team to help "land the jump." My team helped bring this book to life

If I were to name all of the people who helped make this book possible, I'd need to write a whole other volume. My warmest thanks to everyone! I so much appreciate your input and encouragement.

Some key supporters simply *must* be singled out, starting with one of my high school English teachers. Thank you, Nelson, for allowing me to believe that I had it in me to write!

I am incredibly grateful to all the people who helped me contact and connect with the book's many contributors. A big thank you goes out to Bart Connor, P. J. Reynolds, Christina Sheibler, Katrina Ammer, Tim Smith, Randy Doerges, Major Trent Gibson, Deb & Dan Dunham, Mark "Dooley" Ervin, Sue Dorf, Janelle & Ron Adams, Michelle Knox, Stefani Kimche, Susan Hreljac, Heiner Baumann, Hilary & Wendy Reiter, and the Khosla family..

With so many publishers out there, I could not have chosen a better team than Morgan James Publishing to help bring my book to the world. Thank you to Steve Gardner of FIVE STAR Speakers Bureau for recognizing the book's potential and bringing it to Morgan James's attention. Thanks to David Hancock for believing in the project and showing me that there are publishers who truly care. Thanks to Rick Frishman for carrying on the enthusiasm and direction. And thanks to Sherry Duke and Lyza Poulin for keeping me on track in the frenetic final few months.

Thank you to Margaret Carney for her extraordinary editing expertise. Her writing style is so elegant and she knew exactly how to make sure the whole book flowed. Not only is Margaret an amazing copy editor and writer, she's a warm and giving person with a wonderful spirit about her. I'm so glad this book brought us together.

I really needed to make sure that I found a publicist who believed in *When Turtles Fly* as much as I did. I knew, hands down, that Nicole Wool was that person. There is no harder working publicist than Nicole and she always jumps at the chance to do more for me and the book. Nicole's mission has been to make sure the public also falls in love with *When Turtles Fly*.

Acknowledgments

I might not have even gotten to the point of publishing if it weren't for one amazing mentor, Linda Gerber. Being an accomplished author herself, Linda had in-depth insight into the process. Most people offer advice and leave it at that; Linda went above and beyond, taking me under her wing and making sure I developed the best summary, then got it into the right hands.

Speaking of "going above and beyond," Vic Method should have this attribute listed at the top of his résumé. Vic lent his assistance, passion and time throughout the journey. I could always count on him to be just as excited as I was whenever I received confirmation from another contributor. If you want a project to succeed, you can almost guarantee it with Vic in your corner.

The one problem with having so many exceedingly successful contributors is that the rest of the world wants a piece of them as well. I still can't believe that despite how unbelievably busy these individuals are, they took the time to share a part of themselves in *When Turtles Fly*. They have given this book a strong, vibrant pulse and I am honored to share that with you.

Behind many a successful individual is an assistant or two—or a whole group of assistants—who work tirelessly, often in anonymity. I wish I could hug each and every one of them for being the middlemen time and again in bringing each story to completion.

And so that we can see each contributor up close and personal, I thank all the photographers whose talents have come into play. We proudly list their photo credits.

I must share an enormous thank you to my husband, Michael, and our daughter, Zali, who inspired, motivated and tolerated me in a long, challenging, but fruitful process. The two of them make the best cheering squad imaginable. My coach couldn't believe that, in a vast sea of Olympic spectators, we could hear Michael shouting over everyone else. I hear him cheering just as loudly for me today, and now he has Zali to join him. With both of them behind me, I know anything is possible.

Whenever I hear people thanking their parents in an interview or acceptance speech, I always wonder if their folks have come anywhere close to the level of support mine have given. Mom and Dad, you believed in me from the beginning, and allowed *me* to believe I could be anything and everything, and I thank you from the bottom of my heart. For the morals and values you instilled in me long ago, to the editing you did on the book this year, I'm so grateful. Your support has been unwavering throughout, and I dedicate *When Turtles Fly* to both of you.

Lastly, I'd like to thank you, the reader, for purchasing this book, a quarter of the proceeds of which will help support the American Cancer Society. Way too many of us are touched by this awful disease, and I know we are all thankful for any money that goes toward medical advances to combat it.

Chapter 1

Introduction

Introduction

I pushed the enormous rocking chair across the lime-green shag carpet. This would be the last piece of furniture I would need to complete my own Olympic podium. I had just watched Olympic Gymnastics Champion Nadia Comaneci stand on top of the real deal, and I wanted to see how it felt.

I slowly climbed onto the wobbly rocking chair, my pigtails swooshing back and forth. Occasionally a few hairs would catch on my eyelashes and I would pull the strands away from my face so I could continue on my mission. I calculated the chair's rhythm, carefully threw my leg over the back and slowly climbed up onto the lacquered old end table. I pushed myself to my feet and threw my fists toward the ceiling in victory. A huge smile broke across my freckled face as I imagined the crowds cheering around me and the camera bulbs going off left and right. I had my answer. *It felt incredible!*

My mother and father came in from the family room to see what the commotion was. I beamed down at them and stated with confidence, "I'm going to win the 'lympics!"

Now, I think most parents would be a bit leery of giving their five-year-old daughter any genuine encouragement for this giant undertaking, especially seeing that, in all likelihood, she had a better chance of winning the lottery than the Olympics someday. But my parents never flinched. I never saw any reservation on their faces when I declared my goal.

My mom lifted me off the "podium," plopped me down on the plaid easy chair and said, "Well, then I guess it's time for me to teach you about the Turtle Effect."

At the time, this meant little more to me than a chance to potentially hit them up for a pet turtle at Dom's local pet store. But I realized that if I was going to turn those living room chairs and table into a real Olympic podium, I had to learn what this Turtle Effect really meant.

She explained to me that if I wanted to be successful, I needed to be soft on the inside, I had to have a hard shell, and I had to be willing to stick my neck out.

To have a soft inside, I would need a passion for my pursuits. To build a hard shell, I'd have to focus on the task at hand, completely commit to my goals, and develop the ability to overcome any adversity that was thrown my way. And in order to stick my neck out, I'd have to have confidence, take substantial risks, and be a team player in order to succeed. Those seven lessons were key in mastering the Turtle Effect.

As I grew and developed through my years in gymnastics, and eventually, aerial freestyle skiing, I found my mom's advice invaluable. But it wasn't just her words about the Turtle Effect that helped me to become an Olympic champion. It was putting them into action, and experiencing challenges and pitfalls that would eventually help me understand the true depth of their power. Later, I found that by explaining these ideas to others, though motivational speeches, I could help many individuals accomplish their goals.

Galvanized by the possibilities, I decided to create a book that would offer people many profound and amazing stories for motivation, as well as hands-on activities to help them make changes themselves. I sat down and put together a list of people whose lives I found to be truly inspiring, and who'd worked hard to reach the top of their "game". I included accomplished businessmen and women, athletes, politicians, celebrities, authors, Nobel Prize winners, musicians and philanthropists. In telling their stories, these individuals, many of whom I've come to know, all shared a part of the Turtle Effect that helped them find their own success. To continue the inspiration, I've included one more special bonus story on-line that you can view at www.WhenTurtlesFly.com.

Each story is followed by a daily activity that has proved successful at my coaching sessions in changing people's lives in a concrete way, exercises you can use to improve your own personal and professional life. They serve as hands-on tools to help you enhance and develop your passion, focus, commitment, ability to overcome adversity, risk taking, and team building. From my years of experience as an athlete, speaker and peak performance coach, and by studying the habits of many powerful individuals I've encountered, I've come up with highly effective steps to encourage advancement in any career. Each activity includes blank space for you to keep notes on your own transformation.

Whether I'm mentoring future Olympic medalists, motivating hotshot businesspeople, or coaching eager young professionals, I find the Turtle Effect works brilliantly to help people reach success.

It's never too late or too early to pursue your dreams, and you're never too successful to work toward new goals. So get ready for the adventure of a lifetime.

Get ready to *fly*!

Chapter 2

Passion

Passion

It didn't matter if it was Monopoly, minigolf, gym class, or the gymnastics state championship, competition was always filling my soft inside. It got my heart pumping and made me feel really alive. If I put a competitive spin on anything I was doing, my interest was snagged, and I *had* to win.

From ages four through seventeen my competitive passion was for gymnastics. I had an entire wall in my bedroom dedicated to the ribbons and trophies I won in local competitions. My parents thought it was cute until they realized I'd used a staple gun to hang all my ribbons. The other three walls in my room were covered with pictures of Olympic gymnasts I cut out of magazines.

Just after my tenth birthday, I found myself competing in a state championship qualifier. After three events, I realized I was in first place. All I had to do was stick my balance beam routine and I would win the competition and be going on to the championships. *Watch out, Nadia, here I come.*

Well, three-quarters of the way through my routine, my foot slipped off the narrow, four-inch beam and I fell to the mat. I thought I couldn't feel any worse about this stupid mistake until I sheepishly looked at my coach and saw that he'd dropped his head in his hands. I crawled back onto my nemesis, that beam, and finished my routine without a flaw.

I quickly did the calculations in my head and realized that I had not only lost the all-around competition, but I would be sitting at home while several of my teammates went on to the state championships. I ran into the locker room and started to cry.

After a few minutes, I felt a tap on my shoulder. Through bleary eyes, I looked up and found a teammate of mine, Cassandra Wheeler, whom I greatly admired, standing in front of me. Between sobs, I declared that I was quitting gymnastics.

She walked away, and I thought that my role model was turning her back on me and my trivial problems. Then I heard a clanging at her locker and she returned with a small orange card in her hand. She held it out and I read the words, *You Mustn't Quit.*

"Remember why you chose to do gymnastics," she told me. "You love it! And remember that tomorrow is a new day, and you never know what could happen tomorrow, or the next day, or the day after that. If you stick with it and don't give up, you might find that your passions will help you reach your goals."

And she was right. The next year I *did* qualify for the state championships. Without my friend's encouragement to remember my soft inside, that great wall of fame in my bedroom might have remained a small corner of fame.

While I always loved gymnastics, I didn't find my true passion and soft inside until I was eighteen. That was the year I discovered aerial freestyle skiing.

I caught an *Evening Magazine* show on TV, showing athletes skiing down a ramp and flipping and twisting through the air. It looked incredibly exciting, but also incredibly scary. Aerials wasn't one of those things for me that you know right away you want to do, and know you'll love. I probably had the same response that any other sane person does when they see the sport for the first time: "These people are crazy!!!"

But when I saw how the aerialists train in the summer, it appeared relatively harmless. When they make their first attempts, they ski down a sheet of plastic bristles, flip off a jump and land in a swimming pool. And for those landings that don't go exactly as planned, there are pipes underwater that force a layer of bubbles to the surface of the pool to soften the impact. I figured it might be fun to try a single back flip. But that was *all* I wanted to do.

Having a state-level gymnastics background, and growing up skiing recreationally with my family, I found the single back somersault came quite easily for me. That summer, I got to the point where I could do straight-over flips, and back flips with a full twist. My natural abilities started to draw some attention and the national team head coach made his way over to watch me. He pulled me aside, and I should have known by the look on his face that I was in store for something terrifying.

"Are you ready for a double?"

I looked toward the towering double jump ramp and felt my mouth go dry. I turned back to the head coach, gave a nervous little laugh and grabbed my skis, planning to head to the small, comfortable, safe jump.

"I wasn't kidding, Nikki. Let's go."

Well, I knew I couldn't let down the national team coach, so I nervously made my way over to the stairs of the double jump. I clumped up the seventy-two steps and stood atop the platform that led to a strip of white plastic and ended in a ten-foot-tall wall. And I have to say, it really does look like a wall when you're gazing at it from the top!

My hands were sweating, my stomach was in my throat and I didn't know if my legs were going to stop shaking long enough to actually get me off this jump. It's funny, in those moments of sheer terror, how you start to imagine all the things that could go wrong. I could fall on the inrun. Have my legs give out, and hit the jump. Go off the side of the ramp and miss the pool…Or I might not make it all the way around for two flips, and land on my back or head! Through my years as an aerial skier, I actually saw all these things happen.

As I stood up there that first time, debating if I should go shooting down the ramp and into space, I looked around the water ramp facility and noticed that all the other athletes had stopped what they were doing. I would later learn that this was a sort of tradition: watch to see if the rookie would actually take the plunge. Well, luckily for my future career in the sport, my ego was much bigger than my brain. I wasn't going to take the walk of shame back down the stairs.

I turned my skis down the steep inrun, put my arms out for stability and went speeding at thirty-five miles per hour toward this intimidating jump. All the while, I was remembering my coach's advice: "Just think of your takeoff, focus on doing a single back lay-out, take a quick look at the water and pull your knees to your chest for the second flip. I'll yell 'Out!' when you need to stretch your body back out for the landing."

I reached the bottom of the jump, locked out my legs and swung my arms to initiate the flip. I soared off the top of the structure, flipped over once and spotted the water. I must have taken too long a look because I heard my coach shout, "Pull, pull, pull!" reminding me to get into that tucked position for the second flip. I quickly pulled my knees in and spun into the second rotation. I was flipping too quickly to be sure where I was, but I heard my coach yell, "Out!" Almost by instinct, my legs shot out and I hit the water–right side up.

I wanted to scream. Not because I was terrified or even in pain. I was exhilarated! I had never felt such a rush before. In that moment, my life changed. This was no longer a passing whim, this was now my passion. And I was going to find a way to put my heart and soul into this sport.

When people ask me what the single most important factor is in achieving our goals, I tell them that if you don't develop a passion for what you do, you won't be able to vault any of the other hurdles. Our drive comes from our soft inside, so if we develop this, everything else becomes a lot easier.

Lindsey Vonn

Olympic Skiing Superstar

Photo courtesy of Nick Schrunk/Red Bull Photofiles

Lindsey Vonn Biography

Acclaimed as the most successful female ski racer in American history, Lindsey Vonn is one of the few world-class, five-event ski champions.

Lindsey was born October 18, 1984, in St. Paul, Minnesota, and started skiing when she was two. It wasn't long before she was traveling regularly to Vail, Colorado, to train. The eldest of five children—two brothers and a sister who are triplets, and another sister—Lindsey has publicly thanked her siblings for gamely agreeing to move to Vail, largely to further her racing career.

The move was certainly worthwhile, for her dedicated training paid off. Lindsey has been the only American woman to win at Italy's Trofeo Topolino, for skiers eleven to fourteen, and earn Junior Worlds medals and U.S. titles, all while still a teenager. Six weeks after she turned twenty, Lindsey Vonn—then Lindsey Kildow—achieved her first World Cup victory. Two years after making her professional debut in the Alpine Skiing world, Vonn qualified for her first Olympic team.

The 2009 season turned out to be a life-changing, amazing one for Lindsey. She set new records and is now the overall World Cup title holder, the only American woman to have won this twice. As if that wasn't enough, she also earned two downhill titles and a super G, set the record for most downhill victories by an American—ten—and brought her World Championship medal tally to four.

If you work hard, it will pay off in the end, Lindsey claims. It's a philosophy closely connected to another basic rule the athlete has followed throughout her life: when you fall down, just get up again. She has added a footnote: if you fall, get up stronger, hungrier, more ambitious.

Setbacks help you to concentrate, she says. When successes fall into your lap, you lose sight of your goals. With this attitude, and with supporters like her husband, Thomas Vonn, by her side, Lindsey is bound to set more records and secure her place in sports history as one of the world's best skiers.

Please visit Lindsey's website-www.LindseyVonn.com-to learn more.

Nikki's Intro to Lindsey Vonn's Story

No matter how much fun and exhilarating an endeavor is, there comes a moment when it loses its sparkle, and you forget how passionate you normally feel about it. We all have days when we just don't want to get out of bed, and forget why we ever pursued our current path. I've had a number of those.

On my days off from aerial training, I'd sometimes get sucked into the easy lifestyle away from competition and think I was over the whole thing. Life seemed so effortless outside the arena. It wasn't until I experienced an injury and was forced to take a lot of time off that I realized I still loved my sport. With the injury, I didn't know if I'd ever be able to return to finish my pursuit of that illustrious Olympic medal. If I thought there were days when it was hard to get out of bed before, it was a whole new ball game when the goal was gone. There wasn't any driving passion to push me each day.

When I truly realized what I was losing, I had a much greater appreciation for it. And when I finally returned to the aerial hill, my heart was set afire once more. With each training day, I would fall in love with aerial skiing all over again. I found that a love filled with challenges was much better than no love at all.

One woman who knows about reigniting her passions is an athlete we've all come to admire, Ms. Lindsey Vonn…

Lindsey Vonn: My Story

Lindsey Vonn

Passion

The wind whistled through my helmet as I slammed past another gate. My speed was nearing 75 mph and the adrenaline was pumping. I was in the middle of a crucial Olympic practice run for the marquee alpine skiing discipline, the downhill, and was flying down the course and feeling good. I'd later find out that I was leading at the halfway split. But that would be the last split they would clock.

When trouble hits at those speeds, you don't have much time to react. My eyes were locked on the jump just ahead of me when I felt my skis scribble on the icy terrain. My legs scissored apart, and before I knew it, I was flying off the jump backward. The first thing to hit was my back and pain shot through my entire body.

I know it's hard for most people to grasp the intensity of such a crash. Imagine standing on top of a car going 70-80 mph. When the driver suddenly slams on the breaks, you'd go hurtling off the front, onto the pavement. Now, skiers don't land on cement, of course, but plummeting down an icy hill with a pair of skis basically glued to your boots doesn't make for a pretty picture, either.

Despite the stabbing pain, I was still hoping for the best. But let me tell you, there isn't much optimism left when you are being helicoptered off the slopes a day before the start of your Olympic events. Lying there strapped to the backboard, in a world of pain, the only thought I had was that my career was over. My last experience on skis might very well be cartwheeling backward off an Olympic downhill jump. The thought was sickening. Skiing was my *life!*

When I arrived at the hospital, the news didn't improve. The doctors said that I had likely broken my pelvis and back. The excruciating pain I felt told me they could very well be right; particularly because I sensed a growing numbness, too. That awful thought I was desperately trying to muffle returned: How could I possibly deal with never skiing again? No child ever says, "I'd like to be an injured ex-skier when I grow up." But there I was, lying in an E.R. in Italy, with that very prospect in front of me.

The first person to arrive at the hospital was my good friend and mentor, Picabo Street. Picabo loves the sport of skiing as much as I do. And she had been through some frightening injuries that almost sidelined her own career. I was still on the stretcher when she rushed in. No words were needed, because she knew exactly what I was going through. If anyone could relate to what I was feeling at that moment, it was Picabo. I don't know who started crying first, but within seconds we were both drenched in tears.

The support continued as my mother and my husband arrived. I lay there feeling as if I had a gaping hole in my stomach as I awaited the MRI and CAT scan results. By the look on Mom's and Thomas's faces, I could tell they felt the same, and weren't quite sure what to say. What *was* there to say? We were all preparing for the worst.

I couldn't help wondering what in the world I'd do with the rest of my life. I felt lost, trying to wrap my mind around the prospect of not skiing. I had been on skis since I was two and a half years old, and racing since I was eight. Skiing was who I *was*. And not knowing who I might be without it was a scary thing. I'd never had to deal with this thought process before, and just couldn't imagine loving anything the way I loved skiing.

A doctor came into the room and I held my breath as he gave me the news. They didn't see any fractures, just a lot of bruising and swelling.

Did he really say that I was going to be okay and this wasn't the end of my career? *Hallelujah!*

The smile was still plastered on my face when I asked the doctor when I could get back out there. Somewhat reluctantly, he gave me the go-ahead, knowing I had a one-track mind and wasn't going to take the typical advice for extended bed rest. My mom understood as well, but had to add a motherly, "Okay, if you think you can. Just be careful!"

Not only was my career still intact, but with extra work and extra heart, I was back on the slopes forty-eight hours later. The nervousness I'd been feeling just a few days before was suddenly gone. I was surprisingly calm when I skied into position in the starting gate for an Olympic run I hadn't thought I'd take.

The crash and the thought of losing my sport completely changed my perspective. I realized how fortunate I was to be skiing, and regardless of the result, I was determined to take this opportunity to better myself. I didn't want to leave *anything* on the table. I was not going to walk away asking myself if I could have given more.

I had come to the Olympic Games with a mission—so of course was disappointed when I didn't win a medal. But I was still incredibly happy. Believe it or not, the injury scare was actually the best thing that could have happened to me. I finally realized what was most important.

I'd always thought I was one of the lucky ones, never really having any significant hard times in my skiing career. Now I figured I was even luckier, because I did. At last, I had an answer as to why I followed this crazy lifestyle: because I loved skiing. It was that simple. And I would forever appreciate every day I could slap on my skis.

I treasure that Olympic experience in a way that I never expected. I did an interview after my Olympic run and the reporter commented that I must be feeling better, since I was smiling from ear to ear. I guess he didn't think that seventh or eighth place was anything to be smiling about.

But he didn't know what I did: I had found my soft inside. I had found my true passion.

To be successful, you need to...

Be soft on the inside... **Find Your Passion**

Do things you hate first

Nikki's Perspective: Performing triple back flips was something I knew I had to master if I was ever going to win an Olympic medal someday. But doing them terrified me, and I dreaded that part of my training. I would put them off until the end of the day, and if I could, put them off until later in the week. The very thought of doing triples was a weight on my shoulders.

My assistant coach recognized how the pressure was affecting the rest of my training. At the start of the next week, he suggested we do the triples first thing in the morning so I wouldn't have to worry about them all day. Beginning with them didn't make the maneuver any less nerve-racking, but did make the rest of the day much easier. I found everything else a lot more enjoyable.

Your Tools for Success: Our career choices are not always easy and there are times we have to just get through challenging parts. There is often one task we really hate to do. Instead of putting it off until later, do it today, as soon as possible. If we get it over with right away, then we don't have to dwell on it or fret about it. Make that unpleasant call or do that dreaded chore first thing in the morning and you won't have it hanging over you the rest of the day. This will give you more time to enjoy the things you really love.

Be it tackling a pile of laundry or doing triple flips, think of the relief you'll feel, having it behind you.

Below, write down five things you don't like to do. Do each before 11:00 a.m., and check off that you've done them.

TASK	Done!

_____

_____

_____

_____

_____

Chet Huber

Father of OnStar

Photo provided by OnStar

Chet Huber Biography

Chet Huber is the president of OnStar Corporation, a wholly owned subsidiary of General Motors Corporation. OnStar is the world's leading provider of vehicle integrated safety, security, and peace of mind services for retail and OEM customers. Huber has held this position since the creation of the business in 1995, and has been responsible for leading it from its start-up phase to its current position as a nationally prominent brand serving millions of subscribers, with a growing role in supporting the national emergency response infrastructure.

Huber joined GM in 1972 in its Locomotive Group, holding various engineering, operations and marketing roles before assuming global responsibilities for its sales, marketing and product support. In 1994, Huber was selected as the first Industrial Fellow by the U.S. Department of Defense to attend the National Defense University in Washington, D.C., earning a Master of Science degree in national resource strategy from its Industrial College of the Armed Forces, later being inducted into its hall of fame. Upon completion of the program, Huber was assigned to lead a technology and business evaluation effort to explore integration opportunities in the areas of wireless communications, GPS and vehicle electrical architectures, ultimately resulting in the creation and launch of the OnStar business.

Huber also holds a bachelor's degree in mechanical engineering from General Motors Institute and an MBA from the Harvard Business School. He has received the distinction of "Honorary Commandant" from the Industrial College of the Armed Forces, and has been awarded an honorary Doctor of Engineering degree from Kettering University.

Huber currently serves on the Board of Directors of Sirius XM Radio and Engineering College Council of Cornell University. He is a member of the NASA Advisory Committee for PNT—Positioning, Navigation and Timing Advisory Board.

Nikki's Intro to Chet Huber's Story

In 2004, I was invited to go on a volunteer trip to Sierra Leone with *Right To Play*. While there, our group visited a detention center. We were working to establish sport and play programs for boys confined to a small yard and residential building. Many of them were locked up for little more than "loitering" on city streets because their parents had been killed by African rebels.

I was pretty nervous about going to the detention center and even more nervous that the programs we introduced wouldn't be anything that the boys wanted. I knew that what I was doing was important, however, and I just hoped the love I had for sports would be contagious.

When the session ended, the children all filed past us to thank us and shake our hands. I noticed that each one touched his heart before extending his hand to us, and I later learned this was a gesture of great respect and gratitude.

I got to touch the hand of each child who played at the Remand Home that day, and realized how all the fund-raising work I've done over the years has helped touch the hearts of so many more.

Chet might not have had children reach out from their hearts in that way, but he did have someone reach out to him with a letter that would ultimately impact every day he stepped into his office...

Chet Huber: My Story

Chet Huber

Passion

The letter started:

> *"Dear Mr. Huber,*
>
> *We were driving into Atlanta three weeks ago and my wife had an unexpected heart attack. We had the new OnStar in our car and used it to find the closest hospital. My wife died one week later..."*

I dropped the letter and my hands started shaking. My immediate thought was *What did we do wrong?* We were on the cutting edge of technology by installing a comprehensive in-vehicle security, communications and diagnostics system in many new General Motors vehicles. We had been through nearly a hundred prototypes, working to continually improve the product, which had only been available to the public for six months. But I sincerely believed we had a product that was going to profoundly benefit vehicle owners.

It made me sick to think I may have played a role in this woman's death. It was due to people like her that I was initially drawn to the project. I loved my work because I knew the new system would eventually help stranded motorists be brought to safety, contact crash victims, help drivers locate gas stations, track down car thieves who inadvertently kidnapped small children—and, yes, help an ailing woman or man find the closest hospital.

Twelve years before, GM's vice president, Harry Pearce, asked me about heading up a new division that would develop an emergency response system in a number of GM vehicles. I jumped at the opportunity because I knew we would be entering groundbreaking territory within the automotive world. It was a job that was less scripted and templated than most in the core automotive business.

Right from the get-go I realized there was going to be intense pressure to make this system function properly. Because of the accountability toward our customers, there would be no chance of success if we didn't all have passion for our work. When you're toiling endless hours on hundreds of prototypes for a product that could ultimately save lives, you'd better bet that you are counting on that caring, responsive core within you—your "soft inside"—to keep you on track. The brain was always listening to the heart.

We painstakingly went through 350 patent filings. Quite honestly, looking back, I think we might not have even started the project if we had known all the challenges we would encounter along the way. We were on a slippery slope and the pressures intensified with each new patent filing. I knew we were risking our careers, the more deeply entrenched we became. But I was granted a unique form of motivation through General Motors' dedication to improving their customers' lives. I truly believed in the project and was grateful that GM was stepping up to the plate. I was really proud of the company for giving us the broad degree of freedom to do what we all felt was right.

There were countless moving parts to obscure our ultimate mission, but we would continually tap back into our resolve because we knew there was important work to be done. We knew that the results had the potential to greatly impact people's lives. We had the opportunity to influence important outcomes. I don't know how many times in business people have that kind of significance in a job. The emotional connection was undeniable, and it was that underpinning that kept our passion boiling over.

I had never had such love for a project I'd been associated with, and now there was this heart-wrenching letter telling me we had failed. Not only had we failed, but we had cost a woman her life! I went to grab the letter again and found I couldn't keep my hand steady. I wiped the moisture from my brow and released a deep breath, overwhelmed at the incredible physical reaction I was having. But I knew I had to finish the letter, so I slowly picked it up and continued to read:

> *"...I called OnStar, and through Global Positioning they helped me locate the closest hospital. They had doctors waiting for us when we drove up. The doctors told me that our quick arrival was the only reason my wife lived for one more week. I just wanted to thank you and those that helped me have that extra week with my wife. I really needed that time with my wife to get the closure I required to move on..."*

I still get choked up thinking about that letter. That confirmation gave my job meaning. It has continued to help push me through the hard days, and gave all of us at OnStar a real sense of what we were doing here. We finally knew for sure that we *were* making a difference.

I sat down and penned a note to Harry, the man who'd enlisted me on this crusade to revolutionize our customers' safety. The note read:

> *"Harry, we don't have everything right just yet and we're still learning a lot, but I* know *we're doing the right thing here!"*

To be successful, you need to...

Be soft on the inside... **Find Your Passion**

Positive Thoughts

Nikki's Perspective: It was at a World Cup in Madaro, Japan, that I first learned how important a positive attitude can be. The day was warm and the conditions on the aerial hill were deteriorating. The sunny conditions prevented me from getting enough speed on my first jump, and I ended up crashing. Knowing you typically need two good jumps to do well at a World Cup contest, I wanted to throw in the towel.

My next thought: you never know what can happen, and I had to think positively if I wanted to turn things around. I mentally let go of my first jump, knowing I could never get it back. I had to focus on perfecting my second one.

The positive outlook paid off: my second jump was the highest scoring one of the day, and I ended the contest in second place. I learned it wasn't over until the fat lady sang...or at least until the final round was completed.

Your Tools for Success: Today's activity requires a little assistance. Hold your arms out to the side and think of something that really depresses you. Have a friend try to push your arms down while you're thinking this negative thought. Now hold your arms again and think of something that really inspires you and brings you happiness. Again, have a friend try to push your arms down while you're thinking this positive thought. You will be amazed at the difference.

Come up with a list of five positive words, thoughts or objects that you can bring to the front of your mind when you are feeling down or "defeated." Use these words or thoughts to give you strength and bring back your passion.

_____

_____

_____

_____

_____

Johann Koss

Speedskating Olympic Medalist and Founder and CEO of Right To Play

Johann Koss Biography

Johann Koss is one of the greatest winter athletes of all time. The four-time Olympic gold medalist in speed skating made world headlines when he won three gold medals at the 1994 Lillehammer Games in the 1,500, 5,000 and 10,000 meter events. Over the course of his career, he broke a total of eleven world records, won three World All-round Championships and numerous World Cups and National Championships.

Johann's achievements on the ice have since been eclipsed by his efforts on behalf of Right To Play, an athlete-driven international humanitarian organization that uses sport and play as a tool for development of children and youth in the most disadvantaged areas of the world. Johann first became involved with Right To Play, then known as Olympic Aid, in 1993, when he visited the African country of Eritrea. He was profoundly moved by the plight of the children.

Since Lillehammer, Johann has dedicated himself to growing Right To Play into an internationally recognized non-governmental organization (NGO) and a leader in Sport for Development. Sport for Development uses sport and play to enhance the healthy physical and psychosocial development of children and build stronger communities. Today, Right To Play develops and implements child and community development programs in more than twenty countries in Africa, Asia and the Middle East, working with the United Nations and other agencies, including UNICEF, UNHCR, GAVI and WHO.

Johann has a medical degree from University of Queensland, in Australia, and an MBA from University of Toronto, Rotman School of Management, in Canada.

Right To Play's international headquarters are in Toronto, Canada with national offices in the Netherlands, Norway, Switzerland, the United Kingdom, Canada, United Arab Emirates, China and the United State.

Nikki's Intro to Johann Koss's Story

Shortly after my retirement from aerial skiing, I was elected to the U.S. Olympic Committee's Athlete Advisory Council. At my very first meeting, I was fortunate to hear a special Olympic guest talk about a program he'd started to help the most disadvantaged children in the world.

He told us about a young girl so traumatized by seeing both her parents killed in the Rwandan genocide that she became mute. She had, in fact, hidden under their bodies so she wouldn't be killed herself. After being encouraged to take part in this Olympian's sports and activity programs, the young girl finally uttered her first words in two years: "Pass me the ball."

Upon hearing the heart-wrenching story, I immediately knew that I wanted to—no, had to—get involved. Since that day, I have become one of their most avid volunteers. I found that giving back to those in need has filled my life with much greater meaning.

There is a quote I like by Dr. Albert Schweitzer: "I don't know what your destiny will be, but one thing I do know—the only ones among you who will be really happy are those who will have sought and found how to serve." One person I *know* is happy is that Olympic hero who started this phenomenal, charitable organization, and who has become one of my closest friends, Johann Olav Koss...

Johann Koss: My Story

Johann Koss

Passion

I must have looked deep in thought, or as deep in thought as an eleven-year-old can, when my grandmother glanced up from her weeding to ask, "You have something on your mind, don't you?"

"Yes, I was thinking that someday I want to be an Olympic speedskating champion like my hero, Eric Heiden, I want to be a doctor like my parents and I want to help children in Africa."

I immediately knew I had confided in the right person when a knowing smile broke across her face. "Johann, of course! You can do *anything* you want to do!" she said simply. And with my grandmother's staunch support, I set out to pursue my passions.

Fourteen years later, I was positioned to take hold of my first dream: becoming an Olympic champion. The Olympics in 1994 were in my home country, Norway. As I entered the Olympic stadium in Hamar, I wasn't the best athlete, and many had doubts about my ability to perform well. But I had something special working for me. I had a woman in the first row who believed in me following my passions just as much as I did. For the first time ever, my grandmother was going to see me skate.

With minutes to go before my first race, somehow I had a feeling of inner strength, and I knew that I would better all my past efforts and achieve my best ever result.

It happened. Breaking a world record, I clinched the gold, and the support of my country.

As I stood on the podium that I had dreamed about my entire life, a curious question popped into my head. Why me? Why did *I* win, given all the other incredible competitors out there? The reason had to be more than a grandmother who shared a belief in her grandson's dream

The question led me to only one answer: because I wanted to make a difference in the world, and with all the media attention garnered from my success, I could..

I immediately knew what that difference had to be: hope in the lives of the children in Africa. Six months earlier, I'd been invited to Eritrea as an ambassador for Olympic Aid. Throughout the trip I saw the effects that thirty years of civil war had on the helpless children of the region, who never had a chance to just be kids. I remember seeing eight-year-old boys who stood in awe, admiring the posters and statues of the martyrs liberating their country. Eric Heiden was *my* hero, but for these young boys, it was soldiers dying in war.

As I was watching these children, my optimism returned when I saw them cheering for some teenage cyclists who were passing through the town. I was inspired to believe that change could happen. Maybe if these children were able to take part in a more positive activity such as sports, or find new role models in athlete heroes, then their dreams would not be of becoming soldiers.

My newfound optimism surged again after I met a small group of twelve-year-old boys. One was especially popular, and I asked them why. They answered, "Because he has long sleeves." When he showed up, I saw what had earned him his idol status. The long sleeves on his shirt could be tied into a knot, making an impromptu soccer ball for them to play with. I couldn't imagine what it would be like to admire the one guy in town lucky enough to have a long-sleeved T-shirt. Again, I saw the hope that sports could bring these children, not just for their physical health, but for their mental and social well-being.

As I stood on an Olympic podium, I remembered those children standing on a mound of dirt, in awe of a boy with a long-sleeved T-shirt. I vowed in that moment that I would use my accomplishments to somehow help them. Looking around at all the media and fans that had suddenly become my friends, I figured I could use my newfound influence to encourage their support for the children. I made a statement to the press announcing that I was donating my entire prize money to Olympic Aid to help the children of Eritrea and Sarajevo. I appealed to my countrymen's "soft inside" and asked them to share in my mission by donating just one and a half dollars for each medal Norway won during these celebratory games.

There was a much greater force motivating all Norwegian athletes to win medals now. We now had the passion to help these children driving us. Even in competitions where we weren't expected to place, we knew winning a medal would make a profound difference—and it was enough to propel us to the top of the world stage. By the close of the Olympic Games, Norway had won twenty-six medals and we had raised eighteen million dollars for children affected by war.

Over the next six years, I traveled around the world and met countless kids suffering from war, poverty and disease. It came as a disturbing surprise to learn few of them had an opportunity to play; play was a luxury. By the year 2000, I could not accept this any longer. After the Sydney Olympics were over, I followed my passion and built an organization to establish sustainable sports opportunities for the most disadvantaged children around the world. We created sports and play programs that would mobilize children and enhance their healthy physical and psychosocial development and build stronger communities.

While developing this organization, I also kept true to my goal of becoming a doctor, attending med school and earning my medical degree in 1999. At that point I faced the dilemma of choosing which career path to take; otherwise, I would be doing each job only half as well as I could.

In the end, I chose to focus on my charitable work, and develop Right To Play. I realized the organization I dreamed of building could reach more children and affect more change than I ever could as a doctor. In too many troubled areas, no one took sport and play seriously for a child's development. I knew these disadvantaged kids needed someone promoting their holistic development and all the positive effects of sport and play.

Many disadvantaged children don't have the support of a grandma encouraging them to pursue their passions. They often don't even have a grandparent living…or a parent, for that matter. But they now have me and Right To Play in their corner, encouraging sport and play to make a difference in their lives.

To be successful, you need to...

Be soft on the inside… **Find Your Passion**

Look at your achievements

Nikki's Perspective: During my senior year in high school, I decided I'd take up the popular sport of soccer to keep myself in shape during the off-season. Everyone told me it would really help my overall fitness for skiing. I didn't necessarily love soccer, but I was a fairly natural athlete, so thought I could excel at it and be a standout athlete on the team.

No matter how hard I trained, however, I didn't make any great improvements—with soccer or my fitness. I put in a lot of time, but found that my heart just wasn't there at training. The next year I pursued my old love, gymnastics, in the off-season and found that not only were my acrobatic skills improving, but my overall fitness level was, as well. For results, I just needed to follow my passions.

Your Tools for Success: Today, write down your top five achievements in life. You will probably notice that these accomplishments align with what you love. Do you really think this is a coincidence?

If you truly pursue the things you are most passionate about, you will find that doing so helps you attain success. Put your passions at the top of your to-do list every morning and many achievements will likely fall into place.

_____

_____

_____

_____

_____

Michael Lynch

Head of Visa Global Sponsorship Management

Photo provided by Michael Lynch

Michael Lynch Biography

Michael Lynch leads Visa's global sponsorship management strategy and execution, including managing global programs in support of the Olympic Games, Paralympic Games, FIFA World Cup, and National Football League. Lynch and his team are responsible for identifying, securing and managing relationships with Visa's global sponsorship partners.

During his long years of service at Visa, Lynch has led Visa's sponsorship marketing business to the pinnacle of the industry. Visa's innovative sponsorship marketing is renowned for differentiating and building the Visa brand, driving revenue, acquisition, usage and preference for Visa products and services, and providing value to clients and cardholders. In addition to the world's biggest global properties, Visa's U.S. sponsorship portfolio includes some of the best properties in the business—U.S. Olympic Committee, National Football League, NASCAR, Soccer United Marketing, Kentucky Derby, Broadway, and others.

During Lynch's tenure, Visa was recognized by Event Marketer Magazine *as the only financial services company among "the 25 Best Sponsors in America" and was heralded as "the most well-rounded sponsor around."* Brandweek Magazine *ran a cover story on Visa's Olympic Games sponsorship, calling Visa the "poster child" for effectively integrating a sponsorship, and went on to say "nobody does it better." Lynch has been touted by* Sporting News *magazine as one of the hundred most powerful people in sports, and according to that publication, "Visa is everywhere competitors would like to be in sports marketing and sponsorships."* SportsBusiness Journal *recognized Visa as one of the "top five corporate sponsors you most want aligned with your property."*

Lynch also serves on the board of directors for Athletes for Hope, and the advisory board of the World Congress of Sports.

Lynch joined Visa in 1995, after serving as vice president of events for Radio City Music Hall Productions in New York City. He was responsible for the overall development, management and production of Radio City's events business.

Prior to joining Radio City, Lynch was vice president and general manager of ProServ Inc., a worldwide sports management and marketing firm representing more than 150 professional athletes and managing more than 150 events annually. ProServ is now part of Clear Channel. While at ProServ, Lynch was honored with an Adweek *magazine Event Marketer of the Year award for a PGA Tour promotion he developed.*

Lynch has a BBA from the University of Notre Dame, an MBA in marketing from Cornell University, and he's also a CPA. He resides in San Mateo, California, with his wife, Susan, and two daughters, McKenzie and Dylan.

Nikki's Intro to Michael Lynch's Story

I was thirteen years old when the Olympic Games came to Los Angeles, California, in 1984. My family traveled three thousand miles, across the country, to experience the games firsthand. We had always been Olympic junkies, so we were excited to see the events "up close and personal."

I don't think I had the slightest idea how much I would be drawn in by the spectacle. I couldn't believe that I was sitting a few feet away from real Olympic athletes. They no longer felt like movie actors playing parts; these were real people, performing real feats and receiving real medals.

My dreams and passions were no longer a vague concept. They were now a bona fide prospect. I looked at those Olympians with awe and vowed that someday I would become one of them.

Every four years, Olympians step onto the field of play and demonstrate why they are the best in the world at their designated sport. I've been fortunate to know how an Olympian's efforts can inspire an endless number of girls and boys to accomplish great feats. And if I ever forget, I have Michael Lynch to remind me…

Michael Lynch: My Story

Michael Lynch

Passion

I squeezed my way to the front of the crowd to catch sight of one of the early rounds of the 400-meter hurdles. My father had piled me and two of my brothers into the family "woodie" station wagon, and we'd headed north to experience, firsthand, the electric energy of the 1976 Montreal Olympic Games. Being a large family with eight boys, we didn't have money for the bleacher seats, but the standing-room-only tickets were more than enough to stimulate my soft inside.

I was immediately captivated by the world-class athletes, the vitality of the fans, the cacophony of different languages and the patchwork of different cultures all uniting in one common pursuit. I was blown away by the fact that some countries hated each other, yet their athletes, after crossing the finish line, would share a strong handshake or a long embrace, signifying their mutual respect. Regardless, if you were an athlete, official, country delegate or fan, everyone came together in peace.

That one day in Montreal initiated my lifelong personal relationship with the Olympic movement. I had the Olympic bug. However, it didn't take too much thought for me to realize I wasn't really blessed with world-class athletic genes. I wasn't the best athlete in my sport in high school, let alone in the league, state, nation or world. Unless dreaming of one day becoming an Olympian was being added as an Olympic event, I wasn't destined to be at the starting line. But this did not quell my passion for being connected to the movement in some way, shape or form.

After graduating with a BBA from the University of Notre Dame and an MBA from Cornell University, I started working at a sports management/marketing firm and finally had my opportunity to connect with a few Olympic athletes. Though I could now begin ameaningful relationship with Olympic sports, I was still not involved to the extent that I had hoped. I wanted a deeper connection to the event that had so inspired me many years before.

Low and behold, the opportunity dropped in my lap. Fatefully, Visa was looking for someone to run their sponsorship marketing business. Though I knew we would cover a number of sports, I accepted the job with the specific intention of working on the Olympic Games.

And the Olympics quickly became integral to Visa's success. It was the cornerstone of our brand marketing and our long-standing marketing communications campaign, "It's everywhere you want to be."

I felt it was essential that I capture exactly what the Olympic movement meant to me. I wanted to get to the heart of what the Olympic Games were all about. We had to bring the athletes to the forefront. I, along with millions of cardholders, would live vicariously through the Olympians. In doing so, we would help bring the world together in multidimensional, multicultural camaraderie.

By highlighting the athletes, we were bringing the Olympic Games to life at Visa. We created the Visa Gold Medal Athlete Program, enabling key individuals to focus on sport and achieve their dreams.

I knew that our sponsorship would help the athletes, but I had no idea how much it would come back and touch me. While these potential champions were working on capturing their dreams, they were unknowingly capturing our hearts. The Olympic spirit was created in supporting up-and-coming aerial skier Emily Cook, who missed her first Olympic Games after shattering both her feet two weeks before the opening ceremonies, but eventually came back to qualify and compete in the games four years later. And in being the first company to get behind American Women's Hockey, helping the U.S. team to win the first Olympic gold medal in the sport. And in backing women's pole vaulter Stacy Dragila, bobsledder Jill Bakken, boardercross racer Lindsey Jacobellis, and beach volleyball players Kerri Walsh and Misty May in winning Olympic medals, thereby inspiring young girls across the country to pursue their own sports dreams.

Additionally, we were most proud of being the first company to step up and become a global sponsor of the Paralympic Games. In our customary fashion, we provided support to a number of Paralympic athletes, including Cheri Blauwet, Marlon Shirley, Erin Popovich, Manny Guerra and Laurie Stephens.

Through each bead of sweat, Ace bandage and hand over the heart, we all lived the experience with them. They helped drive the passion for what the games are all about. Olympians and Paralympians moved and inspired our bankers and merchants, employees and cardholders to feel good about Visa, our athletes and our country. We achieved our objective of relating the spirit of the games to the spirit of our business. And the partnership could not have been a bigger success.

I'm proud of the way we differentiated ourselves in the marketplace and how the American people supported our decisions. Visa's market share increased 33 percent since we announced our relationship with the Olympic Games. That very same relationship that helped launch my career.

I've now been to eight Olympic Games. And, whenever I see a little boy or girl straining to catch a better view of our heroes, or my daughters getting that telling gleam in their eyes, I wonder if the passion will also drive them to discover their dreams someday.

To be successful, you need to...

Be soft on the inside... **Find Your Passion**

Remember your childhood dreams

Nikki's Perspective: Few kids say, "When I grow up, I want to make X dollars." There was a point in my career, just before my last Olympic appearance, when I started getting sidetracked by the allure of the almighty dollar. Sponsors were all of a sudden interested in aerial skiing, and the money was pulling me away from why I'd started the sport.

I quickly realized this wasn't what my pursuit was about. If someone asked me if I'd rather have an Olympic medal or a million dollars, I'd choose the medal. Even today, if someone offered me any amount of money for it, I wouldn't accept. When I stood on my makeshift podium as a young girl, it was the medal I dreamed of. It was always this desire in attaining that goal that pushed me toward my ultimate success.

Your Tools for Success: We often forget what is most important to us at our core. Today, take the time to remember what you wanted to be as a young child or teenager, and why. Look at your current job, relationship or endeavor and find the parts that resonate with the untainted dreams you had while you were growing up. We often get distracted by money, by what other people think is most important, or by something else on our current path that's secondary. Children naturally act out of their core passions. Find these important elements within yourself to embrace.

_____

_____

_____

_____

_____

William "Bing" Gordon

Top Creative Force behind Electronic Gaming Industry

Photo provided by Bing Gordon

Bing Gordon Biography

Bing was chief creative officer of Electronic Arts from 1998 to 2008, after heading EA marketing and product development off and on since EA's founding. He joined the company in 1982 and helped write the founding business plan that attracted KPCB as an initial investor.

Bing has driven EA's branding strategy with EA Sports, EA's pricing strategy for package goods and online games, and has contributed design and marketing for many EA franchises, including John Madden Football, The Sims, Sim City, Need for Speed, Tiger Woods Golf, Club Pogo and Command and Conquer.

Bing has been a director at Amazon since 2003, and was a founding director of Audible, Inc. In addition to Amazon, Bing serves as a director for Mevio, ngmoco, Inc. and Zynga. He is a trustee of the Urban School of San Francisco, and serves on the Yale president's advisory council.

Gordon earned an MBA degree from Stanford University and a BA degree from Yale University.

Nikki's Intro to Bing Gordon's Story

I often hear people say that I'm lucky to have a job I love. Personally, I don't see how it is luck, when I chose this job. And they have the choice, too. It's never too late to pursue our passions.

I remember my father always telling me to find what I loved to do and then find a way to make money at it. The first time I spoke to an audience of hundreds of people it was terrifying, but also exhilarating. I immediately fell in love with the rush of getting on stage. Public speaking was not, however, a career that fell in my lap. I had to practice endless hours and deliver hundreds of speeches for free to get myself to a place where I felt I could start a career in the industry.

It's not luck that I'm a speaker. It *is* luck—if you want to call it that—that I realized it was important to pursue a career I loved. Bing Gordon, a close personal friend, is a man with that same "good luck...

Bing Gordon: My Story

Bing Gordon

Passion

Most people probably look at a résumé much differently than I do. When I read someone's résumé, I turn it upside down and start by checking the person's interests. I have found that if people don't have interests, then they don't want to participate in their own creativity. And if they don't deem their interests worthy of listing on a résumé, they have already decided they're going to live their lives by what they think they are expected to do, and not by what they love.

I don't want to know that job applicants earned an MBA from Harvard. I want to know what they specialized in and what their favorite assignment was. I don't want to know that individuals worked in a marketing department of a large firm, but I do want to ask what project they are proudest of. I don't want to know if they wrote a screenplay, but rather that they can tell a great story over dinner. I want to know if these individuals are making a habit of following their passions. Are they taking action on their interests? Like the proverbial turtle, are they letting their "soft inside" guide them?

Luckily for me, I had a teacher who helped me recognize that my passions were worth more than a fleeting daydream. One day in my Stanford MBA Decision Support Systems class, Professor Peter Keen ended the formal session early to help us understand our own decisions and how we came to make them. He went around the room asking each student what we would hope to do in five years if money were no object. He wanted us to understand our own decision assumptions, and what weight we put on our real passions.

The majority wanted to handle big corporate takeovers or become investment bankers, even if "money were no object." Several students wanted to open restaurants or day care centers. And then there was me. My vision was not normal. It was a dream I had fantasized about several years earlier, one rainy day working as a commercial fisherman off the coast of Vancouver Island, long before my days of shuffling through MBA classes. I wanted to create an "adult Disneyland" where computers would replace the actors. It would be like a computerized Adventure Land or Tomorrow Land featuring a variety of inventive stories, with computers controlling the characters.

I anticipated viewing a roomful of excited faces or at least nodding heads, but instead my response was greeted by empty stares. The room was silent. Professor Keen gave me what I took as the obligatory "Well, thanks for sharing" and politely moved on. After class, he came up to me and confided that, in actuality, no one really understood what I meant. And even though he didn't fully understand, either, he admired my enthusiasm and encouraged me to "go for it."

Professor Keen told me he had another student who'd told a similar story, and he wanted to connect us. It was a guy named Trip Hawkins, who had a dream of simulating sports games on computers. We talked, then joined forces on a market research project for class credit, on the Fairchild Channel F, the first video game cartridge system. We got the bug.

Four and a half year later, Trip founded a video game publisher, and I joined him as one of the earliest employees. Our small team of dreamers gave Electronic Arts its name and founding business plan. Trip's fantasy eventually morphed into EA Sports, and my own fantasy was eventually realized in The Sims and Ultima Online.

It wasn't until many years later that I realized how valuable those last five minutes of Professor Keen's class were in shaping my future. I have also had the experience of being a teacher at the University of Southern California, and I've found there is an "Aha!" moment when you realize how to spark a student's interest. And if you've really sparked someone's interest, it is a small step to help him or her operationalize it in what philosopher John Dewey called "learning by doing."

Self-awareness is the first step to achieving one's dreams and fantasies. So now when I read a résumé that lists a concept that is beyond my own imagination, all I can think is *Go for it*.

To be successful, you need to...

Be soft on the inside... **Find Your Passion**

Reinvent yourself or change your routine

Nikki's Perspective: Routine is comfortable. Routine makes things so easy, because we don't have to think. But I've found that schedules can keep us in a rut. When I first qualified for the World Cup tour, we would compete in seeds. The top ten women and men would compete in the afternoon, the lower ranked athletes in the morning. I became quite comfortable competing with both women and men throughout the season. We were thrown for a loop one day toward the end of the year when the organizers decided the weather would prevent both men and women from competing, so they would just have all the women compete together.

I was extremely nervous about disrupting the routine, but knew I had no choice. I had to change my whole training schedule and turn my back on some familiar habits. I actually found the new format exhilarating, and at the end of the day, I was standing on top of the podium. The change had infused a new energy that I'd lacked throughout the rest of the year.

Your Tools for Success: Change up your schedule or routine today. Reinvent who you are, or take a path or plan that is completely unexpected by yourself and others. We all find ourselves getting stuck in our habits, and often become bored. Have you ever asked yourself why you have to do things the same way every day?

Even if it feels a bit uncomfortable, try changing the order, style or manner of how you complete your daily tasks today. Take parts of these changes with you into your everyday life. You'll find the "imbalance" actually injects excitement back into your day.

_____

_____

_____

_____

_____

Chapter 3

Focus

Focus

When I qualified for the World Cup tour, I began competing with athletes from all over the world. As an unknown skier my first year on the tour, I had no sponsors, and my parents had to support me financially. I wanted to prove to them that I wasn't going to waste their money. And I didn't.

Four times in that first year I placed in the top three, even winning in my fourth World Cup competition ever. By the end of the season, I found myself in ninth place worldwide. I couldn't wait to take the videotape of my contest jumps home to show my parents how effectively I'd used their money.

I popped the tape in the VCR and we sat down to watch it together. Now, while it seems forever when you are in the air, an aerialist is actually airborne for about three seconds—as compared to the top basketball players, who are airborne for one. I competed in a total of ten contests that first season, with two jumps per event, so the whole tape was about sixty seconds long. After we viewed it, I eagerly sat at the edge of my seat, awaiting my parents' response. We sat there in silence for another thirty seconds. I figured they must be pondering the praise they were going to pile on me, but my father, ever the comedian, had other thoughts. He finally turned to me and asked, "I just spent fifteen thousand bucks for thirty seconds?"

Being caught off guard, I had no clever reply. But I did heatedly explain that a lot of work went into those thirty seconds, and that I had to really make sure I was "on" when it counted most. My dad quickly agreed on the importance of working hard and making sure you bring your "A game" to those key moments. As I've always said, it does you no good to bring a practice session.

Two years later, bringing enough "A games" to the competition hill helped me qualify for my first Olympics. I was so excited that I might have a chance to win the medal I'd dreamed of since I was five years old.

I quickly learned that it wasn't just my expectation, but that of my family, my friends, my hometown, my home state and my country. The hundreds of letters people sent to encourage me unintentionally threw a world of weight on my shoulders. Everyone had expectations about me bringing home an Olympic medal for the U.S.A.

And their hopes had some basis. As I entered the Olympic Games, I was ranked third in the world. There was certainly a chance I might bring home one of those big, shiny medallions. Though some people would find this motivating, I just found it added more unwanted pressure.

I arrived at the games a few days before the opening ceremonies, and had to wait a full two weeks before my competition began. At the Olympics, aerialists have a semifinals contest where all competitors take two different jumps and add their scores together. The top twelve women and top twelve men qualify for finals, starting over with a clean slate.

I woke up on the morning of semis and was blown away by how much greater the pressure felt for this event. The world was suddenly interested in aerial skiing, when most people couldn't have told you what the event was just two months earlier. One of my coaches told me to try to imagine it was like every other day—just like training. Well, the problem was that every other day I didn't have thirty thousand people surrounding the landing hill and another twenty million watching from their armchairs back home. It was pretty hard to imagine this was like every other day.

The random run order listed me last to jump. This meant I had to wait for all the other women to jump before it was time for me to take my place on the hill. Finally, it was my turn to slide into starting position. I somehow managed to calm myself enough to push off for my first ever Olympic jump. I went off the ramp, did two black flips through the air and executed a full twist on my second flip. My form was impeccable, with a perfectly straight position, and I landed the jump with very little impression on the snow. Being the last competitor, I would know my first-round standing right after my score went up on the board.

My score popped up on the scoreboard almost immediately, and in the bottom corner, right under the word *Rank*, flashed the number 1. I was at the Olympics and I was in first place! I started thinking that maybe I could bring home one of those renowned shiny medals. I could follow in the footsteps of some of my Olympic gold medal idols by appearing on David Letterman, and my hometown of Westborough, Massachusetts, would have a parade for me. I wasn't even in the finals yet and I was already thinking about winning a gold medal.

I went back up to the top of the hill with images of medals floating in my head. And with these thoughts of Olympic glory, I forgot about everything else going into my second jump. I did two flips and two twists, and thought my jump was impeccable. But it wasn't *exactly* impeccable... I finished my last flip and realized I was still three feet off the ground. My skis skimmed past the ground and I cascaded on my back along the snowy hill.

I quickly bounced to my feet in hopes of minimizing the judges' impressions of my fall. I skied to a stop at the bottom of the hill and awaited my score. As luck would have it, the electricity went out just then and the scoreboard went dark. I was the last female athlete to jump, so my impending score would tell me specifically if I would be one of those twelve fortunate women going on to finals.

I had to wait a full five minutes before they announced my score. As I was waiting, I thought about how a few other women had touched a hand down on landing, or had poor form in the air. I was in *first* place after the first round, so could literally drop eleven places and still make it to finals, where the top dozen athletes would start over with a clean slate.

After much anticipation, a booming voice came over the loudspeaker. "From the United States, Nikki Stone... Thirteenth place!"

Thirteenth place! I couldn't believe it! I hadn't just missed finals, I'd missed by a mere 0.57 of a point. Less than one point out of over 200 points. It was devastating.

And what was even harder to take was that the woman in twelfth place, the athlete I would have bumped out of finals with just over half a point more, went on to win the first ever Olympic medal in the sport of aerial skiing. That woman was Lina Tcherjazova, an extremely talented aerialist from Uzbekistan. I wasn't disappointed because I thought Lina didn't deserve that medal—she definitely did. I was disappointed because I basically handed it to her.

I had to watch as she took her place on the top of the Olympic podium and had that shiny gold medal draped around her neck. I held back tears as the Uzbekistan anthem started to play. As I sat and listened to her proud national anthem, I realized that I had a very valuable lesson I should be taking away from the day. If I was going to start building my hard outer shell, I had to make sure I was focused on the task at hand.

I was thinking of the "big picture" rather than what I needed to do in order to *achieve* that big picture. My thoughts were bouncing everywhere but where they should be: on the elements of my jump. Lina may have had dreams of gold in the back of her mind, but she had been able to shelve those thoughts long enough to focus on the specifics of the task at hand.

I always hated when life taught me these crucial lessons at such significant moments...before the eyes of the world. Regardless of whether I wanted the lesson or not, it was presented to me and I would be a fool not to learn it. There are so many distractions in life and if we don't build a hard shell to defend against their enticements, we'll be sucked into mediocrity.

Nadia Comaneci

"Perfect 10" Gymnast

Photo provided by Bart Conner

Nadia Comaneci Biography

At the 1976 Olympics in Montreal, Canada, a fourteen-year-old Romanian dynamo captured the hearts and minds of the world with her daring and perfection. We came to know her simply as "Nadia."

By the time the 1976 Olympics ended, Comaneci had earned seven perfect 10s, three gold medals, one bronze, one silver, and countless fans. She appeared on the covers of Time, Newsweek *and* Sports Illustrated, *all in the same week, and returned home to Romania to a heroine's welcome.*

Four years later, at the 1980 Moscow Olympics, Comaneci earned two more gold medals and two silver, to bring her Olympic total to nine medals—five gold, three silver, one bronze. In 1996, Comaneci was inducted into the International Gymnastics Hall of Fame.

In April 1996, Comaneci married American Olympic champion Bart Conner, in a Romanian state wedding. Comaneci now divides her time among appearances, commercial endorsements for major companies, speaking engagements and charity events. In 2003, Nadia wrote a book called Letters to a Young Gymnast, *detailing her inspirational story.*

Currently, Nadia and Bart are business partners with their manager, Paul Ziert, in the Bart Conner Gymnastics Academy, International Gymnast Magazine, *Perfect 10 Productions, Inc., a TV production company, and Grips, Etc., a gymnastics supply company. Comaneci also works as a TV commentator for the World Gymnastics Championships on WCSN, the World Championship Sports Network.*

In 1999, Comaneci was honored by ABC News and Ladies Home Journal *as one of the hundred most important women of the twentieth century. Comaneci, who is also fluent in French and English, continues to travel the world with her various interests. Her charity work is extensive. She is vice chairperson of the board of directors of Special Olympics International. She is also a vice president of the Muscular Dystrophy Association. Comaneci also serves as a member of the board of the Laureus Sports For Good Foundation. Nadia also travels to Romania often to support dozens of charities in her homeland.*

Even though Nadia won a total of nine Olympic medals, five of them gold, she will always be remembered most as the first gymnast to score a perfect 10, leaving her indelible mark on the history of the Olympics.

On June 3, 2006, Conner and Comaneci welcomed their son, Dylan Paul Conner, into the world. Today, Conner and Comaneci continue to travel the world delivering inspirational speeches, as well as promoting their charities, gymnastics, fitness, and healthy lifestyles.

Nikki's Intro to Nadia Comaneci's Story

Not long after seeing my first hero, Nadia Comaneci win the Olympics, I enrolled in a gymnastics class myself. I made great progress, and eventually my babysitter invited me to join her high school team in an exhibition event.

Being so young, I somehow didn't know that I was "supposed" to be nervous. I was just focused on being like Nadia. I was performing with a bunch of girls easily ten years older than me, and I was in an auditorium full of spectators, and all I could think about was being Nadia.

That focus took away all the pressure, and my performance that evening received the lion's share of the applause—though I'm sure the pigtails and freckles didn't hurt. Little did I know that my idol shared a similar experience several months earlier, when her focus helped her make history…

Nadia Comaneci: My Story

Nadia Comaneci

Focus

I never realized that I was going to make history.

I started gymnastics because I had way too much energy and my mom was sick of me breaking the springs on the couch when I launched myself from cushion to cushion. She was relieved when a neighbor suggested a place to try gymnastics. So at the age of six and a half, I was taught my first cartwheel.

It took me a few years to realize that I could be a successful gymnast. I loved learning new things and I loved the competition. But I would be remiss if I didn't mention that I also loved the coaches' attention. They would tell me, "Nadia, you pick things up so quickly" or "Nadia, great balance beam routine." The encouragement made me want it even more.

There came a period where I couldn't see my life without the gymnasium in it. Every thought was focused on the gym. And soon I had expectations of this big event everyone was talking about—the Olympics. I was first introduced to the games in 1972, by way of an eighteen inch, black-and-white television with a fuzzy screen. I imagined the Olympics was just another competition, but with a lot more people participating and a lot more watching.

Eight years after my first cartwheel, I was going to this big event with more athletes and more spectators. Many people say that it must be overwhelming pressure for a young boy or girl to handle. I think it's just the opposite. Quite seriously, I had no clue of the pressure of the Olympic Games. As a fourteen-year-old, I didn't care about pressure and I didn't comprehend the consequences.

I'd attended a competition several months before the Olympics where I had fallen off the beam three times in one routine and scored a meager 7.25. I was determined not to let that happen again. I learned from those mistakes and took those lessons with me to the Olympics. I knew it would take just one wrong angle of my foot to throw me off the beam or one hyperextended knee to miss my dismount on the vault.

I focused my complete attention on doing my routines just as well as I had prepared them. The most important thing was to forget about the extra competitors and spectators and concentrate on transferring what I did in our gym to this competition. There were so many external distractions, so I had to build a hard shell against all the noise and crowds and cameras and the idea of winning, and just focus on my routines. I paid attention to all the mistakes I had made in pre-Olympic competitions to ensure that I wouldn't make the same slipups a second time. A small mistake could be made at any second, so I put my "Olympic podium blinders" up and didn't take them down until my final score was posted.

In addition to the Olympic podium, I had my blinders up to the scoreboard, as well. So when I finished my uneven bar routine, I was oblivious to what the gasp of the crowd meant. I did catch the eye of a teammate who signaled me to look at the score. Across the Longines scoreboard flashed a 1.00. A one?? How had I scored a one? Something must have gone drastically wrong.

My friend explained that it must be a 10.00. When Longines was designing their Olympic scoreboard, they'd called the International Gymnastics Federation and asked if there was *any* chance someone would score a 10. The response was a simple, "Oh no, no way!" So Longines created a scoreboard that could only post 9.95 as its highest score. No one was prepared for a 10. No one knew that a young girl from Romania would see the Olympics as "just another event" and concentrate so hard on perfecting her routines. Ironically, I didn't feel the routine was a 10. But luckily, the judges did, and history was made.

My coach, Bela Karolyi, had taught me this intense focus through our endless repetition of routines. Regardless of whether I knew what the Olympics was all about, Bela did know, and he trained me to be prepared for the routines, but not necessarily aware of the games. He let me go on believing that the Olympics would be just another event, with more people watching. I spent more time around Bela than my parents, so he learned exactly how to shape my focus in order to score a perfect 10. Bela would give all his best effort, then I'd give mine, and together we found success

Success far greater than I ever imagined.

I never thought about making history. I was too busy putting my attention into making it.

To be successful, you need to...

Have a hard shell... **Make Sure You Are Focused**

One step at a time

Nikki's Perspective: When I started college, I had just broken onto the World Cup skiing scene, so I decided to pursue both ventures at the same time. The prospect of trying to find success in both skiing and academics was daunting. Getting through four years of school while trying to qualify for the Olympics was not an easy task. I just had to focus on each step as I encountered it. I put my full attention into academics when I was at school, and my full attention into athletics when I was skiing. I found the focus helped me excel in both areas, and prevented me from having a breakdown on the journey to reaching both my goals.

Your Tools for Success: I know a woman who was going through chemo for cancer when she decided to train for and climb Mount Kilimanjaro—a mountain with an altitude over 18,000 feet. I know how hard it is to climb that high with full energy. A mutual friend asked her how she manages to climb 18,000 feet. She replied, "I don't; I climb one step over and over again until I reach the top of the mountain."

Like this cancer survivor, we need to try to focus on the immediate goal. To tackle a big project, only think about the first step, then the second step, and so on until the project is completed. Keep reminding yourself of this impressive woman, and take it one step at a time.

The great Chinese philosopher Lao-Tzu wrote, "A journey of a thousand miles begins with a single step." Focus on that first step.

_____

_____

_____

_____

_____

Dr. Stephen Covey

Leadership Authority and Best-selling Author

Photo provided by Dr. Stephen Covey

Dr. Stephen Covey Biography

In 1996, Stephen R. Covey was recognized by Time *magazine's as one of the twenty-five most influential Americans, and one of* Sales and Marketing Management's *top twenty-five power brokers.*

Dr. Covey is the author of several acclaimed books, including the international bestseller The 7 Habits of Highly Effective People. *It has sold more than fifteen million copies in thirty-eight languages throughout the world. In 2002, Forbes named* The 7 Habits of Highly Effective People *one of the top ten most influential management books ever. A survey by* Chief Executive Magazine *recognized* The 7 Habits of Highly Effective People *as one of the two most influential business books of the twentieth century.*

Other bestsellers authored by Dr. Covey include First Things First, *with sales over two million;* Principle-Centered Leadership, *with sales exceeding one million; and* The 7 Habits of Highly Effective Families, *the number 1 bestselling hardcover book on family.*

Dr. Covey's business book, The 8th Habit: From Effectiveness to Greatness *(November 2004), has risen to the top of several bestseller lists, including New York* Times, *Wall Street Journal, USA Today—Money, Business Week,* Amazon.com *and Barnes & Noble. The* 8th Habit *was named Best Business Book of 2005 by Soundview Executive Summaries. Dr. Covey's newest book,* The Leader in Me, *was released at the end of 2008.*

Dr. Covey's organizational legacy to the world is Covey Leadership Center. On May 30, 1997, a merger of Covey Leadership Center with Franklin Quest created FranklinCovey, the leading global professional services firm, with offices in 123 countries. Dr. Covey is co-founder and vice chairman of FranklinCovey. FranklinCovey shares Dr. Covey's vision, discipline and passion to inspire, lift, and provide tools for change and growth of individuals and organizations throughout the world.

Dr. Covey holds a BS in business administration from the University of Utah in Salt Lake City, and an MBA in business administration from Harvard University. He also has ten honorary doctorates, and has been given many awards, including Speaker of the Year in 1999, the Sikh's 1998 International Man of Peace Award, and the National Entrepreneur of the Year Lifetime Achievement Award for Entrepreneurial Leadership.

Nikki's Intro to Dr. Stephen Covey's Story

Several years ago I was asked to attend a conference in Rome called the "Glocal Forum." The Forum was a nonprofit organization dedicated to the promotion of international intercity relations in pursuit of a new balance between global and local forces. The organizers asked people from many walks of life to discuss a variety of global concepts and how we might bring them together to help communities on a local level.

In attendance were athletes, artists, politicians, business leaders, students, environmentalists, IT specialists, and more. We shared many valuable ideas that could be applied with universal success. Surprisingly, despite our varied backgrounds, we shared some universal themes for success—not unlike the concept of this book. In compiling my interviews for *When Turtles Fly*, I found that, regardless of whether it was a highway, avenue, major interstate or country path, we all used a similar road to success.

Focusing on recurring commonalities brought some astonishing results to the Glocal Forum. Just as it has brought some astonishing results to my book's contributors, as the accomplished Dr. Stephen Covey can attest…

Dr. Stephen Covey: My Story

Dr. Stephen Covey

Focus

I live life in crescendo. I always believe that the most important work I do is still ahead of me. When I put my attention forward to the vital steps and the valuable tasks I have to do, my life has a pulse.

I don't believe in retirement from the work I do. You can retire from a job, but not from meaningful work that gives you a sense of direction and fulfillment. I sincerely feel that the reason why some individuals live longer than others is because they are continually focusing their efforts on issues that bring them purpose and meaning. When people concentrate their attention on their careers and the resulting dollar signs, it breaks down their immune systems and accelerates the degenerative forces of the body.

I recognized early on that I had to make sure I always centered my attention on increasingly meaningful work. As a young adult, I left home bound for Great Britain on a mission to do volunteer work for my church. After just a few months in the field, I was asked by my mission president if I would train local leaders in fourteen districts and ninety-six branches throughout Great Britain. The prospect was daunting and I was absolutely terrified. But I took the challenge and the experience changed my life. By forgetting about the overwhelming, extraneous factors and focusing on the task, I discovered the thing that gave my life its highest purpose and meaning. Through this leadership role, I found my voice.

When I returned from my mission, my father sent me off to Harvard to develop the skills I would need to enter the family business. The Covey clan had developed a very successful real estate, gas, oil and motel enterprise that spanned four states. The Ivy League education just confirmed what I already knew. I had to tell my father that the prospect just didn't capture my heart, and I would rather focus my life on teaching and training leaders. I was surprised when he applauded my intentions and admitted that the family business had never given him the core meaning he needed, either.

I entered my new career first as a university professor, and later, launching my own business operation, which would eventually expand to 160 countries. I've had the opportunity to train over twenty-two heads of state, cabinet members, administrators and advisors.

When I started, though, I had virtually no experience or knowledge of how to be a great leader. I got my protégés to cumulatively share their best practices with each other. I found that the best way to increase my knowledge was to share it, so that I could gain valuable feedback and learn where people had specific needs and problems. When I put special attention into dealing with their needs and problems, they began to feel I understood them. And when people are understood, they are willing to open themselves to your influence.

I have always believed that we have two ears and one mouth, and should use them accordingly. You don't often learn much from talking. The best teachers are often the best listeners. The books I've written were not produced from sitting around and cogitating about what I learned from others. The lessons I have taught were all whittled down from my experience with the masses. By pooling our knowledge, we come up with a shared direction that ultimately creates a greater result. The essence of winning is to come up with a win-win agreement based on what serves all parties involved.

And with my shared knowledge, I found that, regardless of whether I was studying human nature and the human interaction of business, health care, military, government, education, or nonprofits, the same universal and timeless principles surfaced. I have taught Buddhists, Hindus, Muslims, Christians, Jews and followers of Confucius. And regardless of religion or culture or race, these same truths apply.

My personal ascent as a teacher slowly evolved into the wisdom of principle-centered leadership. This principle demonstrates that self-validating natural laws provide a compass or true north for leaders. Individuals are more effective and organizations more empowered when they are guided and governed by these proven principles. Principle-centered leaders are those who understand and accept the principles by building them into the center of their lives, into the center of their relationships with others, into the center of their agreements and contracts, into their management processes, and into their mission statements. I've directed these leaders to see how this foundation would help build trust and productivity to help empower cultures.

In fact, I recently participated in a leadership summit that was working on building strong relationships between the Arab world and the United States. Everyone was amazed to see how, in a short three-day period, people of profoundly different backgrounds—religiously, politically, and culturally—could achieve alternative solutions to the problems of rebuilding relationships with various world communities.

It's funny how condensing my efforts down to my core beliefs has actually broadened the scope of my results. And the projects I am working on will ultimately affect billions of people around the world. Who would have thought that an overwhelmed young boy who was "destined" to run a family-based business would eventually learn to focus his efforts on people, to help change the world?

To be successful, you need to...

Have a hard shell... **Make Sure You Are Focused**

Know your root focal point

Nikki's Perspective: I've tried to take my own suggested activities and incorporate them into how I would use them in my life now. I originally had a sports-related perspective for this activity, but thought I should see how my lesson could help me in publishing my book. As a result, I spoke to other authors and tried to see if we had a shared core focal point. Through the process, I realized that I was more concerned with presenting what I naively thought publishers would find most intriguing, rather than following my core values. When I refocused my attention toward the amazing stories, lessons and philosophies I found important enough to include in my book, I discovered that I got a much different result with publishers. Narrowing my focus to my core beliefs helped me understand the new direction I needed to take to find success.

Your Tools for Success: If you focus on the whole end goal you will often become distracted and overwhelmed by the process. Pick just one core value or task to focus on for the day, week or month, a step that will ultimately help you reach your end goal. Ask your friends and colleagues what their core focus is, and find the common denominator. Listening to other people articulate their goals, and how they're reaching them, often helps you find your own direction.

_____

_____

_____

_____

_____

Dr. H. Robert Horvitz

Nobel Prize-winner in Physiology or Medicine

Photo courtesy of Bachrach Photographers

Dr. H. Robert Horvitz Biography

Dr. H. Robert Horvitz received the Nobel Prize in Physiology or Medicine in 2002. He is the David H. Koch, Professor of Biology at the Massachusetts Institute of Technology (MIT); an investigator of the Howard Hughes Medical Institute; Neurobiologist (Neurology) and Geneticist (Medicine) at the Massachusetts General Hospital; and a member of the McGovern Institute for Brain Research and the MIT Koch Institute for Integrative Cancer Research.

Dr. Horvitz received Bachelor of Science degrees in mathematics and economics from MIT in 1968. He performed his graduate studies at Harvard University in the laboratories of Drs. James Watson and Walter Gilbert, and received his PhD in 1974 for biochemical and genetic studies of bacteriophage T4. Dr. Horvitz then joined Dr. Sydney Brenner at the Medical Research Council Laboratory of Molecular Biology in Cambridge, England, and there began studies of the development and behavior of the nematode Caenorhabditis elegans.

Dr. Horvitz became an assistant professor in the Department of Biology at the Massachusetts Institute of Technology in 1978, and a professor in 1986. He was named Whitehead Professor of Biology in 1999 and David H. Koch Professor of Biology in 2000. Dr. Horvitz has served on many editorial boards, visiting committees, and advisory committees, and has received numerous awards.

Dr. Horvitz was elected to the U.S. National Academy of Sciences in 1991, the U.S. Institute of Medicine in 2003 and the American Philosophical Society in 2004. He became a Fellow of the American Academy of Arts and Sciences in 1994 and a Fellow of the American Academy of Microbiology in 1997. He has been a consultant to the Novartis Institutes for Biomedical Research and the venture capital company MPM Capital, as well as to a number of biotechnology companies, and he cofounded the biotechnology companies NemaPharm, Inc., Idun Pharmaceuticals, Enlight BioSciences and Epizyme, Inc.

Nikki's Intro to Dr. Robert Horvitz's Story

When I started aerial skiing, it was just a demonstration sport in the Olympics. For these events, no official Olympic medal was awarded. I had always wanted to win an Olympic medal, so many of my friends questioned why I would want to pursue it. When I thought of taking up other sports, however, I just couldn't find the same enthusiasm that I felt for aerials.

So I continued doing what I loved, focusing on the joy I experienced rather than the goal of competing in the Olympics. As my excitement grew, so did the public's, and freestyle aerial skiing was finally accepted as a full-medal sport in the 1994 Lillehammer Olympic Games.

By focusing on my interests, I became the first American aerialist named to that official U.S. Olympic full-medal aerial team. Had I focused on just doing an Olympic sport, I might never have even made it there. And I very likely would not have enjoyed pursuing the path. We can find some amazing results when we focus on *how* we get there and not *what* we're getting *to*. Just ask Nobel Prize winner Dr. H. Robert Horvitz...

Dr. H. Robert Horvitz: My Story

Dr. H. Robert Horvitz

Focus

How does a scientist conceive an idea that leads to a Nobel Prize? There are probably as many answers to that question as there have been science Nobel Laureates. Some have had unique insights or "eureka" moments, but many more simply were trying to learn something new about how the world works, to satisfy their curiosity about nature. I, certainly, fall into this latter category. When I began the research that led to my Nobel Prize, neither the generality nor any possible applications of my work were at all clear. I embarked upon absolutely basic research, directed only at learning something new about biology. Nonetheless, the discoveries made by my colleagues and me now seem likely to pave the way for new treatments for human diseases as diverse as liver disease, neurodegenerative disorders and cancer.

What was my inspiration? I was very lucky to have been surrounded with people who supported and encouraged me. Rather than direct me, they helped me build the confidence that allowed me to find my own way and to explore diverse and admittedly rather diverse areas of interest. My parents were no doubt my major influences as I meandered from thinking about a future in business, law, economics, computer science, medicine, mathematics or biology. My mother and father did not tell me what I should do professionally, but rather helped instill in me a respect for knowledge, a joy of learning and an independence of mind.

My high school guidance counselor was another source of inspiration. She encouraged me to broaden my horizons beyond local colleges and universities, to go east from Chicago and to enroll as an undergraduate at the MIT. There I was exposed to many fields, receiving degrees in mathematics and economics and the equivalent of minors in computer science and psychology.

I received some particularly sage and important advice from Professor Cyrus Levinthal. In my senior year at MIT I was nearing graduation and needed to decide what to do next. The simplest path would have been to go to graduate school in mathematics or economics, or to continue the work in computer programming I had done during the four summers of college. However, six weeks into my senior year, I was intrigued by a new field—biology—from a course taught by Dr. Levinthal. I visited him in his office and asked if, given my background and my ignorance of biology, I was crazy to think of going to graduate school in that field. He smiled and told me that he had received both his undergraduate and PhD degrees in physics, yet he was now teaching my course in biology. Compared to him, I would be starting biology early! His message was clear: Do not be afraid to try something new.

My journey was further shaped by my PhD mentors, Drs. James D. Watson and Walter Gilbert, both Nobel Laureates themselves. They taught me to focus on the unknown rather than dot the i's and cross the t's, to choose problems that have the potential to be important rather than those that are mundane, and to be rigorous in my approach. With them I learned about the fields of molecular genetics and biochemistry and, more important, how to be an experimental scientist.

After my PhD studies I moved to Cambridge, England, staying in the basic field of molecular genetics and joining Drs. Sydney Brenner and John Sulston in their pioneering efforts to solve problems of animal development and behavior by analyzing a microscopic roundworm known as *C. elegans*. In making this transition, I learned that pioneering work may not be popular; I was told by some that my choice of an obscure organism and a foreign country would likely lead to the end of my scientific career. Nonetheless, the problems interested me, and I decided I would take that chance. As our research progressed, our studies of *C. elegans* evolved from being at the fringe to being at the forefront of biomedical research. Our basic work with roundworms led to findings fundamental to human biology and human disease, and led to our shared Nobel Prize.

Today I am concerned that some of the scientific world and much of the public are ignoring the fact that it is basic research—research with no directed practical goals—that has led to many of the most important and unexpected scientific and technological discoveries. Importantly, such basic research cannot be a component of a commercial business plan. Basic research will lead to breakthroughs, but what those breakthroughs will be and what types of companies might be poised to translate them into products that benefit humanity in general cannot be anticipated. For this reason, basic research must be supported primarily through the public sector—in the U.S. this means the federal government—and to a lesser extent through foundations.

The studies of this tiny worm performed by my colleagues and me were recognized in 2002 with the Nobel Prize in Physiology or Medicine. When we were doing our research, I never considered the possibility that we might win a Nobel Prize. Rather, I wanted to do good science concerning a problem that was little explored, in the hope of learning something new. Underlying this work was my belief that some, but not all, studies defined by such criteria would lead to important breakthroughs. I couldn't know if my work would or would not be in this category, but I could know that if done right, my studies would at least advance our understanding of a basic problem in biology.

If I think about messages that emerge from my experiences, I come up with three. First, do not be afraid of trying something new. Second, listen to and learn from those around you, but have a hard shell to protect yourself and your dreams. Third, focus! Whatever you do, do it with determination and to the best of your abilities.

I am indebted to the many people around me who have supplied guidance and support throughout my life. I hope now that I am providing similar guidance and support to others, both to younger colleagues in my scientific life and, even more importantly, to my daughter, Alex, and my stepsons, Joe and Chris, who will no doubt face many alternatives and decisions in their years to come. I hope they listen to my advice...sometimes.

To be successful, you need to...

Have a hard shell... **Make Sure You Are Focused**

Focus on the questions, not the answers

Nikki's Perspective: The year before my second Olympics, my coach put together a training log for me that included a lot of aerobic work such as step classes, running and biking. Coming from a sport where a "run" lasted three seconds and had *nothing* to do with aerobics, I thought the suggestions seemed silly. So if I was running low on time, I would do some extra weight lifting and ignore the aerobic workouts.

As I look back, it seems absurd that I didn't ask the coach why he'd added cardio training to my regimen. It turns out that the aerobic training would help me keep up my stamina throughout the entire season, so I wouldn't fade on tour and have my results drop off midseason. Luckily, I did ask that question eventually, increased my cardio...and didn't fade before I got to February 18th, 1998, the day of the Olympic finals.

Your Tools for Success: We are often so focused on finding answers that we forget to keep asking questions. We need to explore the unknown in order to further our learning. People are sometimes afraid of questions that don't have concrete answers, or answers that may be hard to discover. Kids have it right, constantly asking "why?"

Think up questions that you don't have the answer to. Become a kid again this week and ask people "why?" rather than just accepting their statements. You may find out more on the subject or you may even find out that there really is no sound reasoning to their response.

_____

_____

_____

_____

_____

Summer Sanders

Olympic Swimming Champion and Sports Broadcaster

Photo provided by Michael Lynch

Summer Sanders Biography

Summer Sanders first jumped into the pool because she wanted to be just like her older brother, Trevor. Little did she know she would find her first true passion so early in life. From age four she loved the challenge and the thrill of training and competition.

That dedication resulted in numerous National titles, three gold medals at the Goodwill Games, a gold, silver and bronze at the World Championships, six National Collegiate Athletic Association titles, American records and finally two golds, a silver and a bronze medal at the 1992 Barcelona Olympic Games.

Sanders went to Stanford University, where her team won the 1992 National Title, one of the greatest moments in her swimming career.

After Barcelona, Sanders quickly jumped into her second passion, television work. She has worked for every network, hosting such hit shows as Fox's Skating with Celebrities, *FSN's* The Sports List, *NBA's* Inside Stuff *and Nickelodeon's* Figure It Out. *She has worked for the NBA and the NFL, was a special contributor for the* Today *show and still contributes for* Rachael Ray *and* Good Morning America.

In 1996 Sanders was very honored to become an ambassador for the U.S. Fund for UNICEF. She also actively supports Right To Play.

By far, the roles she is most proud of are mom and wife! She has two beautiful children with her wonderful husband, Erik Schlopy, who just happens to be a three-time Olympic skier.

Her mottos on life are Enjoy the Present, Laugh at Yourself and Age Is a State of Mind. She prides herself on being a professional fourth grader!

Nikki's Intro to Summer Sanders' Story

In 1994, many people in Sweden knew my name because I was the main competition for their country's aerial darling, a phenomenal skier, Marie Lindgren. On the morning of our Olympic semifinals, Swedish cameramen followed both Marie and me around to capture the drama.

Marie later told me about the TV coverage of our differing approaches. She apparently had her game face on and was concentrating deeply. I, in stark contrast, was dancing and waving my arms to every song that blared across the sound system. I didn't want to open myself up to the intensity of the competition.

What the Swedish television captured was the difference in the level of focus between the two of us. Marie had it and I didn't. It must have been great fun for the Swedes to see the dancing fool crash on her second jump while their own Marie Lindgren brought home a silver medal.

Luckily, the lesson was not missed by me. And though she wasn't dancing in front of a Swedish camera crew, the focus lesson wasn't missed by Summer Sanders, either...

Summer Sanders: My Story

Summer Sanders

Focus

Droplets splayed off my arm as I thrust it through the air and drove my fingertips back into the tepid pool. Again and again I made the same motion, slicing my arms through the water and willing my body forward.

I wasn't concentrating on the fact that I was a fifteen-year-old tie-dye-clad rookie going up against seven other girls who each had Olympic experience. I was just concentrating on my coach's advice, "Go as fast and as hard as you can from the start. Just go out there and gain some experience."

It was the 1988 Olympic trial 200-meter medley, and I was a hundred meters into my first Olympic trial finals. I wasn't going to worry about the competition; I was just going to focus on what was happening between my two lane lines.

With three-quarters of the race done, I turned my head to take a breath and saw that all of my competitors were behind me. I was in such disbelief that I took another peak from under the water, and sure enough, I had the lead. Finally, in the last thirty meters, two Olympic swimmers edged passed me, and with just two spots on the prestigious Olympic team, my outside chance of going to my first Summer Games quickly disappeared.

I found out that I'd missed the team by 27 hundredths of a second. But despite the close finish, I was thrilled with the result because I had bettered my time by a full three seconds! I hadn't a clue that I was even going to make finals, and now I had finished *third* against the top athletes in the U.S., if not the world. I went into the competition as an intimidated little girl, but by concentrating on the actual strokes for most of the race, had proved I could be one of the best. That goal was now within reach.

My first Olympic trial taught me a world of good. And four years later, I had the opportunity to relive that moment. I turned all my attention to my strokes and found that I was passing my competitors rather than having them pass me up. No matter what stroke the person next to me was doing, I was racing them to wall. I wanted to continually feel the sensation of catching whoever was in the next lane.

Many people saw my 1988 experience as a failure. Although I was disappointed, I saw the big picture. Looking back, I realize it was a gift. If I had made the team at age fifteen, I would not have understood or even appreciated what it took not only to qualify for the Olympic team, but also to bring home a suitcase full of Barcelona Olympic hardware in 1992.

I definitely learned the most about building my hard shell during the times when I didn't make the Olympic team. This realization came up and smacked me between the eyes four years later, at the 1996 Olympic team trials.

Though I'd retired from competition shortly after the Barcelona Olympics, I decided I wanted to make one more go of it—particularly because the '96 games were to be held in my home country. My aim was not necessarily to win another Olympic medal; it was a personal goal to see how far I could get. I wanted to be reminded what "going for it" was all about. I wanted to challenge myself again.

I called my friends, my coaches, my sponsors and my boss at MTV to tell them of my dreams of returning to high-level competition. I was amazed at their unquestioning support. They understood that I didn't want to look back and regret that I hadn't given it one last try.

I thought that desire was enough to recapture the dream. I can now admit that my mind was everywhere but on my training. My focus went out the door right along with my place on the Atlanta Olympic team. I think that, deep down, I knew ahead of time that I was not going to make the team. It was even evident to those around me. One woman from the U.S. Olympic Training Center came up to me and told me she'd been chosen to talk to me because they saw I was struggling, and they wanted to convey that they believed in me. I was truly honored, but couldn't help but feel that I was going to let them down. I somehow lacked the motivation and mind-set to duplicate my 1992 results. I came back physically, but forgot to pack my mental game when I boarded the plane.

I finished dead last in the finals. I got out of pool and went behind the long curtain to compose myself before everyone saw the tears in my eyes. Sportscaster Jim Gray approached me and told me he was there if I wanted to talk and let my fans know what was going on. It was in that moment I realized there was a reason I had come back. I had returned so that I could fully appreciate what had happened to me in 1992. I would have never known what a valuable tool I learned if I had not experienced the "failure" again.

Many people may not believe me, but this "failure" changed my life in a very positive way. I'm actually glad that I didn't qualify for the '96 games, so that I could have that moment. I gained the closure I needed, and knew I could officially hang up the swim goggles. I no longer needed my swimming to challenge me in life.

I felt that I needed the comeback because there was just something missing from my life. I needed the experience to remember how important focus was. As I look back, it's not standing on the Olympic podium that sticks out in my mind; it's the journey and the experience of appreciating how special my teammates, my family, my coaches, my supporters and my career were. Missing the team made me value all that happened that much more.

My Olympic medals are still tucked away in my sock drawer, because they represent the past. I don't have to look at them every day, for my memories will always be with me. It's not the results, but the process that I truly value. It's not the medals that I wear proudly now, but all I've learned.

The reason I'm most appreciative of this lesson now is because of two small, rosy-cheeked, dark-haired kids named Skye Bella and Spider I see the focus this precious little girl and little boy are developing even now, and I can't wait for it to grow. I long for that day when I can share with my children the valuable lesson that their mommy learned so many years before.

To be successful, you need to...

Have a hard shell... **Make Sure You Are Focused**

It's the process, not the results

Nikki's Perspective: Speedskating champion Bonnie Blair has always been an athlete I've looked up to. Over the years, I've gotten to know her quite well as a friend and colleague, and my respect for her has only grown. One lesson I've learned from Bonnie is that the journey is much more important than the end result. We were once talking about the greatest contest each of us had faced. Most people would assume that hers had to do with winning one of her five Olympic gold medals in speedskating. But not Bonnie. She told me she's most proud of a competition where she finished in fourth place. At that important event, she made key improvements that helped set the stage for many of her future accomplishments...including her five Olympic gold medals.

Your Tools for Success: We need to learn to live in the moment and concentrate on what we have control over. And that's the process, not the end results. For example, we can't control someone else's impression of our work; we can only control what we produce.

Try to complete a task or project today as well as you can—without looking at others for approval. Can you bring something to fruition without worrying about the outcome? If you do feel you have to see your "results", compare them to your own past efforts rather than to what someone else has achieved.

Remember, we can't control someone else's process, only our own.

_____

_____

_____

_____

_____

Barb Schwarz

Creator of Home Staging

Photo provided Barb Schwarz

Barb Schwarz Biography

Barb Schwarz, president and CEO of Stagedhomes.com and the founder and president of the International Association of Home Staging Professionals, created and pioneered the concept of Staging a home back in 1972. She has traveled the country extensively from 1985 to the present, teaching more than a million real estate agents and Home Stagers on the concept of Staging.

Barb has personally Staged and sold over five thousand homes, and holds the federally registered trademark from the U.S. and Canadian governments, Stage®. She is the only individual featured on prime time television segments about Home Staging on ABC's 20/20, *NBC's the* Today *show, the CBS Evening News, FOX News, CNN and PBS, and she's interviewed by major media outlets weekly. Recently, she was featured in* Consumer Reports, Kiplinger's Business Report, *the* New York Times *and* Entrepreneur Magazine.

As a seasoned speaker, Barb Schwarz has logged over eighteen thousand hours on the platform. Over a million people have attended her programs. Her wonderful gift for public speaking and her ability to educate, motivate and entertain was recognized by the National Speakers Association in 1990, when they awarded her the coveted designation of Certified Speaking Professional, earned by less than four hundred speakers worldwide. She has also been a featured speaker at three National Association of Realtors conventions, and is honored to represent the Staging industry at many state conventions.

Barb Schwarz is a bestselling author of her books entitled Home Staging, the Winning Way to Sell Your House for More Money, Building a Successful Home Staging Business, Speaking of Success, How to List and Sell Residential Real Estate Successfully, *and coming out soon,* Staging to Sell in a Down Market. *Her e-book is called the* S Factor. *Her DVDs* How to Stage Your Home to $ell for Top Dollar! *and* How to Price your Home to $ell for Top Dollar! *are also best sellers.*

Barb is a leader, an innovator and a truly gifted speaker who shares the wisdom of her personal triumphs. Those who experience Barb are always struck by her incredible energy, as well as the practical substance of her programs.

Nikki's Intro to Barb Schwarz's Story

I received an e-mail a number of years ago that has always stuck with me. Whether it was a true story or not doesn't really matter. The lesson is real. The e-mail told of a professor who wanted to teach his students about determining the most important things in life.

The Mayonnaise Jar and Two Cups of Coffee

When things in your life seem almost too much to handle, when twenty-four hours in a day are not enough, remember the mayonnaise jar and the two cups of coffee!

A professor stood before his philosophy class with some items in front of him. When the class began, he wordlessly picked up a very large, empty mayonnaise jar and proceeded to fill it with golf balls. He then asked the students if the jar was full. They agreed that it was.

The professor then picked up a box of pebbles and poured them into the jar, which he shook lightly. The pebbles rolled into the open areas between the golf balls. He asked the students again if the jar was full. They agreed it was.

He next picked up a box of sand and poured it in. Of course, the sand filled up all the other spaces. He asked yet again if the jar was full. The students responded with a unanimous "yes."

The professor finally produced two cups of coffee from under the table and poured the entire contents into the jar, effectively filling the empty space between the sand. The students laughed.

"Now," he said as the laughter subsided, "I want you to recognize that this jar represents your life. The golf balls are the important things—your family, your children, your health, your friends and the things you're passionate about. If everything else was lost and only they remained, your life would still be full.

"The pebbles are the other things that matter, like your job, your house and your car.

"The sand is everything else—the small stuff. If you put the sand into the jar first," he continued, "there's no room for the pebbles or the golf balls. The same goes for life. If you spend all your time and energy on the small stuff, you will never have room for the things that are important to you.

"Pay attention to the things that are really critical to your happiness. Spend time with your children. Spend time with your parents. Visit with grandparents. Take time to get medical checkups. Take your spouse out to dinner. Play another eighteen holes. There will always be time to clean the house and fix the disposal. Take care of the golf balls first—the things that really matter. Set your priorities. The rest is just sand."

One of the students raised her hand and inquired what the coffee represented. The professor smiled and said, "I'm glad you asked. The coffee just shows you that, no matter how full your life may seem, there's always room for a couple of cups of coffee with a friend."

I'm fortunate that I met a friend named Barb Schwarz, a woman who really knows how to fill a mayonnaise jar...

Barb Schwarz: My Story

Barb Schwarz

Focus

Life is an adventure. We've all heard that. And mine certainly has been. I've had strokes and have experienced some serious heart issues. Actually, I died and come back to life, but believe it or not, none of these events affected me as much as an incident in 1989. The event changed my life in a way that none other possibly could. Not because it happened to me, but because it happened to my dear daughter, Andrea.

As a ponytailed teenager, my daughter had aspirations of training to be an Olympic skier. And after six years on the slopes, she was definitely on her way. But in 1989 that all changed. One day in autumn, two weeks before her nineteenth birthday, Andrea had wrapped up a great day of competition in the Cascade Mountains in Washington. She climbed into the old Jeep of a boy she was dating, and the two of them started for home. There had been a recent snowfall, but underneath the snow was the slick residue from an ice storm. As he drove the old vehicle around a sharp corner he lost control of it on the icy surface. The Jeep jetted off the road, tumbled over the guardrail and down into a steep ravine.

Tragically, the young man had taken out the seat belt on the passenger side to work on his old car, and hadn't reinstalled it for the ride that day. Without any restraints, Andrea was thrown against the steel dashboard as the Jeep tumbled down the ravine. The intense impact caused trauma to the front lobule membrane in her head, and within a blink, her brain was damaged.

In just two weeks time she was to have started college, but in that moment everything changed forever for her. Time can stop in an instant. And in many ways time stopped that day.

Days and weeks passed, and despite the doctors', and therapists', best efforts, Andrea just wasn't making the progress we all hoped for. But regardless of the brain damage, I felt that there was something behind those vacant eyes.

I decided to look at the solution from another angle, and recognized that we all become an ingredient of the environment we live in. I gazed around Andrea's cluttered hospital room and realized that the hectic atmosphere she was in was likely causing her as much discomfort as the tubes in her throat and needles in her veins. I worked to simplify the space with calming and peaceful elements, and we quickly observed a profound improvement in her overall health and healing. Staging, which was something I had developed years before to help people sell their homes, now helped my daughter in the hospital. Staging her room for calmness worked. There was an awakening in her eyes, and I could now envision my little girl spinning around the living room with her arms stretched out and her head thrown back. In time, Andrea was discharged to my personal care.

After years of doctors' visits, hospital stays, therapy, counseling, prescribed medicines, working with a team of people genuinely concerned about Andrea, caring for her at home and having her cared for in adult family care homes, I have learned so very, very much. My daughter is like an angel on earth to me and many others. Everyone who meets Andrea loves her.

Andrea wasn't the only person affected by her surroundings. Experience had taught me years before to de-stress an environment for people who were trying to sell their homes. I called it Home Staging, and now I apply the same techniques for hospital patients like Andrea. Too much stuff can cause great stress for anyone. And stuff fills too many homes and too many hospital rooms....

It was all about the "stuff." In 1972, way before Andrea had her accident, I developed Home Staging to help people free up the space around them as they were selling their homes, so that potential customers could see and feel it. Individuals need to be able to "mentally move into" a space before they will buy it. Home Staging enables them to free up their mind, their imagination. It allows people to be focused on the important elements in their lives, unobstructed by clutter. Everything else could become the backdrop, the wallpaper in their lives.

I am dedicated to helping people rearrange their surroundings and develop creative solutions with what they already have, a practice that can be taken anywhere and everywhere. I invented it for the real estate industry, where I call it Staging to Sell, or Staging to Live. In offices, studies and shops, I call it Staging to Work. And in the hospital I call it Staging for Wellness. The special attention I put into my daughter's room and environment released the creative juices to see my Home Staging business in a whole different paradigm—in the medical world.

Then one day I woke up feeling horrible. One thing led to another, and the doctors decided to put a pacemaker in my chest to try to stabilize my heartbeat.

The next year, they decided to do another operation, to reduce the extreme atrial fibrillation I was enduring. Specialists had to make an ablation, which meant cutting through the middle of my heart so that the lower and upper chambers could work independently. With the pacemaker installed, you then live totally by battery. If the battery fails, you die.

During that operation, my heart decided to stop beating. I share with you that I experienced what I call "going to the other side." It was an event beyond words. There I felt totally safe and free. If you have lost anyone in your family, I want you to know that, from my perspective, they are safe and happy and free.

I do not know how long I was on the "other side" but I will admit I did not want to return. I feel that I got actually kicked back to life so that I could carry on my work of "Staging the world."

I say that humbly and honestly. I truly feel I am here for a purpose, and that you are here for a purpose, too. My purpose is to help others and share what I know with people striving to help or heal themselves. In essence, I was given a second crack at life.

I feel so blessed to be able to speak and teach Home Staging. I feel so blessed to have such a wonderful loving daughter. I feel blessed to be alive. It has taken me thirty-five years to get on ABC's *20/20,* the *Today* show, PBS, and more. It's taken years to write my bestselling books. Yet that's what our time here is for—for each of us to continue to grow, become more than we ever thought we could be.

The past is gone and the future unknown, so the best we can do is live in the moment. I learned this from Andrea. She taught me to develop a turtle's hard shell in order to block out the detrimental elements, and focus on life's true essence. I call being alive going to "life school," for there are so many lessons to learn here on earth along the way. I was given a gift—to appreciate the simplified, positive elements in our lives. Of course, there are still *concerns* for my daughter, for clients, for my health, for world issues, but I choose to eliminate the *worry*.

I know it's a cliché, but the saying "What doesn't kill you just makes you stronger" is more accurate than anyone could imagine. The other day, when I went to get my prescriptions filled, the pharmacist said to me, "You know why I admire you?"

I replied, "I have no idea."

He continued, "You never complain, you do things you should not be able to do, and nothing stops you."

That is one of the nicest things anyone ever said to me.

My journey, like yours, continues. I share with you that no matter what we feel we've already accomplished, or not, our best is yet to be. Keep on going. Keep on growing. Keep on living your dreams and making them come true.

For the greatest gift you can give others is the gift of you.

To be successful, you need to...

Have a hard shell... **Make Sure You Are Focused**

Reduce the clutter

Nikki's Perspective: I was getting so stressed by many minor issues in my life until my parents were diagnosed with cancer. Abruptly I realized that household chores, arguments over silly problems, what people thought of me, or traffic jams really didn't matter. The diagnoses made me rethink where I should be focusing my energy and concern. Whenever I'm confronted by these insignificant issues now, I'm reminded of what is most important and what really deserves my care and attention.

Your Tools for Success: What in your life is bringing you emotional clutter? Take the time today to really determine the issues that are giving you stress, but don't have an intrinsic value for you, personally or professionally. Try to figure out what the important issues in your life are, and which are just wasting energy.

Pick today to free up your mind and time from these wasted issues. Write them down and see if you can actually cross them off and choose not to let them stress your life anymore. Why not put more time into the things in life that *really* matter?

_____

_____

_____

_____

_____

Commitment

Commitment

The devastation I felt after my first Olympic performance carried all the way into my next season. I dwelled on my poor performance and found my results falling further and further behind those of my peers, further and further down in the rankings. After four discouraging events in a row, I finally got to a competition in Blackcomb, British Columbia, and tearfully told my coach, Frank Bare, that I wanted to quit the sport.

Frank's response was not exactly what I expected.

"That's fine," he said with a shrug. I looked at him quizzically, but before I could get a word out, he continued, "But I first want you to come out to next week's World Cup and give me 110 percent. And then, if you still aren't happy, you can quit."

"Fine," I retorted. He obviously thought I wasn't giving it my all, and that extra effort was going to turn things around. I couldn't wait to prove him wrong.

At Breckenridge, Colorado, the next week, I made sure I was the first person to arrive for practice at the aerial site and the last to leave at the end of the day. After an exhausting day on the slopes, I would still go for a run, then hit the weights in the gym, then work on my flexibility, then review our video from the day, and finally go over my mental imagery training, to perfect my jumps in my head. I was not going to let Frank tell me that I hadn't done enough.

Well, the only shameful part of that week was the crow I had to eat after winning the World Cup. And the crow BBQ didn't stop there because, continuing my intensified, 110 percent training, I went on to win three more World Cups, the United States National Championships, the World Championships and, despite the horrendous start to my year, the season-long World Cup tour.

What my coach was trying to teach me was that, in order to continue building my hard shell, I had to make sure I was completely committed to my goals. I obviously couldn't give more than 100 percent, but Frank realized that I needed to be pushed if I was ever to fulfill potential and find out what I was really made of. I'd thought I was giving it my all, but there was so much more I had to do in order to be fully committed to achieving my dreams.

At my motivational speeches I often get the question, "How do you train the twelve hours a day it takes in order to win an Olympic medal?" I don't think most people truly understand all they themselves can accomplish until they develop their hard shell of commitment. We can all do amazing things when we really commit ourselves to a goal.

George Koblasa

Major Hollywood Cinematographer

Photo courtesy of Photography © Douglas Kirkland

George Koblasa Biography

George's passion for photography dates back to his early teens. Born in Prague, Czech Republic, in 1933, he immigrated to the United States in 1959. His interest in photography and his love of the movies brought him to Hollywood, where he spent forty years working as a film director and director of photography. During this time period he photographed scores of television movies, feature films and thousands of TV commercials. For his work he received numerous national and international awards and nominations. In 1999 Kodak named him one of the world's hundred finest cinematographers.

George is a lifetime member of the American Society of Cinematographers, a nonprofit organization founded in 1919 and based in Hollywood, though its ranks include distinguished cinematographers from around the world. Membership in this organization is by invitation only, reserved for the directors of photography who have shown an exceptional talent in their body of work.

Love of photography has stayed with George throughout his illustrious career. Although his work took him pretty much to all corners of the world, he's always glad to return to his beloved USA. For the past ten years he has made his home in Park City, Utah. With his wife, Maggie, he continues his photographic and video work while exploring the beauty of the colorful American Southwest. Many of his landscape images are displayed locally.

During ski season you can find George teaching skiing at the Park City Mountain Resort. He and his wife have six children.

Nikki's Intro to George Koblasa's Story

The first time I walked in the parade of athletes at the opening ceremonies of an Olympics, my only concern was to make sure I got on every TV camera possible. As I entered the arena, I kept searching for the CBS cameras, and would frantically wave in hopes of connecting with my family and friends back home.

I got about three-quarters of the way around the arena and came into full view of the seating section for athletes, where the majority of the competitors were already gathered. They were all decked out in their countries' colors, and many were waving their national flags. I looked around my own group and saw all the American flags, American colors and American athletes. All of a sudden the cameras no longer mattered, and I burst into tears.

The commitment I had made to get to the games was no longer just about me; now it was about my country. I recognized how fortunate I was to live in a nation that allowed me to work toward my goals. I lived in the land of opportunity, and I had pushed myself to take advantage of that opportunity.

Sometimes we forget how lucky we are to be able to work toward our dreams. Someone I know who has never taken that for granted is George Koblasa...

George Koblasa: My Story

George Koblasa
Commitment/Determination

It's hard to truly understand how unbelievable it is to be free unless you have experienced life without freedom. Growing up in Communist-controlled Czechoslovakia in the 1950s, I experienced those overbearing restraints. There was constant control in nearly every aspect of my life, and endless days when I felt like a caged animal.

My dream was to escape to Hollywood to pursue my passion of cinematography. But greater than that wish was my desire for freedom. To live free! It was the first thought I had in the morning and the last thought I had at night. I was determined to break the chains that were holding me to my native country.

It wasn't going to be easy. With every action I took, I was always thinking of how I could escape. But behind every corner were the Secret Police, waiting to knock me back down. I was even arrested and interrogated about my friendship with a man from the American Embassy. It seemed the Secret Police were onto me, and it was impossible to trust anyone. They wanted to break my hard outer shell, but it was my commitment to reaching America, the golden land of opportunity, that helped keep my shell intact. I reminded myself that there is always a way of reaching your goals; you just can't take "no" for an answer.

I finally saw my best prospect to escape in 1958, when I was granted permission for a tour around the Balkan States. The Secret Police were escorting us from country to country and watching our every move. I was determined that, if I was going to find my freedom, I had to escape now.

As we boarded a ship bound for Greece, I scoped out my possibilities and started to put into place the plans I had dreamed of for so many years. First, I found a waterproof bag for my camera. Then, knowing the water would be brutally cold, I pulled as many clothes from my tattered suitcase as I could, and proceeded to cover myself with layer upon layer. A couple hours into the cruise, I found myself alone on the ship's outer deck, and leaped over the railing into the frigid sea.

The layers of clothes that had been intended to save me quickly absorbed water and started weighing me down. I struggled to stay afloat, barely keeping my head above water. After ten minutes of floundering in the icy saltwater, my arms and legs became weak. I knew I needed my commitment to that hard shell more than ever before. If I could just keep afloat for one more minute, I might be saved, for there was a boat coming my way. I could smell that freedom I had always dreamed about.

The boat crept closer and closer, and I willed every muscle in my body to keep paddling. Then fear suddenly swept over me. What if it was actually the Secret Police, circling back to catch me? I couldn't decide if it would be worse to drown or face the consequences of my criminal actions. I decided I wouldn't surrender in any case.

The boat pulled beside me and I was quickly fished out of the water. I was ecstatic to find myself standing face-to-face with a Greek Coast Guard crew. They took me to the safety of their offices. As I sat in the cramped headquarters, I was offered my first-ever Coca-Cola. I have never savored anything that tasted so much like freedom.

At my request, I was given asylum in Greece. For fifteen months I was holed up in a refugee camp, living on less than a dollar per day. But I never gave up hope that someday I would be given a visa to enter the United States. After months of waiting, I finally received word that I was granted permanent residence in the U.S., and I boarded the ship *Transylvania* for my journey across the Atlantic. I can still vividly recall the lights of New York City and the majestic beauty of the Statue of Liberty as we approached the shores around 2:00 a.m. I couldn't take my eyes off this icon of freedom. I stood on the bow of that ship until daylight, staring at the magnificent statue, knowing this was my new home.

I was finally seeing freedom.

My journey did not end there, but my doubts did. I knew that, if my determination could help me find my sovereignty, it could unquestionably help me find my career. I was on my way to Hollywood…with my camera, my Coca-Cola and my newfound freedom.

To be successful, you need to...

Have a hard shell… **Make Sure You Are Committed**

Not one day or someday…today

Nikki's Perspective: When I retired from competitive skiing, I stopped working out. I just couldn't get myself to the gym. Couldn't get myself to go for a run. Couldn't do anything. I started gaining weight, and lost all muscle tone. I kept setting future dates to restart my diet and exercise regimen, but could always justify why today wasn't the right time to begin.

I had to turn things around in my head and ask why today *wasn't* the day. And I realized there was no real reason it wasn't. I finally grasped the fact that I couldn't wait until New Year's Day to start keeping my resolutions.

Your Tools for Success: People always talk about starting a commitment tomorrow, next week or sometime down the road. Stop the "I'll do it tomorrow" game. Where is that really going to get you? Why won't you choose today to commit to a task or a project or an undertaking?

They say what you do today will predict your future. If this was true, what would you do today?

_____

_____

_____

_____

_____

Steve Young

Legendary NFL Quarterback

Photo courtesy of the San Francisco 49ers

Steve Young Biography

Steve Young's professional football career spanned more than fifteen years in the NFL, primarily with the San Francisco 49ers, where he received numerous accolades, including Most Valuable Player of Super Bowl XXIX, Sports Illustrated *and* Sporting News *Player of the Year from 1992 to 1994, and the NFL's Most Valuable Player for 1992 and 1994. In 2005, Mr. Young was inducted into the Pro Football Hall of Fame, the first left-handed quarterback to be so honored. Mr. Young is also the highest-rated quarterback in NFL history and has the distinction of being the only signal caller in league annals to win four consecutive NFL passing titles.*

Mr. Young is now a managing director of Huntsman Gay Global Capital. Mr. Young is also a member of Huntsman Gay's Policy and Investment Committee.

Prior to his tenure at Huntsman Gay, Mr. Young was a co-founder and managing director of Sorenson Capital, a private equity fund that focused on middle market leveraged buyouts in the western United States. Previously, Mr. Young was a member in Northgate Capital, LLC, the general partner of Northgate Capital Partners, LP, a fund of funds.

Steve Young founded and chairs the Forever Young Foundation, which is actively involved in children's charities worldwide, and he's currently the broadcast host as well as former international spokesperson for the Children's Miracle Network, which has raised over a billion dollars world-wide to benefit children's hospitals.

Mr. Young has also served as corporate spokesperson for companies such as Nike, Visa, Sun Microsystems, Sprint, PowerBar and ICON Health & Fitness, and he's recently been profiled in a variety of publications such as the Wall Street Journal, Business Week, Worth Magazine, Sports Illustrated, People, Inside Sports *and* GQ.

A graduate of Brigham Young University, he earned a JD degree from the College of Law, as well as a BS in finance and political science.

Nikki's Intro to Steve Young's Story

I remember thinking that sports celebrities had it made. They somehow didn't fail like the rest of us. I, on the other hand, had a slew of failures. My parents would remind me that it wasn't a failure, but a "life experience." I wrote in my diary, "I wish I would stop having so many 'life experiences' and finally just find some successes."

A few years later, I came across a book that talked about athletes' failures and commitment. I couldn't put the book down, and quickly discovered that *everyone* has setbacks and challenges. The most successful people just kept *seeing* them as life experiences, and kept at them until they finally turned the tide. I decided that no matter how long it took me, I would learn from my life lessons and welcome them again and again until I found success.

The book I read missed on one count: it didn't include my friend Steve Young, an athlete who truly understood the meaning of commitment and took it to a whole new level...

Steve Young: My Story

Steve Young

Commitment

I pulled my Clam Box baseball cap snug over my ears and slowly walked to the rack of bats. I looked over my shoulder in hopes that the crowds behind me had somehow disappeared to chase down a fallen meteor or search out a leprechaun's pot of gold. I knew it was an absurd thought, but then again, so was my record at bat. I had gone the *entire season* without even one hit.

I had been a standout athlete in Greenwich, Connecticut, and at the beginning of the Little League season, many locals wanted to see where exactly this thirteen-year-old would land. The locally sponsored Clam Box team, coached by Peter and Paul Perry, was the "lucky" recipient.

"Lucky" to have a kid on their hands who would go 0 for 4 in one game, 0 for 3 in the next, and back to 0 for 4 after that. Game after game, after game, after game, getting a piece of that white-stitched leather ball seemed to continually escape me.

I began to dread game day. It was humiliating to step up to bat, hearing the snickering of teammates and feeling all the spectators' eyes boring into the back of my head. Kids started teasing me that maybe I should give tennis or some other sport a try. And though the coaches were encouraging, I knew that they, too, didn't hold much optimism. This, however, didn't prevent them from letting me take another swing.

Eventually, I became horrified at the thought of going to the next game. I went to my dad and told him how embarrassed I was to strike out all the time. I asked him to please not make me go. I pleaded for him to get me out of this repetitive torment. My dad wasn't going to let me just give up, though. No matter how humiliated I felt, he told me that I couldn't quit. And as much as I dreaded it, I knew he was right. Not going just wasn't an option.

So I kept showing up, and my record kept going down. By the last game of the season, I was 0 for 41. I had struck out forty-one times at bat. *Forty-one times!* Even if I had played blindfolded, you'd think I would have hit the ball at least once by chance. But here I was, sheepishly dragging myself over to home plate to take my last swing at bat for the year, and wishing everyone in the ballpark would just disappear.

Looking back, I don't know if I could really put my finger on what worked that final day. What I do know is that I loved the feeling of the ball connecting with the wood, and I wanted to do whatever it took to make sure that wasn't the last time I felt it. I committed myself to an off-season full of training.

My father pitched to me every day—regardless of rain, sleet or snow—to make sure I would never have a 1 for 42 season again. And the commitment paid off. I came back the next summer and had one of the best years of any fourteen-year-old.

There have, obviously, been some profoundly life-altering events I've experienced since my first teenage year as a Little Leaguer, but I truly don't think I've had any that were so formative. That year helped shape my perspective. I learned that if you really want something, you have to fully commit to the hard work to get it. I learned that you can't just show up and hope to hit the ball. I, unfortunately, had to learn all this the hard way. A hard way that made an impression. I don't think I've ever felt as much pressure in my entire life as I did as a thirteen-year-old stepping up to bat.

It was this pressure and difficult lesson that kept me committed to hard work for the rest of my life. This commitment has helped build a hard shell that I will never lose. Even with the natural talent I had, I learned never to rest on my laurels, because a 1 for 42 season could always be lurking around the corner. I took every game seriously; I studied, I prepared and I trained—because I was *not* going back to that humiliation. Even in my seventeenth year in the pros, I didn't want to embarrass myself. That 1 for 42 season has pushed me my whole life.

And I will always appreciate how important persistent effort is in reaching our goals. I owe the Clam Box for that lesson.

To be successful, you need to...

Have a hard shell... **Make Sure You Are Committed**

If at first...

Nikki's Perspective: Parents say that, when you give vegetables to babies for the first time, they often spit them out. They even spit them out the second and third time. But on the eighth try, they will eat them and even seem to like them. We often give up *way* too soon. I found this to be perfectly true with carrots for my daughter, Zali—the tenth time I offered them.

Your Tools for Success: Ask yourself what you have given up on this past year that you might have let go of a little too quickly. Look at the list, pick one and choose today to give it one more try. As children, we seem more determined to make things work. How old were you when you last said, "If at first I don't succeed, I'll try, try again"?

Todd English

World-renowned Celebrity Chef

Photo courtesy of courtesy of Michael Weschler

Todd English Biography

One of the most decorated, respected and charismatic chefs in the world, Todd English has enjoyed a staggering number of accolades during his remarkable career. A graduate of the Culinary Institute of America, he has established one of the best-known restaurant brands in the nation, been recognized by several of the food industry's most prestigious publications, published three critically acclaimed cookbooks, and been featured on numerous television shows.

In 1991, the James Beard Foundation named him their National Rising Star Chef, and subsequently named him Best Chef in the Northeast in 1994. In 2001, English was awarded Bon Appetit's Restaurateur of the Year award. 2001 was also the same year that People Magazine named him one of the "fifty most beautiful people." In 2005, the Todd English Collection debuted on the Home Shopping Network. English has also appeared on countless national television shows from the Today show to Top Chef, and his cooking and travel series, Food Trip with Todd English, currently airs on PBS and won him his third James Beard Award as well as his first Emmy nomination. Most recently Todd became the official chef of Delta Airlines, designing the menu for all domestic coach flights.

Todd English Enterprises includes twenty-three innovative restaurants spanning the country. English's flagship Olives restaurant, located in Charlestown, Massachusetts, has expanded to include locations in New York, Washington, D.C. and Las Vegas. Todd English Enterprises also includes three Figs locations, Bonfire Steakhouse in Boston and New York City, Tuscany at Mohegan Sun Resort in Connecticut, bluezoo at the Swan & Dolphin Resort in Orlando, Restaurant Todd English on Cunard's Queen Mary II and Queen Victoria, and KingFish Hall in Boston's Faneuil Hall Marketplace, Beso in Hollywood, The Libertine in NYC, and da Campo Osteria in Fort Lauderdale. Most recently, he opened Cha in Washington, D.C.

Nikki's Intro to Todd English's Story

On the World Cup tour, there are athletes known as "drifters." They drift back-and-forth between World Cup events and a development tour one level down known as NorAms—North American Tour—until they solidify their spot on the U.S. team or fade into the background. I was determined that, once I made it to the World level, I was never going back. I was not going to drift down and fade away.

There was only one way to ensure my place on the U.S. team, and that was to put in the training. There is a reason for the joke, "Do you know how to get to Carnegie Hall? Practice, practice, practice." Instead of jumping right on to the World Cup team, I spent longer on the NorAm tour and paid my dues. I was adamant about training harder than anyone so that, when I finally made it up there, my placement would stick.

In 1992, I finally qualified for the World Cup tour, and in 1993, I fought my way onto the A-team, the most elite level of the U.S. Ski Team. In the years following, I never went back. I had made it to the big time, and could be proud of my determination to get there.

Making it to the big time of the culinary world is fraught with even more competition. And staying at the top is even more challenging. That's why the journey was never one that Todd English took lightly. He was always shooting for the "A-team…

Todd English: My Story

Todd English

Commitment

When I got into the business it wasn't cool to be a chef. Today, we see hosted cooking shows, reality cooking shows and even whole networks dedicated to cooking. But when I was young, the desire to be a chef wasn't something you proudly declared in your high school yearbook. But regardless of the image, I loved food and I loved cooking. I came from an Italian family—how could I not?

I knew I had to experience other things, so I tried college for a few years. I realized that while it was the traditional next step, it just wasn't right for me. After floating around for a while, I admitted to myself what I knew in my gut—that I was meant to be a chef. I was fortunate enough to be able to go to cooking school and begin my culinary journey.

But school only gives you the foundation. You basically have to make the rest up yourself. I had to find my own way and figure out what my voice was in the culinary arts. How would I set myself apart from all the others starting in the same field?

I decided to venture across the pond. So, with a duffel bag, my guitar, and five hundred bucks in my pocket, I hopped a plane to experience the culinary cultures of Europe. Without much of a plan, I began knocking on doors and asking restaurant owners for work. Those were hard, long, lonely days. But one thing I was never afraid of was hard work. Beyond the work in the kitchen, I had to learn Italian, French and a little Spanish to communicate with everyone in the restaurants. It was a major challenge, but a challenge that drove me.

I returned to the U.S. and, with a touch of naiveté, decided I was going to make a profound statement. I somehow fell into that an opportunity to do so. I was supposed to be the sous-chef of a new restaurant in Boston, but due to an unforeseen circumstance, was thrust into the position of executive chef. So at the ripe old age of twenty-four, I was actually running a prestigious Boston restaurant and receiving all the press to go with it.

I can now admit that I wasn't really ready for this vast undertaking. The restaurant served breakfast, lunch and dinner, so I would arrive around 7:00 a.m. and leave at 1:00 a.m. They were impossibly long days, but I couldn't give up. Since I was already on the media's radar, I had to make sure the headlines weren't going to read "Promising, Young Chef Bit Off More Than He Could Chew." In Hollywood, they say there is no such thing as bad press. This is definitely not so in the culinary world.

And when it came to critics, they were everywhere. We don't all examine rare art every day. And we don't all study X-rays daily. So when an art expert tells us that a Van Gogh painting has exquisite brushstrokes, or a doctor tell us that we have a strain in our anterior cruciate ligament, we don't usually question their judgment. We do, however, all eat. So *everyone* is a food critic. I would toil over the stove for hours trying to create something unique for my three hundred diners that night, and all it would take was one unhappy customer to upset me, regardless of the fact that everyone else loved it. I did not want to fail in anyone's eyes.

No matter what it took, I was going to prove that I could make it as a top-notch chef. It was a huge struggle, but I was committed to the fact that I was *not* going to fail. It just wasn't an option. I played lots of sports growing up and I'd found that the real way to succeed was to put on that hard outer shell, ignore the problems and develop the stamina to go the distance. As a ball player, I was not blessed with much God-given talent, but I excelled because I would always put in one more lap or one more time at bat or one more bench press. I would spend two hours a day in a batting cage hitting baseballs until my hands went numb. I took this same neurotic commitment to the kitchen. Whether on the field or in the kitchen, I knew that the one thing I couldn't replace was hard work. What I lacked in raw talent, I made up for in perseverance.

I'm a perfectionist. Of course, this can make life quite challenging. But I always saw it as a positive, because there was no way I was going to fall short of reaching all my goals. I made Gordon Ramsey, the great but demanding chef from the TV show *Hell's Kitchen*, look like a saint. Ultimately, if there is a failure in the kitchen, it's the chef who has to pay. So if you were part of my staff and you messed up, I was in your face or throwing you out of the back of the kitchen. I expected as much of my team as I expected of myself. The one lesson I did learn, though, was never to fire a dishwasher at 7:00 p.m. on a Saturday night. Because that meant I was going to be the one washing the dishes at two in the morning.

I quickly learned that a chef wears many hats, figuratively speaking. To get the commitment I needed out of my crew, I had to motivate them to want to succeed as badly as I did. We'd all work through the burned food, the cut fingers and the pressure to deliver hot meals on time. I had to feel my staff's pain in order to motivate them to push through the obstacles. And all in all, we succeeded together.

With a pinch more naiveté and a gallon more commitment, I expanded my business and gradually opened one restaurant after another. I convinced myself that I enjoyed the hard work, until one day I realized that I had established my empire.

It was Mario Andretti who once said, "Desire is the key to motivation, but it's determination and commitment to an unrelenting pursuit of your goal—a commitment to excellence—that will enable you to attain the success you seek." Whether you're behind the wheel of a race car or a pot of linguini, dedication pays off.

To be successful, you need to...

Have a hard shell... **Make Sure You Are Committed**

Put in the time

Nikki's Perspective: Nothing replaces hard work. There has not been one thing I've done in my life where putting in the extra time by being the first person to arrive and the last to leave didn't pay off. I had a friend who never understood why I did better than she did in competition. It seemed obvious to others that it wasn't natural talent, it wasn't the opinion of the judges, and it wasn't even the difficulty of my maneuvers. It was the time I put in. If you look at every highly successful individual, I'll bet that 99 percent of the time you'll find they know to put in the extra time needed.

Your Tools for Success: Whether you are going to work, school, practice or a charitable event today, try to be the first person to arrive and the last to leave. Nothing can replace the time you put into your objectives. Make it a game with yourself to see if you can outlast that one man or woman who never seems to leave for the day. A full commitment means full time.

Keith Lockhart

Conductor, Boston Pops and
Music Director, Utah Symphony

Photo courtesy of Christian Steiner

Keith Lockhart Biography

Keith Lockhart, an acclaimed, innovative musical leader, currently serves as conductor of the world-famous Boston Pops Orchestra, music director of the Utah Symphony, and artistic director and principal conductor of the Brevard Music Center.

Lockhart was born in Poughkeepsie, New York, in 1959, and began his musical study at the age of seven. He received Bachelor's degrees in both music performance and German from Furman University in 1981, and a Master's in orchestral conducting from Carnegie Mellon University in 1983.

Named the twentieth conductor of the Boston Pops in 1995, Lockhart is only the third individual since 1930 to hold the position. During his tenure, he has recorded over seventy television performances, including thirty-eight new shows for PBS's Evening at Pops *(one Emmy-nominated), and the annual July Fourth and Holiday spectaculars. He has led the Pops on thirty-two national and four overseas tours, and in the recording of twelve albums, two of which were Grammy-nominated.*

As the Utah Symphony's leader since 1998, Lockhart oversaw an historical merger with the Utah Opera. He conducted three regional television specials, one of which received an Emmy. In 2001, he conducted the orchestra with the Mormon Tabernacle Choir in a national PBS broadcast, and led the symphony for the 2002 Olympic Winter Games opening ceremonies.

In 2007, Lockhart was named artistic director and principal conductor of the Brevard Music Center in Brevard, North Carolina. The Center is one of the nation's leading summer institutes and festivals, hosting renowned guest artists who perform as well as conduct seminars and master classes.

Lockhart has guest conducted symphony orchestras of more than twenty-five major cities around the world, and in 2006, received the Bob Hope Patriot Award from the Congressional Medal of Honor Society. For more information, please visit www.KeithLockhart.com.

Nikki's Intro to Keith Lockhart

Writing a book, particularly with so many intertwining elements, was a challenge. But writing it was not as big a challenge as publishing it. With no experience in the field, I had no idea how involved the process was. The proposal alone had about fifteen different parts, and then you had to figure out where to send it. Do you self-publish? Do you go with a literary agent? Do you send it directly to a publisher? Which firm do you send it to? With so many authors eager to have their books in print, it was difficult just getting a proposal in the hands of publishers.

Everyone seemed to know *someone* in the publishing world, but nothing seemed to pan out. Either I couldn't reach the publisher or agent, it wasn't the right genre for them, or they did not receive my submission. I was hitting roadblocks left and right, and I really questioned if I wanted to continue the process.

My mother reminded me that I didn't win any competitions the first time around, and I shouldn't get discouraged. The one thing I knew was that every time that I told people about the book, they wanted to be first in line to get their copy off the press. I had to keep trying.

So I continued to look for potential publishing avenues and kept working on my book. In one of my final contributor interviews, I spoke to a man who told me that anything valuable is worth pursing with commitment, no matter how long it takes. And about nine months later, I found my perfect publishing partner in Morgan James Publishing.

The man who inspired me to keep going was Keith Lockhart...

Keith Lockhart: My Story

Keith Lockhart

Commitment

I pushed aside the file box of correspondence for my job search. It was filled with seven years worth of rejection letters from various orchestras who didn't want me as a conductor. I had yet to land my first professional gig, and didn't want to think of the box as I sat poised to open my thirty-sixth response.

When I began my job search, right out of grad school, I naively thought I'd send out an application and the jobs would fall into my lap. I think we all would like to believe that the road to success is a smooth one, with few potholes or detours. In reality, I learned that the route is riddled with roadblocks, and it's quite easy to run out of gas along the way.

With the number of rejections I received over the years, my tank frequently read Empty, and I often asked myself if my hope was misguided. If I had inaccurately assessed my own abilities. After seven years of rejections, I began to question whether I should give up the dream and consider going back to law school, or settle for something on the academic side. Whenever this daunting question would arise, something would come back to me, something I had been told early in my conducting training by Murry Sidlin, a conductor with whom I studied at the Aspen Music Festival.

Maestro Sidlin warned us right off the bat that the vast majority of us would not be successful in this profession. His warning came with one caveat: "I do guarantee that every one of you will have at least one opportunity to break through the wall of disappointment. And my only counsel is that you may not be given a second chance, so don't blow the opportunity you are given." Taking this to heart, I realized I'd better be ready when that door opened.

I needed tenacity and a hard shell to keep knocking. It took some serious soul searching each time the door slammed closed, but I hadn't put in a decade of work for nothing. There was no sense wallowing in self-pity, and I cringed when people looked at individuals who had made it and said, "I could have done better than that guy." Such an attitude was pointless and counterproductive.

I realized that, while tenacity could mean the writing was on the wall for that one chance, it didn't mean it would automatically happen. I couldn't just stand around and wait for someone to say, "Wow, he's great!" I had to make a realistic investment in myself and my abilities, and not blindly ignore my flaws. If I was continually getting shut out, it didn't necessarily mean I was going in the wrong direction. It meant that I had to figure out how to improve my skills and be ready when someone eventually did open the door a crack. So I continued to work tireless hours to make sure I was the best conductor I could be.

I was also encouraged to continue on my mission because the competition hadn't started yet; I hadn't been invited to take part. It would have been one thing if I went to the big tournament and lost, but I was still waiting for a chance to compete. I was determined that, until I was given an opportunity to show what I could do, I would never quit.

And I had a boxful of rejection letters to prove my commitment. But I still held out hope that Maestro Sidlin had not been blowing smoke, and that I might be given that one chance to prove my skills. I flipped over that thirty-sixth envelope and stared at it with the same anticipation that welcomed each response. Although I had gotten used to the feeling of rejection, I wasn't going to give up. I tore open the flap and slowly pulled out the letter.

I had to go through it twice just to be sure I was reading it accurately. It was the crack in the door I had waited for. I was overwhelmed at the incredible out-of-body experience I felt as a result of a few words on a piece of paper. Finally, someone was knocking on *my* door rather than the other way around. I was going to have my chance in the arena. I finally had validation for the decade of my life that I had put into this. It was the most satisfying feeling, knowing that the commitment might be about to pay off.

The letter led to an interview, and the interview led to my first professional opportunity with a major symphony orchestra, as associate conductor of the Cincinnati Symphony. I was given that chance that had been promised me, and I took advantage of it when it came. From that opening, things have snowballed and I've realized the dream I pursued for so long—and been warned likely wouldn't come to fruition. I had decided from the day Maestro Sidlin gave us that warning that, when the door finally cracked, I didn't just want to push it open, I was going to find a way to knock it off its hinges. And I did!

To be successful, you need to...

Have a hard shell... **Make Sure You Are Committed**

Put it in writing

Nikki's Perspective: When I made the World Cup team, one of our first responsibilities was to write down our goals. I wrote that my goal was to win a World Cup competition that year. A teammate of mine sneered at me and said that no one wins a World Cup in their first year on the tour. She told me I should pick a more "reasonable" goal, like hers— of reaching one top-ten result, one result better than tenth place.

I left my goal as it was. I took it as a personal challenge, and to keep myself on track, I pinned the goal up next to my bed at every hotel we traveled to.

Toward the end of that first year, we competed at a contest in Inawashiro, Japan, and my teammate finally reached her goal of a top-ten result. But what I think surprised her most was the outcome of my own commitment. I also reached *my* goal that day, and won my first World Cup competition.

Your Tools for Success: Today, either give yourself a challenge or challenge a colleague, teammate or friend to decide on a certain goal with you. Write the challenge down on an index card and tape it to the wall to remind yourself of your goal. This commitment will make you accountable to your goals and responsible for your actions. Read your index card and/or check in with your friend weekly to keep yourself on track. If you aren't willing to put a goal in writing, you probably aren't really committed to achieving it.

_____

_____

_____

_____

_____

Ryan Hreljac

Child Entrepreneur and Philanthropist

Photo provided by Susan Hreljac

Ryan Hreljac Biography

Ryan Hreljac began his life of advocacy for water-poor communities in 1998. He was six years old when he determinedly focused his sights on building a single well for a dry village in Africa. The story touched hearts and launched an avalanche of media reports, films, inspirational book chapters and speaking requests that resulted in more donations and attention to water issues than he could have imagined.

In 2001, with support of family and other volunteers, Ryan established the Ryan's Well Foundation, a registered Canadian charity that helps build wells, educates children about water and sanitation, and motivates people of all ages and backgrounds to perform their own "power of one" miracles. Over the years, Ryan's foundation has received support from people such as Oprah Winfrey, the Prince of Wales, Matt Damon and Dr. Jane Goodall. Where once Ryan's mission was clean water for all of Africa, his activities have taught him more about water needs elsewhere. He has since expanded his dream to a vision of clean water for everyone on the planet.

To date, Ryan and his foundation have raised millions of dollars to support almost five hundred water projects in sixteen developing countries. Ryan's work has helped bring clean water to more than six hundred thousand people, and has triggered innumerable acts of kindness, volunteerism and philanthropy around the world.

Nikki's Intro to Ryan Hreljac's Story

There are some things in life that, no matter how young we are, are worth the commitment. For me, that commitment was helping disabled kids do gymnastics. I was a freshman in high school when I heard that my gym would be teaching young boys and girls with Down syndrome, blindness, autism and a host of other disabilities. Without hesitation, I went straight to my coach and asked if I could volunteer to help.

It was truly one of the most difficult things I ever did as a teenager. The children wouldn't listen, they had a lot of difficulties performing simple maneuvers, and a number of the kids would break down in temper tantrums. But at the end of each day, they would come up and give me the biggest hugs, and all the aggravations would just melt away. No matter how draining it was, I couldn't give up on these kids.

I would recommend that everyone experience the joy of improving other people's lives. It ends up impacting you more than those you help. I will forever value the experience of working with those children.

I can only imagine how much more significant such a commitment would be if it were helping to save people's lives. As Carl Jung wrote, "The sole purpose of human existence is to kindle a light in the darkness of near being." Ryan Hreljac doesn't have to imagine what that feels like. He lived it…

Ryan Hreljac: My Story

Ryan Hreljac

Commitment

Nine steps. That's all it took me to get to the water fountain. Nine steps. And they weren't even big steps. They were the small steps of a six-year-old. I live in Canada, and it was so easy for me to replenish and rehydrate whenever I was thirsty.

I just couldn't get my head around what my first grade teacher, Mrs. Prest, had shared with us. Children in many parts of Africa had to travel nine *miles* to get water. It wasn't even clean, fresh water, but was dirty and bad smelling, and sometimes made people sick. How was it okay for me to go nine steps to get clean water and other people had to walk nine miles to arrive at a dirty puddle that could ultimately lead to their death? I was so conflicted over the discrepancy. People were dying over something that took me a mere nine steps.

Mrs. Prest told us there were organizations that, for seventy dollars, could build a well in these disadvantaged areas to supply clean water to the local villagers. I had a spectacular idea. I would just ask my parents for the seventy dollars that was needed.

My parents, on the other hand, didn't think it was such a spectacular idea. Though they were thoroughly moved by my empathy, they weren't persuaded that there was any real conviction behind my plan. After several days of pestering, I convinced my parents that I was truly committed to helping disadvantaged children on the other side of the world. They understood the importance of the money, but wanted me to grasp the fact that it didn't just grow on trees. I would have to work around the house, vacuuming, cleaning windows and doing other odd jobs, to earn the money I needed.

For four long months I worked harder than I thought any six-year-old possibly could endure in order to earn the money for a well. Finally, my mother directed me, with cash in hand, to the local, not-for-profit organization that helped facilitate clean water projects in third world countries. When I arrived, I thrust out my sweaty palms, which held a cookie tin of crinkled bills and a dream of building a water well in a small village in Uganda. Looking back now, I can only imagine how hard it was for the volunteers there to tell this young boy that his four months of hard work didn't even come close to earning the money needed to purchase a village a well. Somehow, we'd been misinformed. It wasn't seventy dollars needed, but two thousand.

My response was simply, "Well, I guess it just means more chores." It didn't take me long to realize I was going to be an adult by the time I raised that amount of money sweeping the kitchen floor. So I decided to pursue additional means of fund-raising. Seeing my unwavering conviction to the cause, my parents came on board and helped me set up some local public speaking engagements and TV interviews to help promote my fund-raising efforts. And our efforts evidently struck a chord, because with each interview and event, more donors answered my pleas. Within twelve months I had raised the two thousand dollars needed for the well.

If I wasn't sure exactly why I made such profound efforts when I started, the reason resonated clearly with me over the next few years. Our second grade teacher, Mrs. Dillabaugh, decided to further emphasize my philanthropic efforts by setting up pen pal correspondence with the local children in Uganda where my well was built. I was paired with a young boy named Jimmy Akana. Jimmy shared stories of how he and his friends drank from the well daily and how many of them traveled up to five to ten miles on foot to obtain water for their families.

After more than a year of correspondence, Jimmy and I finally got to meet in person. In an effort to promote more awareness of the situation in Africa, I was given the opportunity to visit him and the well in northern Uganda that I had worked to fund. As I arrived, the street was lined with smiling faces. It was incredibly rewarding to see how my efforts had resulted in such joy for thousands of people.

Jimmy took my hand and led me around the village that I had heard so much about over the past year. He showed me the meager homes, the simple classrooms, the barren play yard, and lastly, the well. My well. Scrawled across the cement at the base of it were the words Ryan's Well – Funded by Ryan H. for the Community of Angolo Primary School. I saw the results of the one thing I could do to help keep thousands of people alive. I don't know if I had ever been so proud of anything in my entire life. Something that was relatively simple for me had brought so much value to so many others.

My parents certainly understood the rewards behind a committed endeavor, as well. Several years after I visited Jimmy, we learned that he had been abducted by the Lord's Resistance Army, a northern Uganda rebel group, and escaped to the home of Tom Omach, a Ugandan who worked for a local aid organization. Without much support, my family paid for his schooling, and a few years later he came to Canada and became a permanent member of my family. Jimmy has flourished as an athlete, as a student and as a Hreljac.

Jimmy now knows what its like to take nine steps to the faucet. And it's this thought that keeps me going. There are still so many people who don't know that feeling. It's for these people that I have continued the commitment. Through my foundation, we have now raised over $3 million, completed 461 water projects in 16 developing countries, and helped nearly 600,000 people. All spurred on by a mere nine steps.

To be successful, you need to...

Have a hard shell... **Make Sure You Are Committed**

Just one more

Nikki's Perspective: How many times have you said, "I gave it everything I had"? I know that I am guilty of saying it myself numerous times when there actually was still something left in me. I always picture the marathon runners or cross-country skiers who collapse just after they cross the finish line. I must admit there are many times that, when push came to shove, I really didn't give it that same marathoner finish, and found I still had a little bit more to give. I know that I would not survive if I continually fell over the finish line with nothing left in the tank every day. But I *could* be the person who reached inside to find the strength for one more step. Every time I go to the gym now, I ask myself if I could go just five more minutes—because those three hundred extra seconds each day would make a big difference in the long run.

Your Tools for Success: Go beyond what you think is possible. Many times we believe we're giving 100 percent, but we still have fuel left in the tank. Today, try to push yourself a bit further than what you consider your maximum. Every task you do today, ask yourself if you could give just a little bit more. Sometimes we have to go beyond what we think is possible to find out what we are really made of. Try adding one additional item, step or minute to your list of tasks today. If we added just five more minutes a day, five times per week, we would have put in over twenty-one extra hours by the end of the year. How many times have you said, "I wish I had one more day to finish"? There's your extra day.

Pick five tasks this month where you'll push a little harder.

_____

_____

_____

_____

_____

Brian Scudamore

Founder & CEO of 1-800-GOT-JUNK

Photo courtesy of 1-800-GOT-JUNK

Brian Scudamore Biography

Brian Scudamore is the founder and CEO of 1-800-GOT-JUNK?, a Vancouver-based franchisor dubbed one of the fastest growing companies in North America.

Brian started the company at the age of eighteen, and went on to franchise 1-800-GOT-JUNK? as a way to expand operations rapidly across North America. After several years of hypergrowth, 1-800-GOT-JUNK? now has over two hundred fifty locations in the United States, Canada and Australia.

A leading entrepreneur, Brian has received wide recognition in the North American media and business community. 1-800-GOT-JUNK? has been featured in over three thousand news stories, including articles in Fortune Magazine, CNN, Business Week and the Wall Street Journal. Crowning media achievements include an appearance on the Oprah Winfrey Show in 2003, and repeated appearances on the Dr. Phil and Rachael Ray shows. Brian also contributes a monthly column to PROFIT Magazine.

In 2004, Brian was inducted into the Young Presidents' Organization (YPO) and served as a board member for the Young Entrepreneurs' Organization (YEO). Recently Brian was very honored to have been named the 2007 International Franchise Association's Entrepreneur of the Year. He has also been recognized with a Fortune Small Business Best Bosses Award; been named a finalist in the past five years for Ernst and Young's Entrepreneur of the Year Award; and ranked in the Globe and Mail's 40 Under 40. For the past three years, BCBusiness magazine's "Best Company To Work For" ranked 1-800-GOT-JUNK? in the top two, and for two of those years, the company held the number one spot! 1-800-GOT-JUNK? was most recently honored as the second best workplace in Canada by Great Place to Work Institute Canada, a list featured in Canadian Business magazine.

As a public speaker, Brian enjoys engaging both large audiences and small groups. He was a featured speaker at the Fortune Small Business Magazine national conference in 2004. A strong believer in personal and professional development, Brian graduated from MIT's four-year Birthing of Giants program, and subsequently completed three years of the alumnae program, Gathering of Titans. He has also taken part in the first of a nine-year executive education program at Harvard University through YPO University.

Nikki's Intro to Brian Scudamore's Story

In our senior year, high school students are often invited to share an excerpt of our memories, interests and goals in the yearbook. Among a list of past events and friends' initials, I wrote "Olympics 1992." Because I was a dedicated athlete and made no secret of my dreams, everyone knew that it was my goal to make it to the 1992 Olympics to be held in Albertville, France.

Some guy had the nerve to tell me that every kid wanted to go to the Olympics and it was just a pipe dream to actually qualify. Technically, he was right. I didn't make the '92 Olympics, but it wasn't for lack of trying. But without my "pipe dream" of making the '92 Olympics, I probably wouldn't have made the '94 Olympics. I'll bet that guy didn't make the effort to truly work toward achieving *his* Olympic "pipe dream." And I certainly didn't mind waiting two years to go to the Olympic Games, and waiting four more before actually winning it. I often wonder if he remembers our conversation and regrets what he said. It feels really good to have the last laugh.

I somehow think that Brian Scudamore knows that same satisfaction…

Brian Scudamore: My Story

Brian Scudamore

Commitment

You know the game you played growing up where you would take a small pair of tweezers and 'operate' on a patient by pulling out his heart or spleen or funny bone? You needed a steady hand, because if you accidentally bumped the sides, a buzzer would sound, signaling the end of your turn. I think most parents secretly hoped the game would instill some inner urge for their children to become surgeons someday. This was all too true of my father. He *was* a transplant surgeon and would have liked nothing more than to see his son follow in his footsteps. Unfortunately for him, his son didn't have that same vision.

I've always been the type to go against the grain and take the road less traveled, much to my father's chagrin. One course short of high school graduation, I decided to drop out and start working. With a father who had hoped I'd follow in his footsteps, you can guess how happy he was with this decision. I definitely had to get out there and redeem myself in my parents' eyes. And "redeeming myself" meant at least finishing high school and going on to college.

Knowing that I had dropped out of high school, my parents certainly weren't about to pay for college. So I decided I had to get a job to pay for my education. The next day, I was in line at a McDonald's drive-through and saw a beat-up old pickup truck with plywood sides and junk practically flying out the back. On the side of the pickup, in hand-painted letters, were the words *Mark's Hauling*. I thought to myself, *You know, I could probably get out there and buy a truck of my own and start hauling junk. And I bet that would be a great way to pay for college.*

A week later, I turned eighteen, bought a beat-up truck of my own and formed my new "company"—at the time called The Rubbish Boys. I was ready to pay my way through college.

I started knocking on doors, and when I saw that someone had a pile of junk beside the alleyway or back door, I offered to haul it away for a fee. That became the basic business model.

Well, when I say you sometimes need to go against the grain, it was really my parents' grain I was going against. The business had taken off, and I envisioned how great it would become if I could just commit to the job entirely. My parents obviously didn't want me to drop out of college, but I knew in my gut it was the right thing to do. I wasn't having fun in school. I wasn't learning what I wanted to. I found I learned a lot more about business by running one.

With one year left in my undergraduate program, I made that bold decision to drop out of university. You can just imagine the look in my father's eyes when his eldest son told him, "Dad, I'm going to drop out of college to become a full-time junkman." Though he couldn't see it, I knew it was the right decision for me. He had all his Father-knows-best responses stocked, locked and ready to fire. I really didn't want to disappoint him, but knew in my heart and in my head that I had a vision for running a business, and I was determined to make it happen.

In 1997, eight years into the business, my company had grown to a million dollar enterprise. Even though I was a high school and college dropout, that didn't mean I was a slacker. I always pushed myself beyond what others thought was possible. I wanted the company to grow even quicker and surpass my already established million dollars in sales. I believed that, through franchising, we could create a brand that people in other markets could run, using our established systems.

I knew nothing about franchising, so I got out there and began talking to people with franchising expertise. Every single one told me the same thing: my type of business could not franchise. But I had a very strong determination and faith that I could do it.

I was sure it could be a success because of my clear vision. I've always felt that the best way to make sure something happens in the future is to first create that picture in your mind—just like when an athlete uses "imagery". So I created that image in my mind and stuck to that mission.

I asked the experts why they believed it couldn't be franchised, and they told me it was because of the low cost of entry. Like me, anyone could easily get into the business with a beat-up old pickup. I knew I had to establish something that my franchise partners couldn't create easily for themselves, such as the administrative and customer service side of the business. I worked to create a strong call center and a booking and dispatch system, called "JunkNet," so that my partners could focus on sales, building a fleet of great partners and growing their businesses. When I put this business model in place and went back to my franchise mentors, they all said, "You know, Brian, you may be onto something here. You may have found the answer." And sure enough, it worked.

That Operation game I played as a kid certainly didn't turn me into a surgeon. But it did teach me to build a hard shell around my commitments and go against the grain of what people thought was impossible. And these commitments have paid off. I am now proud to look in my father's eyes and tell him that this college dropout has pioneered a junk removal industry that finished the 2006 year at $106 million in sales.

I can't say that I have gotten a direct, "Brian, I'm really proud of you" from my father. But hearing from friends, family and even random strangers how proud he is of me almost means more than if I'd actually heard the words myself.

To be successful, you need to...

Have a hard shell... **Make Sure You Are Committed**

Drop the anchor

Nikki's Perspective: A few years ago, I realized that I was hiding my workout regimen. Not because I was embarrassed at how little I did. Exactly the opposite. I had a friend who would actually make me feel guilty about how much I worked out.

I'm now more embarrassed by the fact that I let this friend make me feel badly about my committed exercising. I realized that she was just feeling jealous of my efforts, and found it easier to bring me down than to face her own guilt and laziness. I really could have used her support, and I now surround myself only with friends who encourage me to reach my goals.

Your Tools for Success: Today, ask yourself if there is anyone in your life who is actually impeding your commitment. There are a host of reasons why people think you can't succeed, or don't want you to succeed. Either decide to steer clear of those friends or colleagues or tell them about your goal and how you could really use their encouragement. Often time's people don't realize that they're an anchor holding you back.

Chapter 5

Overcoming Adversities

Overcoming Adversities

I quickly learned that you can have all the focus and commitment in the world, but your hard shell isn't really complete if you don't have the ability to overcome adversities. And I ran head-on into that adversity in 1996, two years before my second Winter Olympic Games.

As the '95-'96 season progressed, I found I could almost re-create those same stellar results I had experienced just the year before, but I wasn't always the one standing on the top of the podium. Three-quarters of the way through the year, the coveted yellow jersey bib always worn by the athlete leading the World Cup tour belonged to a woman named Veronica Brenner, from Canada.

In February 1996, at a contest in Oberjoch, Germany, Veronica didn't qualify for finals. Being so close to her in the standings, I hoped this was my chance to pull ahead of her and regain the first-place ranking.

But as the year progressed, I was experiencing some pain in my lower back from a muscle spasm that just wasn't going away. I woke up the day of finals in Oberjoch and went up to my coach, Wayne Hilterbrand, and told him the muscle spasm had returned and my back was hurting quite a bit. He told me we only needed to do four jumps: two training ones and two for the contest. I agreed that I could get through them.

I went to the start of the inrun and got ready to go. I skied down the hill and up the kicker, but as I reached the top, I felt a shooting pain in my lower back as if I had just been stabbed by a knife. Though I finished my jump maneuver, I felt another searing pain upon impact.

I managed to ski away, but collapsed when I reached the bottom of the hill. I found that I couldn't bend forward in order to stand up. Our team physical therapist, Kim Nelson, rushed over to see what was wrong.

"The muscle spasm has probably flared up," he told me. "Give it a little time to see if it calms down."

Thirty minutes went by before I knew it, and Kim was back in front of me. "There's just five minutes left of training. What do you want to do?"

I looked him straight in the eye and replied, "I want to jump."

Kim literally had to brace his hands behind my back and lift me to my feet, since I couldn't bend forward without pain shooting through my body. I somehow made my way back to the top of the hill and got ready for my second required practice jump. With tears streaming down my face, and feeling anything but sure about what I was doing, I headed down the hill with an unsure feeling in the pit of my stomach.

This time, as I hit the apex of the kicker, it felt as if I had ten knives slicing into my spine. It was the sort of pain that typically drops people to their knees…and I was thirty feet up in the air, upside down. Somehow, when your life is in jeopardy, your body goes on autopilot. Pushing through the insurmountable pain, I managed two flips, then felt my feet hit the snow. The surge was excruciating and my back couldn't withstand the force. I collapsed on impact and slid to the bottom of the hill.

As I struggled to get up, I found that not only could I not bend forward. I couldn't move more than an inch in any direction. Tears now soaked my entire face and my sobbing only intensified the pain. There was nothing I could do but wait for the ski patrol to cart me off the slopes.

Because there were no good hospitals close by, the ambulance took me back to my hotel. Even my plush German bed and fluffy down duvet were no comfort. I was holed up in my hotel room for three full days because I couldn't stand long enough to get on a plane to fly back to the U.S. When I finally did head home, I had to make sure I found a flight with an empty row of seats so, I could make the trip lying down.

Once I got home, I began a tour of top spinal specialists. I went from MRIs to bone scans, radiologists' offices to orthopedics' offices, physical therapists to acupuncturists. Each stop seemed more depressing than the last. All the doctors seemed to agree that my injury was not a muscle spasm, but something called Internal Disc Disruption, caused over time by continual compression from hard landings. They explained the injury by telling me to imagine shaking up an egg until the contents became scrambled. The shell would generally remain intact except for several cracks that would leak fluids. This is basically what I did to two different discs in my spine.

The doctors also told me that once a disc was malformed, it would never go back to its original state. Without intrusive intervention, it was an injury I would have for life. Unfortunately, "intrusive intervention" meant fusing the two discs together. If I did this, I wouldn't be able to bend my lower back…which also meant no more aerials.

The alternative was to just deal with the pain. But since sitting for thirty minutes and standing for fifteen was the most I could bear, I could not foresee how I would soon be getting back to a sport that launches athletes fifty feet in the air.

Despite the grim prognosis, I tried every exercise and procedure possible. I did stabilization exercises, spent endless hours stretching my spine out in some medieval torture contraption, bobbed around in a therapy pool with twenty-five other patients three times my age, submerged my back daily in a freezing ice water bath, took fistfuls of anti-inflammatory and pain-relieving drugs, and had a six-inch needle plunged into my spine on three different occasions.

But the worst had to be when one doctor decided it might be beneficial to burn the nerves in my back so that I wouldn't feel the pain anymore. That I actually went through with the initial procedure to numb the nerves, to see if it would work, was proof that I would have done *anything* to take away the pain.

Doctor upon doctor upon doctor told me, "Nikki, you are going to have to face it, you likely won't ever ski again, never mind jump." It was after receiving this same message in my *tenth* doctor's office that I finally broke down. I had tried to remain tough and optimistic until then, but had finally reached my breaking point. I was sick of the doctors telling me a comeback wasn't possible, sick of family and friends telling me to think of the "positives," sick of constantly being in pain. I was sick of *everything*!

So there in that doctor's office, the floodgates opened and I couldn't stop the tears. I kept thinking of the little girl who'd pledged to her parents that she was going to win the Olympics someday. And now I was being told I couldn't even give that dream another try.

When the waterworks didn't subside, the doctor nervously looked around for his pad and scribbled out two prescriptions. The first was for visits to a sports psychologist, and the second was for a mild antidepressant. Despite the endless tears, I had a hard time admitting I was depressed. But it seemed so obvious to those on the outside—and to me, some years later.

As the months progressed, none of the pain subsided. In fact, despite numerous doctors' visits and countless exercises and procedures, the only thing I was losing was *hope*. After months of lying on a mattress in my living room, I started to doubt if I would ever come back from this injury. In addition to my physical and mental state, my relationships were starting to crumble. I was snapping at my parents, my friends stopped coming by, and my boyfriend and I were constantly fighting. No one wanted to be around a depressed individual.

The truth was, no one was going to pry me out of my depression until I somehow faced it myself.

The man who forced me to face it was someone I didn't know, and who didn't know me. I was flipping through a magazine one day and saw a picture of Joe Frazier, a legendary boxer who won a gold medal in the 1964 Tokyo Olympics. The caption under his picture revealed something many people don't know: that Joe had won his gold medal with a broken wrist. I figured this man needed his wrist for boxing as much as I needed my back for jumping. If he could come back from his injury, why couldn't I come back from mine?

Around the same time I came across the picture of Joe, I also stumbled upon an old, familiar poem. I was rifling through a draw and found a little orange card that I had wrapped Scotch tape around many years before. It was the poem "You Mustn't Quit," the one given to me by my role model, Cassandra Wheeler, when I was a young, struggling gymnast. I reread the poem, hoping it would offer me the same wisdom it had fifteen years earlier:

YOU MUSTN'T QUIT

When things go wrong, as they sometimes will,
When the road you're trudging seems all uphill,
When the funds are low and the debts are high,
And you want to smile, but you have to sigh,
When care is pressing you down a bit,
Rest! if you must–but never quit.

Life is queer, with its twists and turns,
As every one of us sometimes learns,
And many a failure turns about
When he might have won if he'd stuck it out;
Stick to your task, though the pace seems slow—
You may succeed with one more blow.

Success is failure turned inside out—
The silver tint of the clouds of doubt—
And you never can tell how close you are,
It may be near when it seems afar;
So stick to the fight when you're hardest hit—
It's when things seem worst that YOU MUSN'T QUIT.

-Author Unknown

I realized that if I was going to get better, I had to take action myself. Doctors and cures weren't going to magically search me out; I had to find my own solution. The poem and picture gave me the fire to start seeking out new doctors. After a great deal of searching, I found an eleventh doctor who came highly recommended and seemed quite promising. Dr. J. Rainville was based in Boston, Massachusetts.

I knew I had found the right doctor when, after explaining my injury, my sport, my aspirations, and all I had been through, Dr. Rainville never questioned if I would get back to competing. Most doctors didn't want to come within fifty feet of an athlete who regularly tossed herself off a steep ramp. But Dr. Rainville was ready to tackle this obstacle with me.

He put himself on the line by suggesting that I push through the pain, lifting heavy weights to build up the muscles in my back that would help protect those injured discs. The real issue was that I risked blowing out my discs completely by lifting these heavy weights. Dr. Rainville told me it would be the biggest undertaking of my life and I was going to have to suffer through incredible pain in order to come back.

Injections and simple stabilization exercises just weren't working. I knew I would have to take drastic measures if I was ever going to return to aerial skiing. As sure as Dr. Rainville was that I could do so, I was just as certain that I could suffer through the pain. What did I have to lose? Things didn't seem like they could be much worse.

So I met with Dr. Rainville's physical therapist and learned my newest torture regimens. Dr. Rainville wasn't kidding when he told me the process was going to be incredibly painful. To be honest, I don't think *incredibly* was a strong enough word. I was on the verge of screaming through every dead lift, back extension and rotary torso. I think this may have been the time that my teeth grinding began, because I would clench my jaw and think about that Olympic gold medal every time I had to push through the agonizing pain.

Within five months, I had built up the muscles in my back and was ready to take to the slopes. The pain never really dissipated, but it was manageable, and my spine was now strong enough to withstand the continual pounding of multiple thirty-foot-high jumps. I was back, and no one was going to tell me my dreams were impossible!

Whether it's the economy, jobs, academics, family issues or health, absolutely *everyone* has adversities. We have the choice to be the victim or the challenger, be weak or strong, have a hard shell or soft exterior. Which do you choose? There is a way around every obstacle; we just have to be tough enough to keep searching for it.

Gabe Adams

Inspirational Youth

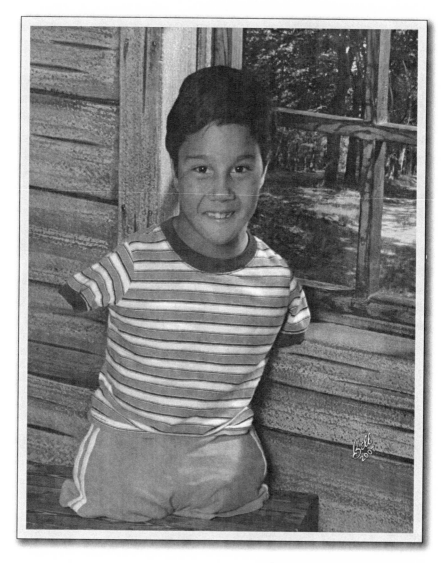

Photo provided by Janelle Adams

Gabe Adams Biography

Gabriel Leal Da Costa was born on November 16, 1998, in São Paulo, Brazil. He was born without limbs. His birth mother stated that she was in no financial or social condition to assume Gabriel's care. His father did not live with her and had another family. Gabe's mother said she hoped someone would adopt her baby.

LIMIAR, an American child advocacy organization that specializes in assisting Brazilian children, put Gabriel on their website. A psychologist for LIMIAR, Helena Sarahan, saw Gabe on March 18, 1999. She described him as "smiling!" and noted, "This is a very special child! He should not continue to live in the hospital much longer. He stays alone in his room and is therefore deprived of stimulation."

Gabriel went to live with Ronald and Janelle Adams and their family in Utah in July 1999. The Adamses had seen pictures of Gabriel on the LIMIAR website and been so impressed they decided to bring the child to live with them. There was an immediate connection, and in 2006, he was adopted by the Adams family.

Gabe has faced many challenges in his short life, apart from the obvious disabilities. At age two he had surgery for a submucous cleft palate and went through extensive speech therapy to learn how to speak clearly. He also has hearing problems and struggles with short-term memory loss. Through it all, Gabe keeps on smiling. He tackles each new challenge with hard work and determination. Gabe has learned to walk, hop, climb stairs, dance, write, draw, sing and swim, all without the use of specialized equipment. He does have a beautiful, automatic wheelchair that he loves.

Gabe is very thankful for all of the loving help he has received over the years from LIMIAR, his family, his friends, and his teams at both Shiners Hospital and the Davis County School District. There have also been many anonymous donors over the years who have blessed Gabe's life.

Nikki's Intro to Gabe Adams's Story

Several years ago, I saw a news piece about an eight-year-old boy and it blew me away. He had no arms and no legs, but he wasn't letting this adversity stand in his way. I found the clip on the Internet and forwarded it on to everyone I knew, asking for help in tracking him down. I had to meet this little boy. I tried all my networks and even tried to reach the local news station that had broadcast the story. With my contacts leading me nowhere, I swept the Internet. I couldn't find the child, but there was something impelling me to continue the search.

As a last-ditch effort, I took his last name and the town he was from and called Information myself. Maybe the old-fashioned route would work. On the second try,

I reached and spoke to Gabe Adams's mother. It had taken me months to track Gabe down. I had an easier time finding Fortune 500 CEOs and fashion icons. It seemed only appropriate that I had to jump through endless hoops to track down a boy who has had to jump through hoops since he was born.

Meeting him in person was much greater than I could have ever imagined. Gabe rolled or hopped wherever he needed to go. He wiggled his way up the stairs, and could flip a cup up with his mouth to get a drink. Regardless of the task, a smile never left his face.

Before I left, Gabe drew a picture of me with skis by holding a pencil between his shoulder and ear. I actually think it was a better depiction than I would have drawn as an eight-year-old. I still have the drawing on my fridge as inspiration to remember that absolutely *anything* is possible…

Gabe Adams: My Story

Gabe Adams

Overcoming Adversity

I sat at the end of the diving board and stared down at the water, which, quite frankly, seemed miles below. From the side of the pool came cheers from my mother, father and many brothers and sisters. "Come on, Gabe!" "You can do it!" "You're not going to quit now, are you?"

The commotion had drawn the attention of all the other swimmers. The local pool was typically abuzz, but at that moment you could hear a pin drop. Apparently, an eight-year-old boy without arms or legs, dangling off a diving board, draws a lot of attention.

I've found that attention seems to follow me. Wherever I've gone, people always see me as different. Well, not everyone. Not my family. They never let me look at myself as disabled, despite the Hanhart Syndrome I was born with. They helped me see myself as a normal boy who could find independence. I just needed a different approach to accomplish things. And maybe, more importantly, they let me figure out what that different approach might be.

I guess my parents decided that, with thirteen brothers and sisters, I'd better be able to fend for myself. It didn't mean that they had no concerns for how an adopted son was going to work his way into this active family…never mind how I would get around. But my mom told me that, even when I was very young, I wasted no time figuring out how to get what I needed. When I was eight months old, my brother Landon took my pacifier and crawled across the room to taunt me with it. With my first physical challenge in place, I rolled across the room and bit Landon on the leg until he dropped the pacifier. The "getting around" issue had already been solved.

My physical limitations were often compounded by additional challenges. With Hanhart Syndrome, I also had short-term memory loss. One day, I'd learn to climb the stairs by putting my head on a step, then slowly squirming and thrusting my torso after it. The next day, I would yell and cry at the bottom of the stairs because I had forgotten how to navigate this impossible barrier. With the help of my family, physical therapists and a whole lot of repetition, climbing stairs eventually became second nature.

Without any other people like me around to copy and learn from, I often had to invent the tools I needed as I went along. When I saw kids playing jump rope, I figured out I could hop where I needed to go. I realized I could write and draw with a pencil tucked between my head and shoulder. I even found a way to dive onto a skateboard, because that wasn't a thrill I was going to miss. Life became one huge experiment.

Everything took me a little longer to learn, but the reward was always that much greater. There were always people who assumed I couldn't accomplish something. The frustration drove me to work that much harder and prove them wrong.

Very few people thought I could swim without drowning. But my father took me to the pool again and again, and let me battle through the hard days. I adopted a motto that I carry with me for every challenge I encounter: I Can Do It with a Smile on my Face. Not only will I embrace the challenge, I'll stick with it until I have it mastered. And nearly every day, I'm supplied with a whole new challenge.

On that particular day, my challenge was plunging off the diving board. Teetering out there on the end, I had to admit it was one of the scariest adversities I'd ever had to face. I looked around at all the disbelieving people responding to the now almost jeering shouts of my family. My parents and siblings knew I wouldn't feel fulfilled until I had this checked off my list of accomplishments, until I built up my hard shell against one more adversity. And they knew I'd be even more fulfilled knowing I had proved all the cynics around the pool wrong.

I took a deep breath and bounded off the end of the board. Seconds later I splashed into the chilly water below, and that water had never felt so satisfying. I broke the surface with the always-promised smile on my face. But when I came up for air, it wasn't the silence of the other swimmers or the shouts of my family that I heard, but the overwhelming sound of applause. A sound that reminded me it was no ordinary task I had just accomplished. It was the sound of gaining my independence.

So what do I want to be someday? I really liked flying in an F16 at the Hill Air Force Base, and I loved wearing Nikki Stone's Olympic medal. So perhaps one day I'll be a jet pilot or a world-class athlete. Or maybe a teacher who inspires his students to believe that, despite their apparent limitations, the world is their oyster...arms and legs or not.

To be successful, you need to...

Have a hard shell... **Overcome Your Adversities**

If I couldn't fail

Nikki's Perspective: I hate failing. Obviously, no one likes to fail, but one event made me see that I actually feared failing, so much that I missed key opportunities.

When I first made it onto the U.S. Ski Team, I was terrified to do any interviews. The vice president of communications for the team asked me if I would do it if I knew I wouldn't fail. It seemed like a ridiculous question—until I realized I so feared failing miserably in front of the camera that I was avoiding valuable media opportunities.

I had to adopt a new attitude, so I volunteered to do the ski team's next interview. To be honest, I don't think that first interview went much better than I expected, but I really wouldn't say I failed. And the experience opened up a whole new world for me. I never would have thought that shy girl in front of the camera would now be someone who loves to get up on stage and speak to huge audiences.

Your Tools for Success: Ask yourself, "If I knew I couldn't fail, what would I try?" After you answer this question, ask yourself why it would be so awful to fail at the task or activity. We learn much more from our failures than we learn from our accomplishments.

Remind yourself that everyone fails at numerous things in life, and it's the failures and setbacks that help us grow and improve. Go out there and attempt that thing you would try if you knew you couldn't fail. Even if you do fail, you might succeed the next time.

What things would you be willing to do if you didn't worry about failing?

_____

_____

_____

_____

_____

Louis Zamperini

Olympian & WWII Prisoner of War

Photo provided by Louis Zamperini

Louis Zamperini Biography

Louis Zamperini finished eighth on the track at the 1936 Berlin Olympics, receiving special attention from Hitler himself, and was America's best finisher in the 5000 meters. His world record in the mile for school-age students lasted almost twenty years.

With the cancellation of the 1940 Games due to World War II, he joined the U.S. Air Corps, where he served with distinction in the South Pacific. When his plane went into the ocean during a reconnaissance run, he floated in a life raft on the Pacific Ocean for forty-seven days, enduring difficult weather, starvation, strafing runs by enemy planes, and shark attacks. He drifted more than two thousand miles before finally being captured and imprisoned in a Japanese prisoner of war camp. Louis endured mental and physical abuse for two and a half years before being freed at the end of the war, and returned to the United States a true American hero.

Because of a spiritual conversion during a Billy Graham crusade, Louis returned to Japan to preach the gospel of forgiveness to some of the same guards who had held him captive. As a result of his attitude and service, Louis was honored by the Japanese people and asked to be a distinguished Olympic Torch bearer during the 1998 Olympic Winter Games in Nagano. He carried the flame through his former POW camp in Souetsu, and laid flowers at the Japanese World War II memorial. Louis was featured in a forty-five-minute story of his life during the CBS network coverage of the 1998 closing ceremony. He was recently inducted into the USC Sports Hall of Fame.

The script for a feature length movie of his life is currently being produced. Ninety-two years young and still in great health, Louis regularly skis "double-diamond" runs, is learning how to play better golf, and maintains an active lifestyle in Southern California, just a stone's throw from the famous Hollywood sign. Laura Hillenbrand, the Pulitzer Prize winning author of Seabiscuit, *is writing his life story.*

Nikki's Intro to Louis Zamperini's Story

In summer training, it's tough to simulate the experience of skiing off a snow jump. The closest thing we can find is a hard-bristled plastic surface, like a big upside-down scrub brush, that we call "the meanies"—for obvious reasons if you fall. Aerial skiers are all apprehensive every time we make our way down the unstable plastic material.

I was training for a summer water-ramping competition one day, about to perform a difficult maneuver, when I caught an edge of my ski on the meanies, sending me off the side of the jump. Because I was knocked off-kilter, I didn't perform the maneuver I was intending. My coach, who was supposed to make the call on what I should do, was thrown off by my change in flight plans. I was disoriented in the air, so remained in a tucked position until I heard him yell for me to come out for my landing. His call came a second too late and I completely missed my feet, plummeting to the water on my back from fifty feet in the air.

Many people think that a water landing is much more forgiving than snow. I can tell you otherwise. I felt as if I'd been dropped on a slab of concrete. The wind was knocked out of me, I gasped for air, and proceeded to cough up blood…for two days. Unfortunately for me, the contest was also in two days, so I had no time to nurse my wounds. And there was no time to soothe my nerves. I was sore and achy and scared.

It turned out that the impending competition was all I needed to get "back on that horse." I had no time to complain; I *had* to get back up there right away. I can't imagine how hard it would have been without the urgency of a competition. It still wasn't easy mounting that "horse" again. But it was much easier for me than that *dragon* Louis Zamperini had to mount…

Louis Zamperini: My Story

Louis Zamperini

Overcoming Adversities

IN GRATEFUL MEMORY OF *First Lieutenant Louis S. Zamperini, A.S. No. 0-663341*, WHO DIED IN THE SERVICE OF HIS COUNTRY *in the Central Pacific Area, May 28, 1944.*

These were the condolences my parents received from the U.S. Army in June 1944, thirteen months after my plane went down in the Pacific during a rescue mission for a planeful of World War II American soldiers. In reality, at that time I was being tormented in my first of three Japanese POW camps.

I admit there were times when I'd wished the army was right. But now, at age ninety-two, I have vivid memories to remind me otherwise. Some people go through one life-altering event that makes them cherish their existence with a greater exuberance. I have far exceeded my quota of life-altering events and they forever changed my outlook on life. I think a cat would envy the number of lives I've had.

One life was "given up" when my plane went down, and steel wires pinned me to the wall of the cabin as it began to sink toward the ocean bottom. Another life was used up during the almost seven weeks I spent with two other survivors, afloat in two small, lashed-together yellow rafts in the middle of the Pacific, without any food or water. Another life would be "given up" in the forty-three days I spent imprisoned and beaten in a tiny island POW cell, six feet long, six feet high and thirty inches wide.

Perhaps ten to fifteen lives were "given up" to the guards that tortured me during the two years I spent in prison camps on the Japanese mainland.

I think the most improbable of the endless times I escaped death came twenty-seven days after our plane, the *Green Hornet*, went down. The only other two men to survive the crash were pilot Russell "Phil" Phillips, and tail gunner Francis "Mac" McNamara. We had been stranded on our tiny rafts for nearly four weeks when we heard the promising sound of a plane approaching. It was the third aircraft we had seen since the day we crashed. Our first two attempts to signal passing planes had ended in disappointment, but with the path and altitude this one was flying, we were hopeful we would finally be rescued. We quickly voted whether to use two flares and a packet of water dye to try to summon rescuers. Since we had already wasted several flares and a few packets of dye in the last two fruitless attempts, I decided I should also use a mirror to try to signal the plane.

Our hearts leaped as the disappearing plane circled back and started to descend. They had spotted us! We were going to be saved! We started bouncing about, flailing our arms and waving our shirts like crazed children.

What happened next was the worst thing I could imagine. The plane opened fire and we heard the sound of machine guns and the hiss of bullets piercing the raft, some missing us by a fraction of an inch. My first thought was that the idiots believed we were the enemy. Then I realized we *were* the enemy. As the aircraft approached, I saw big red circles on the wingtips, the Japanese symbol of the rising sun.

We were immediately faced with the dilemma of whether to hunker down in the rafts and risk being riddled with gunfire, or abandon ship—raft, in our case—and becoming a tasty snack for the two seven-foot sharks that perpetually circled our tiny vessel. I decided the latter was the safer option, and threw myself over the edge. Phil and Mac quickly followed suit.

After the bomber passed, we scrambled to get back in the rafts. Phil and Mac were so exhausted by the effort that I had to muscle them both in and then hoist myself after them. Unfortunately, the Japanese bomber hadn't had enough, and circled around for another go. I slid back into the water, but in Phil and Mac's weakened state, they knew they'd have drowned if they submersed themselves again.

I grabbed the raft's rope to secure my bearings, and plunged several feet below the surface. I was determined to live as I watched the bullets penetrating the canvas raft and studied the two persistent sharks circling for their dinner. I cocked my free arm back and shot my fist right into the nose of one shark, all the while trying to keep myself vertical in the ocean currents to more easily avoid the bullets.

Fearing my friends' demise, I quickly clambered back onto the now deflated raft, and was overjoyed to find that neither Phil nor Mac had been harmed. I encouraged them to sprawl out and pretend to be dead so that the bomber would finally give up. It would be another half hour before the crew finally left us alone.

On the last pass, I saw the bomb bay doors slide open and a depth charge tumble out. They obviously wanted to be fully satisfied that they had completed their mission. I held my breath, waiting for the device to explode. Not fifty feet away, the bomb hit the water, and we heard nothing but the sound of the Japanese Sally bomber sputtering away. Fortunately for us, our luck had been placed in the hands of an incompetent bombardier. He apparently hadn't armed the charge correctly, so our lives would be spared one more day.

The question was: would it be *just* one more day?

With pass after pass, continually firing, the Japanese gunners had shot out the bottom of one raft and left forty-eight bullet holes in the other. Miraculously, none of us had been hit, but we were far from safe. We all quickly realized that if we were to survive any future adversities, we would have to abandon the bottomless raft, and toil for days to patch up the other one. With the arrival of just one big storm or one adamant shark, we would have all been "goners."

Just as one fight for our lives ended, another would immediately begin. Fortunately, we had a small survival kit that included some patching material and a pump. Without a knife, and with whitecaps crashing over the sides, patching was nearly impossible. What made the task even more difficult was that we had to continually pump air into the raft in order to stay afloat.

We had to work day and night: patch and pump, patch and pump. The effort continued for eight wretched, endless days. With Phil still overcoming a head wound from the crash and Mac quickly losing hold of his sanity, I bore the brunt of the task and did most of the pumping. I don't know if I have ever worked so hard in my life.

Knowing the alternative as I did, there was no question that I would do whatever was required in order to survive. We might die someday soon, but it would not be because I gave up! Before my military career, I had competed as a runner at the 1936 Berlin Olympics. Just as in my Olympic running experience, no matter what got in my way, whether it was exhaustion, sharp elbows or sharp cleats, I would always find a way to finish the race.

We perched unsteadily on one side of the raft as we folded the opposite side over to repair the bottom. I would work on the patching and pumping, Phil would hold up the folded raft, and Mac's job was to ward off oncoming sharks with the oars. The repairs took a great deal out of all of us. With only the water we collected from rainstorms to drink, and the occasional fish or bird we caught to eat, we were losing weight rapidly. While the conditions might savage my body, they could not take away my will or my spirit. My desire to survive kept me surging forward. I'd been raised to face down any challenge.

Some people thrive in dire conditions and others fall apart. Mac, unfortunately, fell apart. After the Japanese bomber's attack, he was never the same, and slowly became weaker and weaker. On our thirty-third day at sea, Mac relinquished his last efforts for survival, and passed on quietly during the night.

Two weeks later, Phil and I floated into the Marshall Islands, which we soon found were occupied by Japanese military. We tried our best to keep out of sight, but two skeletal men rowing a half-deflated raft were no match for the patrol ships. Once we were spotted, we were immediately fished out of the drink and taken prisoner. Of course, our journey didn't end there, but we had survived our ordeal at sea. And that victory gave us strength to soldier on through any future hardships that would be thrown our way.

I knew that my years as an Olympic athlete were a large contributing factor to my success out there in the ocean, and subsequently in the POW camps. I knew it gave me the fortitude to build the hard shell that I needed to conquer all these adversities. The strength I gained through my years of running, and the commitment and discipline that I learned from my endless training, were originally meant to bring me an Olympic gold medal. But as luck would have it, it brought me something much greater—my life.

During several escapes from death, my life never "passed before my eyes," as people talk about. But when I heard the gospel from Billy Graham during my postwar years, my life *did* pass before my eyes. And when I heard the Good News, I realized there was something missing in my life, and that something was the Son of God.

"For God so loved the world, that He gave his only begotten Son, so that whosoever believeth in Him, should not perish, but have everlasting life." John 3:16

To be successful, you need to...

Have a hard shell... **Overcome Your Adversities**

Bounce back

Nikki's Perspective: When my doctor told me I was going to have to push through agonizing pain if I was ever to get back to jumping again, I knew I needed some external focus to remind me to keep my tough outer shell. The "bounce back" activity below explains why I took a Super Ball with me to the gym every day as I was working on my comeback. When I thought I reached as much pain as I could take, and wanted to give up, I would bounce my Super Ball and remind myself to stay strong.

Your Tools for Success: General George S. Patton stated, "Success is how high you bounce when you hit rock bottom." We all reach that low point at times, and need to know we can rebound. If you don't stay strong when adversity hits, you certainly aren't going to bounce back very well.

Buy yourself a Super Ball today to use as a visual reminder to keep yourself strong. When challenges present themselves, bounce your Super Ball to remind yourself to have that hard outer shell so you can bounce back. You'll notice that a cotton ball doesn't bounce back quite as well!

_____

_____

_____

_____

_____

Lance Burton

World's Leading Magician

Photo courtesy of Francis George

Lance Burton Biography

World Champion Magician Leads Magic into the Twenty-first Century!

Lance Burton's achievement is an American success story that has brought him to be known by his peers as a "magician's magician." His introduction to the world of magic began at age five, after attending a Christmas party where the featured performer was magician Harry Collins. Collins mentored Burton.

Lance entered his first competition as a junior magician at a convention in 1977 and won first prize. In 1980, Lance became the first winner of the coveted Gold Medal for Excellence from the International Brotherhood of Magicians. Lance left his Kentucky home and moved to California. Bill and Milt Larsen signed him up for their annual It's Magic! *show, which led to an appearance on* The Tonight Show *with Johnny Carson.*

Lance performed for nine years at the Folies Bergère. He entered the competition at "FISM," the Fédération Internationale des Sociétés Magiques in Lausanne, Switzerland. He honored his country on July 10, 1982, by winning the Grand Prix that recognized him as a World Champion Magician.

Lance was brought back to The Tonight Show *with Johnny Carson nine more times, and has appeared six times with Jay Leno. He was twice awarded Magician of the Year by the Academy of Magical Arts. He was honored to have performed for the late President and Mrs. Reagan in Washington, D.C. He also performed and met Her Majesty, Queen Elizabeth.*

He opened his own show at the Hacienda Hotel in Las Vegas in 1991. On May 12, 1994, Lance Burton was given the honor of having the "Mantle of Magic" passed on to him. On August 11, 1994, Lance entered into a contract to star in, produce and direct a new and lavish version of his magic show at the Las Vegas Monte Carlo Resort & Casino, which opened on June 21, 1996. In nearly every poll, Lance Burton has been voted "Best Magician" and was voted "Nevada's Best Entertainer." His charitable work mainly includes the Shriners and the Variety Club.

Lance has starred in and produced five TV specials.

Nikki's Intro to Lance Burton's Story

When I was five years old and my sister, Laura, was seven, she decided to hold a magic show, with me as her assistant. My job was to sit hidden under the cloth-covered table and make it "levitate" when I received her cue. I heard half the neighborhood file into our living room to watch the big event as I nervously waited, curled up on the floor.

Laura performed a number of tricks, to the amusement of a roomful of elementary-aged girls and boys. By the oohs and aahs, I could tell everyone was impressed. Then I heard Laura signal it was time for the big finale… "I will now make this table float in the air." Between my nerves and the heat of waiting under the tablecloth for so long, my hands were completed covered in sweat by then. I went to lift the table and it slid right off my fingertips, toppling over. I slowly looked up to see my sister's disappointed glare as the room erupted in laughter. Laura was pissed, I was humiliated, and our parents' table lay in shambles.

It was years before Laura asked for my help with a performance again. But this time she had me plan ahead for any unexpected mistakes. And luckily, no tables were harmed. I always felt that we were lucky we weren't working with any animals. Lance Burton wasn't quite so lucky...

Lance Burton: My Story

Lance Burton

Overcoming Adversities

All children have the desire to do magic—and firmly believe in it. But as we grow up, magic loses its sparkle and fantasy no longer fits our rational lifestyle. Day after day, week after week, we start making logical decisions, and eventually grow old and pride ourselves on having lived a secure life.

Thank God I never grew up!

I think as kids, we have an innate awe of magic. Love the mirrors, trapdoors, sleight of hand. Magicians are seen as sorcerers, because of how they fluidly move and speak. How they can deceive a roomful of intelligent, skeptical critics. And how they can work through mistakes and make them looked planned.

But as kids, we also accept that there will be challenges. We know it's okay if people see the bunny under the table, or the card fall out of your pocket. It's all part of experimenting. As young children, we know it's okay to fail.

This is what magic taught me. If there is ever a chance something could go wrong, it likely will. And I think I've been through them *all*. I've fallen. Split my pants. Dropped a prop. Just about anything that they say not to try, I have tried.

None was more humiliating than a performance I did in Phoenix, Arizona, back in 1984. I had been working at the Las Vegas Tropicana Hotel for nine years, and every now and then their parent company, the Ramada Corporation, invited me to perform at charity events they put on around the U.S. At this particular show in Phoenix, I decided to do a few tricks with birds. Of course, everyone says don't work with animals because they are so unpredictable. It turns out "everyone" was right.

In the middle of my act, the bird flew off into the audience. And before I knew it, a roar of laughter erupted—laughter like I'd never heard before. Knowing I needed to go find my bird, I signaled for the orchestra to stop. I ducked under the spotlight and wound my way down into the audience, and there, in the front row, found a man sitting perfectly still with my bird on his head.

I proceeded to do all I could: I grabbed the bird and pulled out a handkerchief to wipe off the man's head. Once again, the audience burst into laughter. I figured my face had to be beet-red.

After the show someone rushed up to me and asked how I planned it so perfectly to have the bird land on *that* man's head. Who *was* that man? Turns out it was Richard Schnell, the chairman of the board of the Ramada Corporation. My immediate thought was, *Uh-oh. Do I still have a job?*

During the party afterward, all anyone talked about was that bird. They all claimed it was the best magic show they'd ever seen. I found out that sometimes, when things look like a disaster, they can actually be a blessing in disguise. Here, I unexpectedly triumphed, for an incident I feared was about to ruin my career.

Once a year, I work with a youth convention, and fifty or sixty children attend my seminar. I teach them all the lessons I've learned from living through my own adversities. I remind them that failures can be minimized if you try to figure out what could go wrong and have a plan B, C and even D in mind.

But sometimes the adversities can't be helped, and in those situations, I want the kids to understand that it's okay to give ourselves permission to fail. We've all done it, and many times the setbacks teach us much more than succeeding would have. I tell the kids to ignore the adult mentality and embrace their failures.

And for those times, make sure you have a handkerchief handy.

To be successful, you need to...

Have a hard shell... **Overcome Your Adversities**

Plan for the unexpected

Nikki's Perspective: Preparing for the 1998 Olympic Games, I decided to ready myself by making every day the Olympics, regardless of whether it was a training day, a World Cup competition or the real deal. Whether I was feeling sick, the site wasn't up to par, I didn't have enough sleep or there was poor weather, I still had to imagine it was the day of the big event. I had to prepare for the unexpected. That way, I would be ready for any eventuality the Olympics actually presented. And it was a good thing I did, because those eventualities were all thrown at me when the big day came.

Your Tools for Success: Redirect your failures so they work for you. My neighbor is a pilot and he told me that a flight overseas is off course the majority of the time. The reason it gets to its destination is because the pilot is constantly readjusting to put the plane back on course.

Be a pilot who keeps making corrections to get the job done. Today, pick a project or activity you are working on and come up with three alternate plans in case something goes wrong. As with fire drills in grade school, it helps to plan several escape routes in case of an emergency. Expect the unexpected and you will never be thrown too far off course.

_____

_____

_____

_____

_____

Chris Klug

Giant Slalom Snowboard Olympic Gold Medalist and Organ Transplant Recipient

Photo provided by Chris Klug

Chris Klug Biography

In July 2000 Chris Klug received a life-saving transplant to rid himself of primary sclerosing cholangitis (PSC), a rare liver disease affecting one in ten thousand. Never one to take much time away from his competitive snowboarding career, he was back on the World Cup podium in Italy five months later. Chris is the first-ever organ transplant recipient to compete in the Olympics and win a medal.

Born November 18, 1972, in Vail, Colorado, Chris took to the slopes as soon as he could walk. The 2002 bronze medalist in Parallel Giant Slalom, he is a two-time Olympian, with many competitive credits to his name, including the 2009 U.S. National Snowboarding Champion PGS *title, ten-time* U.S. National Champion *and five-time* Snowboard World Cup winner.

In addition to snowboarding, Chris is dedicated to promoting the life-saving message of organ donation awareness in all that he does. In 2004 he founded the Chris Klug Foundation, *with the mission of educating people about the importance of organ and tissue donation. In 2009, CKF hosted fifty "Donor Dudes" high school and college campus awareness events across the country to promote the donation message.*

Chris had the honor of lighting the torch to open the 2002 U.S. Transplant Games *in Orlando, Florida. He was keynote speaker at the* 2009 World Transplant Games *in Brisbane, Australia, the largest organ donation awareness event in the world. Chris is also a* U.S. Olympic Spirit Award *winner, was named one of* Outside Magazine's *twenty-five most extraordinary people, and was voted one of "the sexiest men in sport" by* Sports Illustrated for Women.

As if he wasn't busy enough,, Chris has been working as a filmmaker and producer, first on Ride of your Life, *a documentary about what is possible after organ transplants, and currently on* Carve, *a documentary film project showcasing the sport of alpine snowboarding. In 2004 he released a book entitled* To the Edge and Back: My Story from Organ Transplant Survivor to Olympic Snowboarder.

When he's not on the mountain or working on one of his many projects, Chris is an active surfer, kiteboarder, skateboarder, mountain biker and sand volleyball player.

Nikki's Intro to Chris Klug's Story

After my second Olympic Games, I was invited to visit several children's hospitals. I still remember my first tour of St. Jude Children's Research Hospital just outside Boston. As an Olympian, I couldn't wait to inspire the young patients. I wanted to do more to raise their hopes than any celebrity they had ever met.

I was handed a mask as staff there explained the children's vulnerability to germs and diseases. Then I walked from room to room, activity to activity and conversation to conversation, expecting to find a bunch of somber faces. But a somber face was the one thing I *couldn't* find. These children had the most amazing outlook on life, though many weren't expected to make it through the year. They had all gained a new perspective on life, and weren't going to let the adversity of ill health take away the time they had here.

I'd met everyone from celebrities to Olympians to the president of the United States, but I walked out of that hospital feeling more inspired by those children than by anyone I had ever met before. Since that day, I visit children's hospitals and cancer wards every chance I get, and never cease to be inspired.

A few years later, I met a snowboarder named Chris Klug. I didn't know anything about Chris's background, but, as with the children, I was immediately drawn to his spirit. I soon learned why...

Chris Klug: My Story

Chris Klug

Overcoming Adversity

Weird numbers? What did the doctor mean when he said that my physical was showing some "weird numbers"? I was a world-class athlete. World-class athletes didn't have "weird numbers"...did they?

I'd been snowboarding on the World Cup circuit for a while and was feeling perfectly healthy when the doctors told me I had primary sclerosing cholangitis, or PSC. They didn't know if it would be in one, five or ten years, but they told me I would eventually need a liver transplant. I had never paid all that much attention to transplant lists, but I knew that bodily organs weren't on sale at my local pharmacy. Being asymptomatic, I figured that I had plenty of time, but they decided to put me on the transplant waiting list in 1994.

My dreams had always been to follow in the footsteps of my Olympic idols, speedskating greats Dan Jansen and Eric Heiden, and downhill skiing champion Bill Johnson. Four years later, it finally looked possible, as alpine snowboarding was included in the Nagano Olympics in 1998. My teammates and I were all thrust into the limelight overnight and were overwhelmed with the Olympic spirit.

After a devastating second run in Nagano, I dropped from the silver medal position down to sixth place, arriving home afterwards with an empty, unfulfilled feeling. But my experience at the games spurred on the motivation to come back in four years to capture one of those illustrious Olympic medals. However, the path to that medal would be a rocky road, and would rely on one of the bravest families I've ever met.

After the 1998 games, I was still feeling healthy, but the doctors continued to tell me the horrifying fact that this autoimmune disease was causing my body to attack itself, and the continual scarring of my liver would eventually lead to cancer. Each year, I would undergo medical procedures to clean out my bial ducts and keep me going a little longer before the inevitable transplant. Despite the repeated test results, I was sure they somehow had the wrong guy. I felt fine.

In the spring of 2000, my stubborn denial finally came to an end as my first symptoms appeared. I started feeling a bit crummy just as I was getting ready to leave for a Hawaiian surfing trip. After a few days, I realized this was more than your common flu when a shooting pain sliced deep into my lower right side. I knew exactly what sat below the layers of skin and muscle there…my liver. Apparently, the doctors didn't have the wrong guy.

Further tests would show that my liver was so scarred it was barely doing its job. Without any arguments from me, the doctors immediately advanced me to the more critical stage on the liver transplant list. I was sent back to Aspen to start my "training" for surgery. I prepared for it just as vigorously as I did for any snowboarding competition I'd ever entered. As in my snowboard races, I did visualization daily to ready myself for the race for my life.

I tried to keep up with regular exercise, but each week found I was getting sicker and sicker. I dropped from 220 pounds down to 186. Each day I lost more energy, and I was forced to think about the stats. There were 86,000 people across the country waiting for organs and fifteen died each day waiting for a transplant. I just prayed that I would be fortunate enough to make it off the list and get a second chance. And if I was given that second chance, I was certainly going to do something valuable with it.

I still remember the day I received the call that I would receive my chance. They had a liver transplant candidate for me. On July 28, 2000, I found out the candidate was a match, and the next day I would be receiving his liver. I went into the hospital on a Saturday, and by the following Wednesday, I was discharged, without any signs of infection or organ rejection. I was kept on a short leash for about three weeks and, miraculously, seven weeks later I was on my snowboard again. Any initial qualms I had about bouncing back were quickly put to rest.

Six months after that, I found myself atop the World Cup podium, and ended the competition season with four World Cup top-three finishes. A year and half later I was standing on the podium and receiving a bronze medal in the Olympic Games… in my home country. Standing on that podium, I had a wealth of emotions running through me as I remembered all it took to get to that spot.

I couldn't help but think of the family who had given me a second chance. The family who had lost a loved one but granted me a new life. Shortly after the Olympics,

I had the opportunity to meet my donor family. I was more nervous about our meeting than I had been for my Olympic race. How do you thank a family for life itself?

It took unimaginable strength to turn the tragic loss of their thirteen-year-old son into the most profound gift you could offer to five different families. None of the adversities I conquered could compare to the challenges that family faced. They were the real heroes of this process, and I am humbled daily by their decision. They gave the biggest gift you could give, and they gave it to a complete stranger.

It was a truly emotional encounter. We all shared laughter and tears. I got to hear stories about the little boy who had touched them all so deeply. They got to hear how, ultimately, he had done the same for me. And in the end, I think they understood how incredibly grateful I was for the difficult decisions they'd made, and how the Olympic medal was as much his as mine.

My experiences now have become much less about demonstrating my athletic prowess and more about proving what someone can do with the gift of life, and about encouraging everyone to share their decision with their family. One donor can save up to twenty-five lives–I'm here today because of it.

To be successful, you need to...

Have a hard shell… **Overcome Your Adversities**

Stop the downward spiral

Nikki's Perspective: While I was recuperating from my spinal injury, depressive and negative thoughts were the biggest anchor dragging me down. Because I was feeling low, I didn't exercise as much as I should, and because I didn't work out, I was feeling down. When I forced myself to do the things I typically loved, however, I found that endorphins energized the rest of my day.

Many years later, during that tiring period after my baby was born, I discovered that taking the same "me time" helped me to be more motivated and more productive throughout the rest of the day. I found I could be a better mom, businesswoman and person in general.

Your Tools for Success: Stop the negative cycle that adversities can provoke. When we get down on ourselves, we tend to spiral lower and lower, until it's difficult to pull out of the depression. When you find yourself thinking negatively this week, choose one activity—such as exercise, meditating or writing in a journal—do until you're thinking positively again. Taking a break can also help you clear your head and come in with a fresh attitude.

Many people worry about "wasting time" in performing such an activity, but you'll discover that much more time is wasted thinking negatively. Besides, feeling sorry for yourself never got anyone anywhere.

_____

_____

_____

_____

_____

Orrin Hudson

Chess for Life Lessons Teacher

Photo courtesy of BeSomeone.org

Orrin Hudson Biography

Orrin C. Hudson owes his life to a teacher. The seventh of thirteen children, Orrin found his early years difficult. He was in and out of foster homes and involved in petty crime, until James Edge, a white teacher in an all black high school, saw the potential in Orrin. Mr. Edge sat him down and showed him that his actions had consequences. He taught Orrin how to play chess and win in life. Voted "Most Likely to Succeed" and "Outstanding Student" in his senior year, Orrin stepped into the world and began to exceed those predictions.

When Orrin made the move to develop his potential, life took on new meaning for him. As an adult, he served as an Alabama state trooper for six years, developing the discipline needed to become a winner. He later owned and operated a car dealership, succeeding once again, as a business and community leader. Being the best continued to be a large part of Orrin's personal developmental strategy. He gleaned back-to-back victories when he defeated the Alabama State chess champion two years in a row, and later beat one of the top Russian grand masters, a chess player who had won more tournaments in the U.S. than anyone at the time.

Orrin began to teach others how to think strategically, plan effectively and build self-confidence, using chess as his vehicle. Remembering how Abraham Lincoln's mother's advice, "Be someone," had helped Lincoln aspire to the White House, Hudson used that simple, yet monumental concept to his fullest advantage, naming his non profit organization Be Someone, Inc. *Focusing his talents on children, he began teaching others to "be someone" through his award winning, highly effective and much lauded presentations.*

Nikki's Intro to Orrin Hudson's Story

Through my work with Right To Play, I met an amazing gentleman named Safari. Safari lived through the Rwandan genocide of 1994, where nearly a million people were killed, including many of his friends and family. Safari had to hide out so as not to be slaughtered as well, and he desperately tried to escape several times. Finally, after much hardship, he fled to a refugee camp in the Congo.

Though he was now safe, his life continued to disintegrate. Safari turned to drugs, stopped attending school and basically dissociated himself from society. The trauma had taken away his will to survive and fight for what once meant so much to him.

Life in the refugee camp was quite dismal. But the one bright part of Safari's day was when he joined some of the other refugees for pickup basketball games. Through playing basketball, Safari began to remember the importance of goals, cooperation, confidence, teamwork, respect, responsibility, commitment and fair play. He couldn't believe how much the sport gave him. Basketball turned his life around.

Safari eventually went back to Rwanda and worked with Right To Play to set up and run sport and play programs in refugee camps. He wanted to give back to sport and help other children overcome their horrific past.

Those disadvantages don't just exist half a world away. I recently met a man who wants to make that same difference for children in the United States. I guarantee you'll see a movie made about Orrin Hudson someday…

Orrin Hudson: My Story

Orrin Hudson

Overcoming Adversities

"Breaking news," I recall the reporter saying. And her tragic report that day would change my life.

It was May 24, 2000. The images flashed across the screen. Seven people had been shot in the head during a robbery…for a meager two thousand dollars. And that said it all.

I had been a state trooper for six years and was continually being sent in to pick up the pieces after people made the wrong choices and wrong decisions. But after so many years on the job, I didn't see the penal system making a difference for these individuals. They would go into prison and come out with a harder edge and a more criminal mind.

I just couldn't stand by and wait to see how someone who shot seven people for two thousand bucks was going to come out the backside of the legal system. I had to do my part. I had to take preventative action. So, shortly after I heard that jarring news report, I set out to create a crime prevention program that would force young adults to think about the moves they made before their actions landed them behind bars.

And, remembering an experience I had had thirty years before, I immediately knew what I could do to make a difference for these youths. As a young boy in the South, I attended an all-black high school. When I walked in my introductory day, the first person who approached me was a Caucasian teacher named Mr. James Edge. I would come to learn that his race didn't matter, but his words would. I must have looked completely hopeless, because before I knew it, he had pulled me aside, grabbed my shoulders and told me, "Every move you make has consequences." My forehead crinkled as I asked him what he meant.

"Well, I can show you." He smiled, pulled a chair up to a chessboard and invited me to join him.

Over the next several months, he showed me how the moves on a chessboard could be directly related to life. He showed me that if you make every move count, you can find success. He explained that on a chessboard and in life, black and white are the same—no one is better than you are, and it's all in the moves you make. If you make good decisions, you get good results. Mr. Edge's lessons taught me that no matter what my background was, I could make the right moves to be someone.

Be Someone. It was the perfect name for my new program. Be Someone would engage children to learn chess rather than the ways of the street. I was going to make a difference by teaching kids to think it out, rather than shoot it out—and push pawns rather than drugs. But the main reason I started the program was to teach these young adults that the new currency on the planet was KASH with a "K". Knowledge, Attitude, Skills and Habits. And when you get this type of cash, no one can take it away. It was important for youths to realize that we don't have to cheat in order to get the things we wanted in life.

All the life lessons my students needed were falling into place:

- **Stay focused**: If you are distracted from the board or your goals in life, you are the one who pays.

- **Resource management**: In chess and in life, you hear all about the resources everyone else has, but it's about how you use *your* resources that counts.

- **Time management**: In chess there's a clock, and in life there's an hourglass measuring out our seconds on this earth. You have to develop and use what you have where you are. You can't worry about the past; you have to deal with what is in front of you *now*.

Be ready for change: Situations are constantly changing in chess and in life, so you have to deal with what is in front of you.

- **Make advances:** You have to continually move toward your goals. When you stop moving, the issues you don't want are the ones that take over.

- **Maintain:** It's important to know that you just can't give up. The main concept is to stay in the game. Many kids fear that if they make a mistake, they're going to lose. It's vital for them to understand that it's okay to lose, because you are actually learning through the process. You often gain more from losing than you do from winning.

- **No one is better than you:** If you make the right moves, you get the right results. You have to want to reach your goals just as badly as your competitors do theirs, if not more so.

- **There's always more to learn:** School is never out. Chess and life are all about learning, and you succeed from learning. There is always more to master.

- **Have fun:** Maybe most importantly, kids needed to know that learning can be enjoyable.

If I ever had any doubts about whether the initiative could work, they've been all laid to rest. The continual stories of my kids' success keep me motivated, none more than that of an eighteen-year-old boy with a rap sheet as long as my arm.

Several years ago, the boy's father had just been released from prison after twenty years behind bars. When he arrived home, things became heated and a fight ensued. The boy nearly killed his father and almost went to jail for attempted murder. After hearing his story, I knew I wanted to help that boy. Each day, I taught him the lessons of the chessboard, and not long after we began working together, he won first place in the statewide Georgia Association for Alternative Education program. The boy is now a productive citizen rather than behind bars. It was all about teaching him that if he picked the right move, he could get the right results.

I can now proudly say that I have taught thousands of kids like my young prodigy to think it out rather than shoot it out. And, as rewarding as I originally thought it was to bring troubled youths to jail, that was nothing compared to curing their troubles.

I no longer wear my state trooper badge, but I'm continually inspired by the prospect of instilling a sense of justice in our youths. I have seen the results of putting kids on the right side of the track by timely intervention, helping them turn their lives around. I couldn't possibly think of anything more important to do.

I'm living my dream. And I'm helping these youths see the advantage of getting their names on the lists of America's Most Accomplished rather than America's Most Wanted.

To be successful, you need to...

Have a hard shell... **Overcome Your Adversities**

Reward the comebacks

Nikki's Perspective: Through personal development coaching of people in business, I worked with a client who was discouraged over losing a big customer because of the failing economy. Instead of harping on the loss, I congratulated my client and applauded his ability to keep his other clients despite his difficult situation. Too many people look at the negative rather than the positive. Putting the attention back on the positive allowed my client to keep forging forward to overcome future obstacles, rather than crumbling under their weight.

Your Tools for Success: Try rewarding yourself or others today for overcoming a particular setback. Things could always be worse, and we should be proud of averting disaster.

We continually applaud the successes in life, but don't spend much time rewarding the comebacks, which are often harder to accomplish. By rewarding ourselves and others for overcoming adversities, we are more likely to stick with a project and not give up when faced with challenges. And in offering praise to others, you will find that praise is returned.

_____

_____

_____

_____

_____

Chapter 6

Confidence

Confidence

After a year dealing with my injury, I was back on the slopes in time for the 1997 World Championships in Nagano, Japan, site of the following year's Winter Olympic Games. I couldn't wait to show the world that Nikki Stone was back. What I didn't realize was that the world hadn't waited while Nikki Stone was recuperating.

Competing with the same jumps I had perfected before my injury, I found that many of my fellow athletes had increased their degree of difficulty and were performing more advanced jumps. Even if I executed my maneuvers perfectly, it would still be a long shot for me to make it to the podium. I ended the World Championship finals in eleventh place.

Now, I'm not stupid. I knew eleventh place was a long way from where I needed to be in order to stand atop that dreamed of podium.

Rubbing salt in my wounds, a sports journalist wrote, "Nikki Stone will never stand on the podium again." *Ouch!* I had two options: feel sorry for myself and fall victim to what the reporter had to say. Or prove him wrong by sticking my neck out and believing in myself.

I decided to take that second option and prove that journalist wrong. I was going to build my confidence to do some of those more difficult jumps so that he would have to eat his words. *No one* was going to count me out.

Coming back from such a severe injury, I had a big task in front of me. I was trying to instill confidence in myself at a time when I was just rebounding from my lowest low. I had to remember that I was actually jumping again when ten doctors had told me it wouldn't be possible. That alone was something to be proud of.

But I did know that, to accomplish my goals, I needed to step up my game. Doing harder jumps was going to prove to be just as big a challenge since I was so afraid of heights. Double flips require you to jump thirty feet high. To do triple flips, I would have to launch myself fifty feet in the air—the height of a five-story building. I felt queasy looking down from such a height. How was I going to tackle this timidity? I had to concentrate on my successful acrobatic and landing abilities, and try to ignore my fear of heights.

As I continued preparing for the Olympics, I realized the jumps weren't the only thing I needed to change. My practice had to be much different than it was four years earlier. I knew it was important to keep my peripheral vision on the competition, but if I was only worrying about *their* training, I wouldn't be focusing enough on my *own* practice. If I was in a sprinting race and turned around to see what the other runners were doing, they would blow by me. I had to keep looking forward and worry about my own progress, pushing full steam ahead.

Finding my strengths and determining my most appropriate preparations gave me the confidence I needed. And my confidence gave me a shot at proving that journalist wrong.

Confidence is *not* something we are born with. It's something we develop. We all have the ability to develop confidence. We have to be willing to stick our neck out, knowing that we may feel a bit uncomfortable at first. But it will pay off.

As Peter T. Mcintyre said, "Confidence comes not from always being right, but from not fearing to be wrong."

Tommy Hilfiger

World-famous Fashion Designer

Photo courtesy of Richard Phibbs

Tommy Hilfiger Biography

For over twenty years, Tommy Hilfiger has brought Classic American Cool apparel to consumers around the world. His designs give time-honored classics a fresh look for today's consumers, and his discerning taste has provided the foundation for the growth of a global brand. Under Hilfiger's guidance, vision and leadership as principal designer, the Tommy Hilfiger Group has become one of very few globally recognized designer brands offering a wide range of American-inspired apparel and accessories.

Born the second of nine children, in Elmira, New York, Hilfiger first realized his philosophy in 1969, in high school, when he opened his own small chain of stores called People's Place. His goal was to bring big-city fashion from New York and London to his local community in upstate New York. Self-taught, he soon began designing the clothes that his customers wanted but could not find, and in 1979, he moved to New York City to pursue a career as a fashion designer.

In New York, Hilfiger caught the eye of Mohan Murjani, a businessman who was looking to launch a line of men's clothing and believed that Hilfiger's entrepreneurial background gave him the unique ability to approach men's fashion in a new way. With Murjani's support, Hilfiger introduced his first signature collection in 1985 by modernizing button-down shirts, chinos, and other time-honored classics—and immediately struck a chord with consumers. The relaxed, youthful attitude of his first designs has remained a distinctive hallmark throughout all of Hilfiger's subsequent collections.

In 1995, Hilfiger launched the Tommy Hilfiger Corporate Foundation to enrich the physical and intellectual well-being of youth, with a major emphasis on education and cultural programs that impact a diverse population.

Hilfiger is actively involved in a number of charities and causes, including the Washington D.C. Martin Luther King, Jr. National Memorial Project Foundation and the Anti-Defamation League. He has also served on the board of directors for the Fresh Air Fund, a New York-based group that has been sending underprivileged children to summer camp since 1877, and the Race to Erase MS (Multiple Sclerosis) since 1994.

Nikki's Intro to Tommy Hilfiger's Story

When I returned to competition following my spinal injury, I found sports journalists were not the only people who had written me off. I had to convince my sponsors that I was still worth my salt. Believe me, sponsors don't just take your word that they should bank on you with their valuable marketing dollars. And since my injury, I had yet to produce any results to demonstrate that I might be an Olympic medalist a short nine months later.

I knew I had to prove that I still had it in me to be the best, which meant I had to first believe it myself. I had to learn to do the more difficult jumps, perfect the maneuvers and land them, in less than three-quarters of a year. I think I may have been one of the few people who actually believed that I could do all that in such a short time.

To prove how confident I was, I had to be creative with my contracts with sponsors. Before my injury, the majority of my contracts were "retainers," where sponsorship dollars were set in advance and delivered up front. Sponsors knew my abilities and were willing to pay for the likely results. To prove my belief in my own post-injury skills, I had to accept a "victory schedule" contract, where they would pay me each time I ended with a top-three finish, the big bucks coming if I landed on the Olympic podium.

With my only source of income being my sponsor payments, and absolutely no recent podium finishes, it took a large amount of bravado for me to choose this path. I couldn't wait to prove to sponsors that they should have banked on me with the advanced set retainer, because I had every intention of landing on the podium every week.

I bet there are a great many people who wish they had banked on Tommy Hilfiger way back when…

Tommy Hilfiger: My Story

Tommy Hilfiger

Confidence

Sitting on the New York subway, I could feel the wad of cash tucked in my back pocket—one hundred fifty dollars. I was eighteen years old, and it was my life savings. Everyone had told me the money was barely enough to buy a couple knockoff Rolex watches, but I was headed into the Big Apple to prove them all wrong. I was going to open my own blue jean shop.

The only people who weren't mocking my meager bill roll were the ones assuring me there was no way I could open a store without any retail experience, schooling or knowledge. The train screeched to a halt at Grand Central Station and a smile spread across my face. I was confident that I could somehow make it work.

I wound my way through the bright yellow cabs in search of the garment district. I spent the better part of the day searching for the best product, and before I knew it, my bundle of cash had been turned into an armful of jeans—twenty pairs. Satisfied with my purchases, I hopped the train back to Elmira, New York, and started the exciting task of setting up shop. I began with grapevine, word-of-mouth marketing to spread the word that my jean shop, People's Place, was going to be open for business the following Saturday.

By Sunday evening, I had sold every last pair of jeans. I took my profits and restocked the store for my next surge of customers. People's Place had made its mark and the denim was flying off the shelves quicker than I could hop the train back to New York City to replenish my supply. Within months of my eighteenth birthday, I had a thriving business that stunned all the naysayers.

The quick success of my business gave me the extra boost of self-esteem I needed to tackle the next round of skeptics. I just knew that I was destined to do more. I wanted to start my own designer line. My critics scoffed that I may have been successful with a little denim shop, but starting a fashion line without design school training and a large supply of cash, I would never be able to compete against the top names.

As hard as people tried to suck the life out of me, I fought even harder to stick my neck out and prove them wrong. I sold my business, for very little money, and set out to get the "required" experience that everyone said I needed. I was quickly hired to work at Jordache Jeans, and just as quickly fired when they found out I didn't have any structured design education. Shortly after my stint at Jordache, Bonjour Jeans decided to jump on the bandwagon and fire me as well. The only thing I was proving was that I was one of the most fireable men in design.

You wouldn't believe how many people told me I had to do everything by the book. But Bill Gates never cracked that "book," Einstein didn't know it existed, and I chose to follow them and leave "the book" on the shelf. I realized that many of my critics might just have lacked the confidence they needed to step out of the "structure," so it was easier for them to try to hold others back from doing so. Fortunately for me, I had always sensed I didn't need to do what everyone else did in order to be successful.

I felt in my bones that I could make this design business happen. We all have the choice to see the glass as half empty or half full. I always saw it as half full, with a refill on the side. I would set lofty goals, picture myself achieving them, and once I set the next goal, find myself landing the first one.

The same positive energy that propelled me to release the Tommy Hilfiger design line just a few years after selling my little Elmira jeans business gave me the motivation I needed to make sure the line succeeded. And within six or seven years, I was competing with, and surpassing, those companies that had fired me for inadequate experience several years before.

It's that same confidence that has pushed me through every new challenge I encountered. I know the critics will be back to try once again to break me when I work to shatter the next mold—by creating the Tommy Hilfiger Hotel. Luckily, I've got a spirit that can't be easily broken.

Sticking to my guns has changed my life. I can now say that the pocket of my pants has become much more important than the cash it holds.

To be successful, you need to...

Be willing to stick your neck out... **Believe in Yourself**

Positive affirmations and visualization

Nikki's Perspective: When I was training for the Olympics, one of the activities I did was to run, trying to build up my stamina for the entire season. Running became my sanctuary, and I used the time to remotivate myself for the upcoming year. I would rebuild my confidence by visualizing a perfect Olympic performance. But I wouldn't stop there. The real inspiration came through the thoughts of standing on the Olympic podium and receiving my medal. I imagined the crowds, the noisemakers, the music playing. I even imagined the interviews I would do after my exhilarating win. I often found myself smiling as I was running through the streets. When I finally got to the Olympics, my positive visualizations helped set the stage for an experience that was more exciting than my wildest dreams.

Your Tools for Success: Pick a positive future goal or thought to repeat today to instill confidence in yourself. This doesn't mean you have to spend the day chanting in front of a mirror, "I feel good. I feel great. I feel wonderful"—unless, of course, this works for you. But you should continually imagine a positive outcome to your goals. Successful individuals often visualize a perfect outcome hundreds or even thousands of times before they actually attempt a task.

Try to visualize a scenario today where you are reaching your ultimate objective. You need to imagine the sights, smells and sounds. Try to internalize the situation and see the scene through your own eyes rather than watching yourself from outside. You can literally break apart perceived walls and change your perception of the possibilities. You become the director, producer and actor of your own outcomes, from academic to career to healthy lifestyle goals. It's amazing what you can accomplish with positive thoughts.

Bob Baffert

Kentucky Derby-winning Thoroughbred Trainer

Photo provided by Jill Baffert

Bob Baffert Biography

Bob Baffert is widely recognized as one of the most successful trainers in the history of horseracing.

Through the years, Bob Baffert has registered numerous major stakes victories, earned a multitude of awards and received accolades galore, all stemming from his drive to succeed and his knack of being able to elicit the very best that an equine athlete has to give.

Bob Baffert, along with owners Bob and Beverly Lewis, struck gold with Silver Charm. An $85,000 purchase, Silver Charm earned $6,944,369 before being retired to stud. Silver Charm's racing career was highlighted by victories in the Kentucky Derby and Preakness Stakes in 1997, and the rich Dubai World Cup in 1998.

After coming within three-quarters of a length of sweeping the coveted Triple Crown with Silver Charm in 1997 for the Lewises, Bob Baffert came even closer to Triple Crown glory the following year, with Mike Pegram's Real Quiet. Real Quiet won the Kentucky Derby and Preakness before losing the Belmont Stakes by a scant nose.

Bob Baffert thus became the first person in the history of Thoroughbred racing to train Kentucky Derby and Preakness winners in back-to-back years.

Captain Steve became another success story for the owner-trainer team of Baffert and Pegram. A $70,000 purchase, Captain Steve won the Dubai World Cup in 2001 and earned $6,828,356 during his racing career, helping Baffert become the United States Champion Trainer by earnings for the fourth year in a row.

In 2001, Bob Baffert again won two-thirds of the Triple Crown—the Preakness and Belmont—this time with Point Given. That year he became the first Thoroughbred in history to win four straight races worth $1 million or more.

War Emblem likewise won two-thirds of the Triple Crown for Bob Baffert in 2003. War Emblem won the Kentucky Derby, as a 20 to 1 longshot, the Preakness and the Haskell Invitational Handicap.

Bob Baffert's winning history continued in 2007 and 2008, with horses winning the Breeders' Cup Juvenile Fillies in 2007, the Breeders' Cup Juvenile in 2008 and the Breeders' Cup Sprint in 2007 and 2008.

Bob Baffert was voted the Eclipse Award as the sport's outstanding trainer three times—1997, 1998 and 1999—and in 2007, Baffert was named to the Lone Star Park Hall of Fame.

Nikki's Intro to Bob Baffert's Story

My first World Cup competition was in Blackcomb, British Columbia. Because the U.S. team had too many athletes, I was allowed to compete to gain experience, but my result wouldn't count. Being the rookie of the tour, I wasn't familiar with any of the common practices. I felt I was constantly in people's way, and timidly stood off to the side, feeling as if I didn't belong.

The contest was on Saturday and I couldn't wait for the week to be over. When I finally got to the competition, my jumps felt fair, but certainly not my best. Because my score wouldn't count, the organizers decided not to announce my results. I left the hill feeling not much better than I had all week.

That evening, our coach came up to where I was sitting in the restaurant and said, "Congratulations." It was obvious from my puzzled look that I had no idea what he was talking about, so he added, "Your score would have been good enough for third place."

In that moment, everything changed. I was no longer that lost, out-of-place girl, I was an athlete who had the potential to win a World Cup. I'd been unsure of myself, but then found out I could have been third, and realized I might have what it takes to win. Suddenly I belonged.

It seems funny that, with all his accomplishments, Bob Baffert ever shared that unsure feeling. It's nice to know that I'm in good company...

Bob Baffert: My Story

Bob Baffert

Confidence

The Kentucky Derby has always been my Mount Everest, the pinnacle of success. I remember reading when I was growing up about legendary trainers like Charlie Whittingham and Laz Barrera. Never in my wildest dreams could this cattle rancher's son believe I would have that kind of success.

Even as I gained experience, I still couldn't imagine playing with the "big boys" as a Thoroughbred trainer. So when I started out, it was with my first love, quarter horses. In 1986, my horse Gold Coast Express won the Champion of Champions quarter horse race against some more experienced horses. That win gave me the confidence I needed to start believing I might have what it takes to rub shoulders with some of the training greats. Winning that race the second time around solidified my feelings. Anyone can win once by luck, but when you win twice you have something concrete to feel confident about.

The Kentucky Derby wasn't even on my radar screen when I made the transition to training Thoroughbreds. The first one I bought was a big gray horse named Thirty Slews. His name came from the fact that I paid thirty thousand dollars for him as a yearling. It might as well have been thirty million, considering I didn't really have an owner for him and it was a huge amount of money at the time. I was in the game, but on the ground floor. I was competing against the best horses and most established trainers. It was hard not to compare myself to them and their successes, so I committed to sticking with a game plan that would work for me.

It paid off when Thirty Slews won the Breeder's Cup Sprint in 1992. My first Thoroughbred purchase had taken me to the big dance and I was hooked. It was an unbelievable confidence builder. Race by race, with steady strides, I began building my foundation in the Thoroughbred business.

Four years later, I found myself on that grandest of stages, the Kentucky Derby— racing's Holy Grail. That year a gelding named Cavonnier had shown great promise, but after a series of defeats I was losing faith in his ability. I decided to give him one more chance in the Santa Anita Derby, the final prep race in California for the Kentucky Derby. Like people, horses need their confidence boosted from time to time. I was hoping a good showing there would be just what my horse needed.

Cavonnier was coming into the race in great shape. During the race, he sat just off the leaders. Coming into the far turn he was stuck behind a couple other horses. I saw that his jockey, Chris McCarron, had a ton of horse and that Cavonnier was crying out for more distance. When they turned for home, Cavonnier was still behind and I was thinking *Please let something open up so he can get by.* Finally, McCarron found the opening needed and ran by the other horses. Cavonnier won by four or five lengths. He had just punched our ticket to the Kentucky Derby.

A week later I headed east to Louisville. When I drove up to Churchill Downs and got my first glimpse of the famous twin spires, I felt like a kid in a candy store. It literally sent chills down my spine.

Any nerves I was feeling during the two weeks leading up to the big day were easily overshadowed by my overwhelming excitement. I was at the Kentucky Derby! Not only that, but reporters actually wanted to talk to me about Cavonnier's eye-catching win at Santa Anita. Unbridled's Song was the favorite that year. For every three or four reporters outside my barn, there were two hundred outside his. Even so, their presence validated the confidence I was feeling in my horse.

You can't imagine the energy at the Kentucky Derby. When the big day finally arrived we walked onto the track to the sound of thousands of cheering fans. Never mind that they were cheering for Unbridled's Song, who was walking beside us. It was surreal to me. Here I was, this guy from Nogales, Arizona, walking into the Kentucky Derby next to a champion racehorse. Reality shook me. I was living my dream.

They say the Derby is the most exciting two minutes in sports. When you have a horse in the race, it's also the longest. As the gates opened, Cavonnier took up his familiar position just off the leaders. When the field turned for home, he made a powerful move. Seconds later Cavonnier was in front and I was in shock. I kept thinking, *Oh my God, we could win this thing!* When your horse takes the lead in the home stretch of the Kentucky Derby you just aren't prepared for the overwhelming emotions. A feeling of elation took over my whole body as I gripped the rail in front of me and let out a bloodcurdling roar. It was the hardest I have ever cheered for a horse in my life.

As quickly as it started, my euphoria turned to disbelief. With less than a hundred yards to run another horse was coming like a shot down the center of the track. I prayed for the finish line. When they reached it the horses were head to head. Had Cavonnier held on? I wasn't sure. It seemed like an eternity as the crowd stood silently waiting for officials to hang the photo. In those moments, I thought to myself, *I may have won the Kentucky Derby!* Right then, I understood why people are willing to pay so much money for Thoroughbreds. You can't put a price tag on what I was feeling.

They showed the replay over and over while we waited. Each time, I came to a different conclusion. Chris McCarron was making his way back around the track on Cavonnier. The minute I saw his face, I had my answer. Cavonnier had been beaten. After five agonizing minutes, the tote board made it official. Cavonnier was second. It was the cruelest of defeats.

I couldn't stop the wrenching pain in my gut. I can't imagine anything worse in this sport than thinking you've won the Kentucky Derby, then finding out you haven't. I didn't think I'd ever be able to stop asking myself "What if?"

Rarely in life are we given more than one chance to get it right. I felt I had been given an unbelievable opportunity and let it slip through my fingers. I never lost confidence in my ability, but in my heart I knew how hard it would be to get that perfect combination of luck, talent and timing that it would take to get me back to Louisville on the first Saturday in May. Instead of wallowing in self-pity, I jokingly told anyone who would listen that I might not have gotten the roses, but I walked away knowing what it felt like to win the Derby, if only for a moment.

The next few months were hard. Little did I know a cure for my Derby blues was already in my hands. His name was Silver Charm.

I had bought the gunmetal-gray colt the week of Cavonnier's Derby. And it didn't take long for me to realize he was something special. Almost unbelievably, we found ourselves back in the Derby the next year. This time I had a raging fire burning in my belly that wouldn't be quenched. I put all doubts aside and trained with as much confidence as I was capable. I didn't have the Derby favorite, but now I had the faith.

When the field turned for home, jockey Gary Stevens had Silver Charm in a good spot. At the sixteenth pole, they took the lead. When I looked back, I couldn't believe my eyes. The favorite, Captain Bodgit, was gaining ground with every stride. "Please don't do this to me again," I heard myself saying. But Silver Charm was a warrior, and I knew he wouldn't let the other horse so much as look him in the eye. As soon as

Silver Charm saw Captain Bodgit, he leaped forward with an extra surge. When he hit the wire, there was no doubt. We had won! Vindication was mine!

It was an extremely emotional day. The feelings of disappointment and regret that had been gnawing at me for a year were gone, replaced by sheer happiness. I had won the Kentucky Derby. That day, I stood alongside my parents and felt a profound sense of gratitude to them. They had instilled in me, and my six siblings, a strong work ethic and the confidence of knowing that hard work will be rewarded.

The very next year I won the Kentucky Derby again, with a seventeen thousand dollar horse named Real Quiet. And in 2002, I won my third Kentucky Derby, with War Emblem. I would never again doubt my belief in myself or my ability to stick my neck out.

By winning both the Derby and the Preakness, those three horses each gave me a shot at winning a Triple Crown. Each time, victory eluded me in the Belmont. Even though I walked away from those losses—and a five million dollar bonus—with a certain emptiness, I can honestly say nothing in my career has hurt worse than Cavonnier's loss in the Derby. I'm thankful for that experience and the lessons it taught me.

Life and horses have been good to me. For that I am truly blessed.

To be successful, you need to...

Be willing to stick your neck out... **Believe in Yourself**

Personal Strengths

Nikki's Perspective: Softball is definitely not my forte. When my husband and I first met, he asked me to come play in the local softball league because they needed more women. I was so bad that I would ask to be put at the end of the roster in hopes they wouldn't make it to my turn at bat. If I just looked at batting abilities, I'd feel like a failure as an athlete. But, luckily, I have my own capabilities—and ball sports aren't it! It took me awhile to realize I was much better at strength, agility and acrobatic sports than I was at ones requiring hand-eye coordination. When I figured this out, I found that as long as I could get to first base, I was quite good at stealing bases and actually had something I could contribute to the team.

Your Tools for Success: Focus on your own strengths. We all have our strong points and we need to remind ourselves of these attributes. Create a list today of all the personal traits that give you confidence. Everyone has strengths and weaknesses, and knowing your strengths will help you compensate for your shortcomings.

It also helps to know your personal capabilities when you are working with others. You will find a group is much more productive when everyone knows where and how they can contribute the most. And you can learn how to improve your weaknesses by watching someone else demonstrate a task in a more effective way.

_____

_____

_____

_____

_____

John Naber

Olympic Swimming Medalist and Motivational Speaker

Photo provided by John Naber

John Naber Biography

John Naber is more than a champion swimmer. After earning five Olympic medals in 1976, he was honored as the nation's outstanding amateur athlete, was inducted into the U.S. Olympic Hall of Fame, and served as director and Olympic flag bearer at the games in Los Angeles. He has carried the Olympic Flame in four different Olympic Torch Relays.

He was twice elected as president of the U.S. Olympians, and was chosen in a USA Today *nationwide poll as the male captain of the Xerox 100 Golden Olympians, an all-star collection of the country's greatest Olympic champions.*

Professionally, he is an "observer of excellence." As a celebrity, he's met with business and political leaders, and as a television announcer, he's covered over thirty different Olympic sports, filing reports from nine Olympic Games, including the recent Olympic Games in Athens, Greece.

Along the way, John has discovered the method champions in all walks of life use to reach their goals, and he shares this process with audiences around the globe. His books Awaken the Olympian Within *and* Eureka: How Innovation Changes the Olympics and Everything Else *have earned rave reviews from the Olympic and professional community, as well as various bestselling authors and motivators.*

Nikki's Intro to John Naber's Story

A year after I retired from aerial skiing, I was asked to go on a promotional barnstorming tour for Delta Airlines. We traveled from city to city, and I would say a few words to the press and audience at each stop. Landing in Los Angeles, we were joined by a few other Olympians, one of whom was John Naber.

After hearing me speak, John asked me if I'd consider pursuing a career as a public speaker. I didn't know if I had any talent in that area, or if I had a story to tell. He invited me to come hear him speak, offered me a world of advice and encouragement, and assured me I had a lot to offer. John helped launch my career as a motivational speaker, and all he asked in return was that I pass on advice and encouragement to others.

John evidently learned how to "pay it forward" from *his* experiences as an unsure, young boy in high school…

John Naber: My Story

John Naber

Confidence

I started my swimming career as a high school freshman, because I happened to be sitting in Algebra class next to Jeff Stites. He was a silver medal winner at the recent Junior Olympics, thereby earning the title of the second fastest thirteen/fourteen year-old backstroker in the country. I was in awe of the kid, and when he invited me to join the swim team, I jumped at the chance.

That first season, I avoided swimming the backstroke, as that was Jeff's territory. Besides, I wanted to win races, not swim in Jeff's shadow. That year I earned my first Most Improved award, and later that summer, the club coach suggested in earnest that, due to my flexibility, I might be a great backstroker if I just gave it a try. Sure enough, in my first two backstroke races, at a "B" level competition, I turned in two "AA" times, winning both novice events. My times were so fast that a parent of one of the other swimmers lodged a protest, assuming I was a ringer in the meet.

The coach had been proved right, but I still had Jeff to contend with.

During my sophomore year, I closed the gap a little, and earned my second Most Improved award, but Jeff was still the "big man on campus." Over the summer, I showed some serious improvement, and was looking forward to training with Jeff in the varsity lanes. Sadly, due to mandatory school busing, in our junior year Jeff enrolled in the crosstown high school. Now we were going to be opponents, not teammates—and though I still held Jeff in high regard, I thought I'd have to improve without help from him. That spurred me on in practice.

Sadly, the day before the first dual meet of the season, I was clowning around on a diving board, and fell off it sideways, landing on the concrete gutter and breaking my right collarbone. The doctors declared that I would not recover before the end of the season.

Not wishing to be a drain on the team, I volunteered as an assistant swim coach, and helped run workouts and plan lineups, all the way to the league championships.

As expected, Jeff Stites won the backstroke title, and I watched his swim from the bleachers, sitting next to his girlfriend, Corinne. After the awards presentation, he sat down on her other side, holding the gold medallion in his hand.

"You know, John," Jeff said carefully, "I'm sure that if you had been in the water this season, you most certainly would have won today's race, so I think you should have this." And he placed the gold medal in my hand.

Stunned, I shook my head. "I can't keep this, Jeff," I protested. "You earned it, and it's rightfully yours."

At that moment, Corinne leaned forward, and with a tear in her eye, said, "John, you have to take it. It's all he's been talking about for the past three weeks."

When Jeff gave me that medallion, he wasn't merely conceding the race. He was urging me to think of myself as the best backstroker in the area and, by extension, someday the best backstroker in the state, nation and world. It was almost as if he was saying, "Stick your neck out. You can do this! Go on! Swim like the wind!"

On that day, Jeff gave me the confidence to see myself as "the man to beat," not the man trying to climb the ladder. Jeff gave me the gift of self-esteem, and the support of a teammate who wanted me to go further and faster than he had ever gone before.

I thought of Jeff as I won my medals at the Montreal Olympic Games. His selfless tribute in high school started me on a path that ended with four Olympic medals. His gesture was a gift of faith. To this day, that medallion means more to me than any national or world title I ever earned.

To be successful, you need to...

Be willing to stick your neck out... **Believe in Yourself**

Confidence Log

Nikki's Perspective: Leading into my second Olympics, I read that one of my greatest role models, Dan Jansen, kept a journal of everything he did: how much he slept, what he ate, energy levels, emotional stress, pain felt, communication, etc. I learned that Dan kept track of each training day and each competition so that he could look back and see which things were enhancing his performance and which things weren't. I adapted the journaling for my personal needs, coming up with a log where I could input what went well and what I could improve. I found doing so forced me to think more positively and gave me a point of reference when I looked back to important milestones.

Your Tools for Success: Let today be the day you start journaling to recognize what you do well and what you can improve. Each day, write down one thing you did well that day and one thing you could improve on. It's often easy to see the achievements and improvements others make, but we have to take the time to recognize that regardless of what we are going through, we can change, too. Build your confidence by getting to know and appreciate yourself.

Day	What did I do well today?	What can I improve?
Monday		
Tuesday		
Wednesday		
Thursday		
Friday		

_____

_____

_____

_____

_____

Rick Searfoss

NASA Astronaut and Certified Speaking Professional

Photo provided by Rick Searfoss

Rick Searfoss Biography

Colonel Rick Searfoss shares with only a handful of people in history the sublime joys of flying in space. In his career he has led many different teams, including commanding the most complex science research space mission ever, the STS-90 Neurolab flight on Columbia. He also piloted two other space flights, including a joint Russian-American mission to the Mir space station.

Prior to becoming an astronaut Colonel Searfoss was a fighter pilot and test pilot in the U.S. Air Force, with over 5800 hours flying time in 71 different types of aircraft. A distinguished graduate of the U.S. Air Force Fighter Weapons School and the U.S. Naval Test Pilot School, he currently is director of flight operations for XCOR Aerospace (www. xcor.com), where he has test-flown two unique rocket-propelled prototype aircraft, and works with the development team of the Lynx suborbital space plane, for which he will be the first test pilot.

Rick is active on the corporate speaking circuit as a high-content expert on leadership, teamwork, innovation and peak performance (www.astronautspeaker.com). He is among an elite group of professional speakers awarded the National Speakers Association's highest designation, Certified Speaking Professional. His mission: sharing the teamwork, leadership and innovation lessons of human space flight, while bringing the wonder of space down to earth for all to enjoy.

Colonel Searfoss completed a Bachelor of Science degree in aeronautical engineering from the USAF Academy, and a Master of Science degree in aeronautics from the California Institute of Technology on a National Science Foundation Fellowship. He attended USAF Squadron Officer School, Air Command and Staff College, and Air War College.

His numerous awards include the Harmon, Fairchild, Price and Tober Awards as the number one overall, academic, engineering, and aeronautical engineering graduate in his USAF Academy class; USAF Squadron Officer's School Commandant's Trophy as top graduate; Tactical Air Command F-111 Instructor Pilot of the Year; Outstanding Young Men of America; Air Force Meritorious Service Medal; Defense Superior Service Medal; NASA Exceptional Service Medal; NASA Outstanding Leadership Medal; Distinguished Flying Cross; and the Legion of Merit.

Nikki's Intro to Rick Searfoss's Story

Experienced athletes often like to say that we could execute a maneuver or skill with our eyes closed. Aerialists have to perform each new trick hundreds of times into a pool before we're ever allowed to perform it on snow. So by the time the end of the summer rolls around, we've done so many jumps most of us feel our bodies could almost respond automatically…even while blindfolded.

Despite this confidence, no aerial skier would actually try doing so. Well, no one except Eric Bergoust. My teammate and fellow gold medalist decided he was going to prove that his abundant training could allow him to jump blindfolded.

Another jumper wrapped a scarf tightly around Eric's eyes and pushed him onto the inrun. The rest of us thought Eric was crazy, but with reckless abandon he demonstrated his faith in his training. He soared off the jump, flipped over twice in the air and landed on his skis in the water.

Eric performed his stunt again in the weekly aerial show. This time, in addition to the blindfold, he had his wrists handcuffed behind his back.

Sometimes in life we don't get to plan when the death-defying maneuvers are going to come. Just ask Rick Searfoss...

Rick Searfoss: My Story

Rick Searfoss

Confidence

We were all plastered against our seats at three g's—three times our normal weight—and I was hoping for a textbook launch so I could basically keep my hands in my lap as the Shuttle *Atlantis* approached orbit. With the powerful engines pushing us, we were all along for the "ride."

It was 1996 and my second space launch. I was the pilot for this crew of veterans. We had all been through the challenging years of preparation. Been through the demanding, endless hours in the simulator. We had all felt the burden of the pressure suits, weighed down with seventy pounds of gear. We had all experienced the phenomenon of space, and had survived past missions.

The thousands of hours spent in the simulator were meant for the very rare occasion when the possibility of surviving was thrown into question. And that became reality on this launch, moving at twenty-two times the speed of sound just thirty seconds prior to the planned shutdown of the main engines.

As the pilot, I was responsible for the main engine performance, the small rocket engine, plus the hydraulic, electrical, reaction control and orbital maneuvering systems. If you think a jet pilot has a lot of procedures to be aware of, try stepping into the pilot's seat on a space shuttle. I was expected to be on top of *everything*.

We were seconds away from the main engine scheduled shutdown, and still pressed against our seats, when the radio crackled. "PLT, execute hydraulic leak procedure of system two," a voice from mission control said. Team members on the ground have much more detailed information than we do in our cramped cockpit. There's at least one person monitoring each system. Evidently, we had a leak to take care of, and since "PLT" stood for "pilot," it meant the problem fell on my shoulders. I pulled the information about the hydraulic system up on the primary system monitor to look at it. Sure enough, the data showed a potentially catastrophic leak.

So, at three times my normal weight, I began to execute the hydraulic leak procedure. Everything needed to be executed perfectly. Every switch had to be right, every movement exact. There were three different systems, and if the wrong one was shut down…well, put it this way, I wouldn't be here telling the story. There was absolutely no room for screwing up, and it all required critical split-second decisions. The scene was right out of a box office thriller—alarms going off because we had lost so much fluid, while I was simultaneously conversing on the radio and flipping switches. Under the g forces, I had to move my head slowly and methodically to avoid vertigo. Further, with the bulky pressure suit, my movements were limited. Despite the impediments, I managed to stop the leak. And, working with mission control, developed a plan to safely operate the remaining hydraulic systems for reentry.

When I finally had a chance to exhale, the thing that surprised me most wasn't that we'd encountered this system failure, but that I hadn't had one iota of fear in the process. Like a professional athlete, I was "in the zone." So much preparation went into the mission that the result was like that Nike slogan—you Just Do It! You simply don't have time to think about anything but executing your job perfectly, and your training has prepared you to do just that.

Two months prior to the launch I had grown somewhat tired of the constant training and retraining. After one fourteen-hour day, I vented to our commander, Kevin Chilton, saying, "Can't we cut back on the simulations? We're all way ahead of where we need to be."

Without hesitation, he responded, "No, this is an opportunity to get even better. We need to overprepare. We need to leave no stone unturned. When you think you've got it all figured out, then hit it from another angle."

Even at the time, I knew he was right and that this extensive training would ready us for any type of emergency we might encounter.

The benefit of all that training was that the response was almost mechanical. It needed to be a 10.0, with no time to calculate the possibilities. I had to be hyperaware of the subtleties, and I executed just what I was trained for. An athlete making a minor error might lose a medal or a trophy. If I made a minor error, I could have lost the lives of my shipmates.

It wasn't until the drama ended that I actually got nervous. I was just so relieved that I had had the confidence to quickly and decisively take the necessary action. The confidence to stick my neck out when I needed to.

I've come to realize that we are continually challenged with high-tension situations, and success is completely reliant on whether we can perform effectively when they're thrown in front of us. I developed a process for dealing with such challenges, summarized by the acronym PACE:

Preparation
Awareness
Confidence
Execution **E**xcellence

I used PACE to guide my teams and me to achieve at the highest levels, when it really counts, regardless of how dynamic, difficult or even dangerous the situation.

The best foundation for meeting any challenge is having a solid knowledge base and depth of experience—in my case, as an astronaut, my many previous years as a fighter pilot and test pilot, coupled with the most intense crew training imaginable. Only with excessive *preparation*, whether managing the complexities of a spacecraft with over two million parts, or a modern, complex organization, will a leader have sufficient *awareness* to rapidly, yet effectively, analyze every nuance of potential actions. Over time, that leads to the right balance of maintaining and exuding *confidence* in the heat of battle, so one develops the keen analytical capabilities to properly assess the situation—threats, opportunities, ramifications—and make the correct choices. I found that confidence must be tempered with the recognition of our own imperfections. We need to constantly fight complacency or overconfidence, because there is always someone out there taking things one step further. In my business, complacency means you die.

The result is *execution excellence* in closing that last little gap between an adequate and an exceptional performance. I've found that it's in the toughest last couple of percentage points where people usually fall short and don't close the execution gap. When you're 95% done with a project, you have 50% left to go. We can't slack off at the finish line.

Our journey on *Atlantis* didn't end after those tension-filled first few minutes. We still needed the confidence and awareness to get our hides back home. The space shuttle was intended to reenter and land with all three hydraulic systems helping. Although we could reenter with just two, we would at that point be just one failure away from almost certain disaster. We had only enough fluid remaining in our third system to support the most crucial part, the landing itself, so we reentered the atmosphere and flew most of the way home on two systems. Just before landing, I completed yet another "off-nominal" procedure to repower the third system for touchdown. Again, the rehearsals came into play, and with our belief in one another, we landed *Atlantis* safely. To this day, Mission STS--76 has been the only time a space shuttle has reentered using just two of the three hydraulic systems, making it perhaps the riskiest return ever.

There were high fives all around as we made our way out of the cockpit. You can only imagine the excitement of seeing your family after such a dramatic mission. I always think of how challenging it must be for those left waiting for their father, mother, husband, daughter or son to come home. I'm grateful that through a robust, intense preparation process I was able to build the awareness, confidence and execution excellence to do my part in bringing my crewmates home safely to their loved ones.

To be successful, you need to...

Be willing to stick your neck out... **Believe in Yourself**

Practice for Pressure

Nikki's Perspective: I had never been more nervous about making a speech than I was at my hometown parade after my Olympic win. My old high school was filled with family, friends, teachers and a townful of supporters. It was the first time I was given the opportunity to publicly thank all those people who had supported me along the way. I didn't realize how much pressure I would feel or how emotional I'd become. At the first "thank you" I uttered, the tears began to flow and my mind went completely blank.

Knowing how much these acknowledgments meant to me, I didn't want to forget to thank *anyone*, so I had put in a full day of additional speech practice. Despite the pressure of the moment, I felt confident that I could get through the presentation because of all the preparation I'd put in. Without a pause, the names came pouring out of my mouth. Not one person was forgotten, and I walked away having learned the best secret for combating pressures: practice.

Activity: People often lack confidence when it's most important: in the heat of a critical moment, when the adrenaline is really pumping. It's much easier to demonstrate self-assurance when the pressure isn't on. Ask yourself if you have what it takes to perform when you're in a truly stressful situation. How many dry runs have you been through to ensure a resounding yes to that question? If something is important enough to be nervous about, then it's important enough to rehearse repeatedly. Before your next nerve-racking event, try rehearsing your performance three to five more times than you normally would. You will be amazed at your self-confidence when you walk into a situation fully prepared. And when your nerves kick in, it feels much better knowing you have rehearsed to a level where you're almost going on autopilot.

Bill Drayton

Top Social Entrepreneur and World Changer

Photo courtesy of Yusuke Abe (Japan)

Bill Drayton Biography

Bill Drayton is a social entrepreneur. As a student at Harvard, Balliol College in Oxford University, and Yale Law School, he founded a number of organizations, such as Harvard's Ashoka Table, an interdisciplinary weekly forum in the social sciences.

In 1970, he graduated from Yale Law School and began his career at McKinsey and Company in New York. From 1977 to 1981, Mr. Drayton served as assistant administrator at the U.S. Environmental Protection Agency, where he launched emissions trading—the basis of the Kyoto Protocol—among other reforms.

In 1981, while working part-time at McKinsey and Company in New York, he launched both Ashoka and Save EPA, and its successor, Environmental Safety. With the support he received unexpectedly when elected a MacArthur Fellow in 1984, he was able to devote himself fully to Ashoka. Mr. Drayton is currently chairman and chief executive officer of Ashoka: Innovators for the Public. He is also chair of Youth Venture, Community Greens, and Get America Working!

Mr. Drayton has won numerous awards and honors throughout his career. In 2005, he was selected as one of America's Best Leaders by U.S. News & World Report *and Harvard's Center for Public Leadership. In 2006, he was recognized as being one of Harvard University's hundred most influential alumni. In 2007, he received the Duke University Center for the Advancement of Social Entrepreneurship's (CASE) Leadership in Social Entrepreneurship Award, the University of Pennsylvania Law School's 2007 Honorary Fellow Award, and the Goi Peace Foundation's Peace Award. In 2008, he was recognized by Tuft University's Institute for Global Leadership with the Dr. Jean Mayer Global Citizenship Award, and Americans for Informed Democracy's Social Innovator in Smart Investing Award.*

Nikki's Intro to Bill Drayton's Story

When I was thirteen years old, I went through the rebellion that most adolescents do. I got in a big fight with my family and told them I didn't care if I lived or died.

My grandmother was sitting there, and the comment floored her. Nanny looked me straight in the eye and said, "Don't ever say that, because the reason I'm okay with passing on someday is the fact that I know I'll be carried on through you. You have too many things still to accomplish.

It was one of those statements she likely doesn't remember saying, but it stuck with me all these years. Her words gave me a confidence I'd never felt before. She had put power in my hands and I had to do something with it.

I know that, when my grandmother does pass on, she will be proud of the fact that I didn't let the belief she instilled in me go to waste. No doubt Bill Drayton will also be proud of the legacy he someday leaves behind…

Bill Drayton: My Story

Bill Drayton

Confidence

"I want to change the world!"

It's a statement every young person believes is possible. But somehow, as we grow into adulthood, we lose the confidence to believe we can make a difference in society. Our mission must be to make sure that children and young adults don't lose this conviction. We need everyone to know he or she can be a changemaker.

I was given that gift growing up. No one squashed my dreams. I knew before leaving grade school that I could organize and build things, that I could make a difference. I set my own goals, and fortunately, no one ever shook my confidence by telling me achieving them wasn't possible. My family sometimes worried, but they hid it well.

In elementary school, I started a newspaper that eventually served multiple schools. It gave all of us a voice, and helped build my confidence. In high school, I established the Asia Society, to expand our school's cultural horizons and familiarize students with the needs and challenges of two-thirds of the world's population. Later, I organized a third of my law school classmates to provoke change by serving legislatures across the Northeast, through Yale Legislative Services.

It became increasingly obvious that a big idea is the most powerful force in the world—if it is in the hands of a strong, confident entrepreneur. Many people have this potential. What if we could tear down the walls that tell people they cannot change the world? What if, instead, we encouraged them to dream and helped them to fly? In 1980, we created Ashoka: Innovators for the Public, with the goal of generating this profound transformation in society.

Ashoka seeks out changemakers who are looking to create new, pattern-changing solutions for improving the lives of millions of people. We knew these social entrepreneurs would, in both very hands-on and highly collaborative ways, make hugely valuable changes actually fly. To succeed, they must persuade thousands of others in thousands of communities to give themselves permission to organize and press the entrepreneur's vision forward. They also are pulling the world's citizen sector up to an entrepreneurial and competitive level equal to that of the world's business sector.

We've now helped thousands of individuals run with their ideas. For example, Ashoka Global Academy member Muhammad Yunus, who founded the Grameen Bank in Bangladesh and was awarded the Nobel Peace Prize in 2006, has more recently shifted his focus to encouraging social business. In 2003, Ashoka helped bring him together with Ashoka social entrepreneurs working in this area, which is key to long-term poverty alleviation. The results, including shared insights that helped accelerate change on several continents, illustrate why our community of social entrepreneurs working together is so much more powerful than the sum of the parts.

It's magical when we can help individuals see the horizon and make their dreams the new reality. They have the ability to change institutions, people and emblematic thinking. The essence of that ability is that they know they can. They believe in a vision, and they know they will make it happen. They also draw power from the deep satisfaction of knowing they will be leaving something that will last beyond their years on this planet.

All of us gain strength as we get to know these marvelous changemakers. One example is Ashoka Fellow Zackie Achmat, in South Africa. He founded the Treatment Action Campaign, which holds the state accountable to its constitutional obligation of assuring all citizens a right to life by providing affordable AIDS medications. A second Ashoka Fellow, Rodrigio Baggio, founded the Committee for Democracy in Information Technology. Rodrigio equipped young people in low-income Brazilian communities with computer skills, and therefore much greater job opportunities and access to modern technology. His organization has expanded to fifteen countries on two continents.

Like me, almost all our Ashoka Fellows started out as young teenagers who felt they could make a difference in the world. So many people worry about putting this power of change in children's hands. I am more fearful of putting it in the hands of adults who have lost the confidence to feel they can change the world. We need to help all young people ignore the barriers that adults unwittingly put up for them.

Young people with confidence are highly contagious. Peer pressure can become a hugely positive force. If we act now, in ten years we could well see twenty to thirty percent of the world as social changemakers sticking their necks out, rather than the one percent that exist today.

Every young person can be a changemaker. Through Ashoka's Youth Venture, I have seen thousands of cases. Take Jesse Fuchs-Simon and Nick Cuttriss, who in 1994 traveled to Ecuador and were inspired by the story of a six-month-old boy, José Gabriel, who went into a coma after being diagnosed with insulin-dependent diabetes. Jesse and Nick began a support group for children with diabetes in Ecuador in the only space they could find, the hallway of a public hospital. Inspired to serve as agents of change for other youths, they then founded American Youth Understanding

Diabetes Abroad, Inc., AYUDA. Nick and Jesse will not be cogs in society. They will upset society's existing arrangements and bring big changes no one else thought possible.

Imagine what we could accomplish if we all felt our dreams and visions were feasible. Too many people shake their heads when a young person asks if he or she can change the world. Don't be one of them. Simply say, "Why not?"

To be successful, you need to...

Be willing to stick your neck out... **Believe in Yourself**

Short Term Goals

Nikki's Perspective: No matter how many defeats I experience, I can always point to one great accomplishment: my daughter, Zali. I might have a bad day at work. I may feel like a failure for my dismal domestic skills. I could make a poor financial investment. But when I see how well my daughter turned out, I know there is a great deal that I have done right. She always gives me the confidence to feel that, with her as an accomplishment, everything else is just around the corner.

Your Tools for Success: Remind yourself of all the short term goals you've reached. Write down five of your past accomplishments. It's often easier to remember our failures than our achievements. When we are lacking confidence, it helps to recall that we have achieved a great deal already. Recognize that many people out there haven't managed these same accomplishments. You had to be doing a lot right in order to find success in the past, so you know you have the potential to find success again in the future.

_____

_____

_____

_____

_____

Chapter

7

Risk

Risk

My newfound confidence helped me qualify for my second Olympic Games. This time, when reporters came up, thrust a microphone in my face and asked what my Olympic goals were, I proudly responded, "To win!" That was my goal, and I was going to make myself accountable to that objective.

This did not, however, mean that the nerves were gone. In fact, going into the Olympics I was ranked number one in the world, and that only added to the tension. To give a visual of how intense the pressure was, I ground right through a night guard my dentist gave me because I was grinding my teeth at night. The protective piece was about half a centimeter of very hard plastic, and I ground all the way through it in the month preceding the Olympics. Surprisingly, the dentist gave me another night guard following the games, and I still have it!

That pressure got the best of me during my Olympic semifinals performance. I executed an advanced triple-twisting double back flip called a "full-double full" on my first jump. The maneuver went well in the air. But on landing, I touched my hand down as a small safety check, to stabilize myself. When the scores were posted from the first round, I found I was sitting in twelfth place—and only twelve skiers would qualify for finals. I had missed the cut four years before.

I went back to the top of the hill to talk to my assistant coach, Kris "Fuzz" Feddersen, before my second jump. "All right, we have two options," he stated. "We can go for a double-twisting double back, which is an easier jump. You know you can land it and make it into finals. Or you can go for your new triple back flip—which is obviously more difficult. You've probably landed only 15 percent of them this year, but if you do land it, you'll likely be ranked higher going into finals, get a better placing, and prove to yourself that you can do it."

I thought about my options, turned to Fuzz and replied, "The gold medal doesn't go to the conservative." I wasn't there to end up in twelfth place...or even fourth. I had a goal—and my goal was to win. If I was going to do that, I had to pull out all the stops and take the risks needed. I was determined to take the subjectivity away from the judges and prove that I was the hands-down favorite.

A smile broke across Fuzz's face and I could immediately tell that was the answer he was looking for. Being a three-time Olympian himself, he knew I was going to have to take some risks in order to stand on the Olympic podium.

And I was on my way there after my second semifinals jump. I landed the single-twisting triple and found myself in *my* first-ever Olympic finals.

The officials gave us a day off before finals "to rest or further prepare". *I* think they gave us the time just to build anxiety. For me, it was one more day to let anticipation mushroom.

To add to everything, I woke on the morning of Olympic finals to find the wind howling outside my window. I decided I had to make sure I had everything working in my favor…and that included all my stupid superstitions. Just the week before, I had read that speed-skating legend Bonnie Blair—one of my top role models—would eat peanut butter for good luck before every competition. I didn't know if I could keep any food down, I had such butterflies in my stomach, but if Bonnie ate a peanut butter sandwich before her comps, then I was going to somehow get one down myself.

I made my way out to the aerial venue and saw that the flags were standing sideways in the strong winds, which were gusting up to 40 miles per hour, the officials told us. In conditions like that, an aerialist can become a kite rather than a competitor. Training would be slow because we would have to wait to take our jumps between gusts. I made it through the agonizing, drawn-out training and got ready for the competition.

The wind continued to play havoc with us, and the two skiers right before me in the run order pulled off the course just before they reached the kicker, postponing their jumps. Both claimed that the headwind was too strong and they didn't have enough speed to complete their jumps. I could tell my coaches were trying to decide if they should let me start, or if I should also stop just before the jump, to get a reading on my speed. I quickly turned to Fuzz, who was standing at the start with a walkie-talkie, and told him I wanted to take my jump. He called down to Wayne Hilterbrand, who was once again my head coach, and told him I wanted to go. They both agreed, but encouraged me to stay in a tuck until I reached the jump so that the wind would whip over my head and there would be less surface area to slow me down.

The bells sounded over the loudspeaker, signifying that the judges were ready. I looked to Wayne, who checked the wind and gave me the all-clear sign. I pushed off from my starting position, pulled myself into a tight tuck and waited until I was about twenty feet from the jump. I stood up, swung my arms over my head and skied up the ramp. Flipping and twisting through the air, I performed my triple-twisting double back flip. My height and form were right on the mark, and as I spotted the landing, I made sure to have both hands in front to prepare for the impact. I was determined not to let my hand drag across the snow this time.

After the first round, I found my name at the top of the scoreboard, but knew from my experience at my first Olympics that a medal was far from won. I mustn't think of the David Letterman show or parades yet. I had a second jump to perfect. I grabbed the rope tow to make my way back to the top of the hill to prepare for my triple back flip.

With the changing winds, I had to make sure my speed was going to be adequate to execute the maneuver properly. For each trick we did, we needed to make certain our speed was right on the mark, within one to two kilometers. To perform a good lay-tuck-full, I needed a speed of at least 61 kilometers per hour. We had speed guns to register our speed.

I had a little time before my second jump, so I took a speed check to see how the conditions had changed. Starting at exactly the same spot as my practice jump, I went through the speed guns at 57 kph. With a little time to spare, I headed back up for another speed check. The higher up the hill I started, the more speed I'd have. So I took a big step up the inrun, turned, and went through the speed guns at 58 kph—still 3 kph too slow. I turned to Wayne for guidance.

"We don't have time for another speed check. You are just going to have to take a *big* step up and be confident that you can do this jump no matter what your speed is," he instructed.

It wasn't exactly the reassurance I needed, but I knew it was the only option I had. I gave him the best look of confidence I could muster and slowly nodded. I found myself still nodding ten seconds later and realized I wasn't just trying to convince Wayne that I could do this, I was trying to convince myself as well. I skied over to the rope tow and latched on for my last and final trip up to the top of the Iizuna Kogan ski mountain.

It was only minutes before they announced that I would be the next to compete. I slid across the slope and made my way to my newly adjusted starting point. That morning had been so cold that the hill was a sheet of ice. Volunteer workers had to take chainsaws to saw little slots into the slope so that we wouldn't slide down the hill before our jumps. I thought to myself that this wouldn't be the Olympics if Mother Nature didn't throw in as many challenges as she could.

I took my place in my slots and looked down to where Wayne was standing next to the jump. Not many people realize it, but our coaches are allowed to call to us while we're in the air, to help instill confidence or give us corrections for adjustments, since we are rotating so fast we have trouble seeing the ground. I'd been amazed earlier to learn the meaning of a word the Japanese coach kept calling to his athletes, time and time again: *danger.*

As I prepared for my contest jump, I felt reassured that *my* coach would actually give me specific instructions for what to do if I was ever in trouble. My eyes darted back and forth between him and the fluttering windsocks. Wayne was holding his arms crossed on his chest, signaling for me to hold off until the wind died. I stood there for a full three minutes, waiting for a lull, knowing that when it came, I would be expected to take off at a second's notice before the wind picked up again.

Three minutes feels like a lifetime when you are waiting to execute a performance you've been preparing for all your life, and which could alter the rest of your life. As I stood there, I tried to block out the forty thousand people blowing horns and whistles at the bottom of the hill. I tried to block out the gusting headwinds. I tried to block out the fact that my feet were sliding out of the chiseled slots in the ice. I tried to block out the fact that I'd been much too slow on my two speed checks. And I tried to block out the television cameras, which were now six inches from my face, likely filming how my heart was pounding out of my chest. I just kept mimicking the arm motions I would need to perform my triple back flip.

Finally, Wayne threw his arms into the all-clear sign, meaning it was probably the best time to go. I quickly pushed out of my slots and thrust my skis down the inrun. I got back into my tucked position so that the wind would again whip over my head, and stood up just before I reached the jump. I swung my arms in a circle in preparation for the ramp, and felt the force of the incline as I locked my legs to counter the compression. I swiftly launched off the kicker and squeezed my legs in a straight position for my first flip. As I came back around to vertical, I pulled them into my chest for the second flip. Reaching my third rotation, I stretched out my body and wrapped my arms across my chest to initiate a full twist.

As I spotted my landing, over the din of the crowd I heard Wayne call out, "Reach now, reach." It was my cue that the landing was coming up quickly and I had better have my hands in front in preparation for the impact.

Now, as I've mentioned, I wanted to be going through the speed guns at 61 kph. I later found out that I went through them at 65 kph—4 kph faster than I had ever gone through them before. With the extra speed, I had gone higher in the air than ever before…which also meant I was coming down to earth with a greater force. Upon impact, my knees accordioned into my chest and my chin hit my knee. The excessive force felt like a grand piano had landed on my shoulders. I had to use all the strength in my legs and back to throw off that "grand piano" and ski down the hill.

When I reached the bottom, I broke into an unplanned dance. I can't say that my windmilling arms would win me a spot as a rock star's backup dancer, but they did demonstrate my exuberance. It was an enthusiasm I just couldn't contain.

I was holding my skis up for the cameras when I heard someone calling my name. I looked over and saw that my boyfriend, Michael—now my husband—had somehow sneaked into an area that was supposed to be restricted to media and competing athletes. I rushed over and threw my arms around him, so excited that I forgot to drop my skis, and nearly decapitated him. I hugged him as hard as I could and whispered into his ear, "I did it. I did it. I did it."

A reporter overheard me, and later asked me whether "I did it" meant that I had just won the Olympics. I had been so focused that day that I hadn't seen one other athlete jump. I didn't know what kind of lead I had. I didn't know that I was the only aerial skier performing the more difficult triple maneuver because the others had backed down due to the gusting winds.

To me, "I did it" meant that I'd come out here and proved ten doctors and one sports journalist wrong. "I did it" meant that I'd done the best I could that day, and that was all I could ask of myself.

There were still three skiers left to go: Veronica Brenner from Canada, Alla Tsuper from Belarus and Nannan Xu from China. I watched Veronica's final jump, then Alla's, and found that my name was still holding at the top of the scoreboard. It was down to just Nannan. I heard people saying that she had the best chance to snag the gold.

I was pacing as Nannan took her place for her final jump. Her coach gave her the all-clear sign and she was on course. She executed a beautiful full-double full, the same jump I had performed in the first round. Nannan skied to the bottom of the hill and squealed with excitement as she jumped into the waving arms of her teammates. I hadn't been following the scores, so didn't know what she needed to surpass my own. It was just a waiting game now.

Since Nannan didn't speak much English, I went to her side to give her an enormous hug. But I still peered over her shoulder, never taking my eye off the scoreboard. I looked to that familiar spot on the bottom right corner that would soon be flashing Nannan's ranking—and my ultimate fate. It seemed like forever before the scoreboard held her name, and then finally flashed a giant "2". At that moment I knew I had won Olympic gold.

The officials had given me a bottle of water for the upcoming drug testing, and I was so excited by the results that I spun around and poured half the water over myself, not even realizing it. I kept shaking my head because I couldn't believe that *I* had just won! Me! Nikki Stone was going to receive her own Olympic medal. I now know why people ask to be pinched to make sure they are really awake and not dreaming.

Officials grabbed me almost immediately and dragged me over to the awaiting CBS camera crews. Their question was simple: "How do you feel?" The answer wasn't so easy to articulate. How do you capture the feelings of slaying a dragon and achieving your lifelong dream in a fifteen second interview? My response was heartfelt and genuine as I declared, "I'm just so happy! I'm just *so* happy! *I'm just so happy!!*"

I can guarantee that my happiness would not have come without the risk. We are often so focused on the potentially negative results of sticking our neck out that we never reap the rewards of actually taking the risks. Some people are okay with being stuck on the merry-go-round. And if that's you, then don't worry about it. For me, I love the roller coaster. Sure, it's riskier, but what a rush! What happiness!

Corporal Jason Dunham

Marine Hero Awarded the Congressional Medal of Honor

Photo provided by Deb Dunham

Corporal Jason Dunham Biography

The birth of the United States Marine Corp took place on November 10, 1775, early in the course of the American Revolution. On November 10, 1981, Jason Lee Dunham was born. Being in possession of twinkling hazel eyes, towhead-blond hair and a smile that dazzled your heart, Jason was much loved by all who met him.

Being in possession of these assets became quite beneficial and he used them to his advantage. His mother found it nearly impossible to discipline him when his smile appeared. Teachers were also hard-pressed to reprimand his impish behavior. Growing up in rural, small-town Scio, New York, Jason attended the same school building from kindergarten through high school graduation. This created an easy environment to continue the close connection he had with his three siblings. Justin, a grade behind him, was involved in many of the same social and athletic activities. Kyle and Katie, several years younger, ran into him often throughout the day in the halls.

Jason excelled at athletics, especially soccer, basketball and baseball. These sports were not only a place to hone his physical and competitive skills, but gave him a chance to learn leadership, sportsmanship and teamwork, all characteristics that would serve him well in his future career choice. With encouragement and blessings from his parents, the summer before his senior year in high school Jason signed with the Marine Corps in the Delayed Entry Program.

Growing up on a dairy farm and working with his father, Jason learned the value and need of a strong work ethic. From his mother he learned empathy and the ability not to ask others to do things you weren't willing to do yourself. These were life tools he took with him to Parris Island in July 2000, where he completed his marine basic training. Jason entered the Marine Corps with great potential. The marines polished his skills and added more, and he graduated a young man who embodied the core values of Honor, Courage and Commitment. Jason was born to be a marine.

Nikki's Intro to Corporal Jason Dunham's Story

I have a friend who's always been afraid of fully committing to a relationship. I would tease him that he wasn't a risk-taker like I was. I risked flipping and twisting fifty feet through the air with skis on. I risked overcoming a career-threatening spinal injury. I risked traveling to third world countries to volunteer time with disadvantaged children. I risked putting my heart on my sleeve to find true love. And I risked braving a consulting business as a motivational speaker in a world dominated by men.

My friend was all too quick to point out that this self-proclaimed risk-taker still hadn't taken the risk to have children. I knew that I wanted children someday, but the thought did scare me, so I always managed to put it off every time my husband brought up the notion. I realized I was being a hypocrite and wasn't taking the risks I so proudly claimed. So the next time my husband brought up the topic of kids, I decided I would just go for it and take the plunge. Ten months later, I gave birth to a little girl who changed my life and never allowed me to question these big decisions again.

There are very few instances in life where you have just a split second to decide if you'll make a profound difference for others. I have yet to make such a grand decision, but if I'm ever presented with that kind of choice, I hope that I could respond like Corporal Dunham...

Corporal Jason Dunham: My Story

Corporal Jason Dunham

Risk

Quite honestly, I'd be a fool if I hadn't been apprehensive about going off to war. But with three siblings at home and not enough money for college, I enlisted in the marines, knowing they would help pay for a good education, provide me with the most challenging training, and allow me to represent and defend my country at a time when it needed it most.

Being so close to my family, I was nervous and reluctant when I was first deployed to Iraq, but I knew there were marines there that needed me. It was the greatest honor to be entrusted with the training and lives of fellow Americans, and with protecting my country.

This opportunity was so important to me that, despite being scheduled to return from Iraq in May to end my enlistment, I decided to extend my tour of duty until September 2004, because I wanted to stay with my "brothers" until their own combat tour was up. I was well aware this wasn't something everyone did. But I had made a promise to my men that I was going to bring them back alive, so I had to take the risk to stay on and ensure that happened. As their squad leader, I had a responsibility to these marines, and nothing was going to stop me from living up to it

With each new mission, I was more proud to be wearing the cloth of my nation. But I was even prouder of those who wore it with me. Evidently, they thought quite highly of me as well, because I was selected by Kilo Company's platoon commanders as one of the twelve best noncommissioned officers to lead one of Captain Gibson's twelve rifle squads. Captain Gibson was our company commander, and it was an.

honor to serve under his command. I had been chosen to lead marines into harm's way; I had been chosen to make a difference, and to train and protect my men.

I don't think I completely understood how much trust and respect they had for me until the night of April 13, 2004. Two of my team leaders, Lance Corporal Hampton and Lance Corporal Carbajal, took the time to prepare a plate of hot chow for me, because I was working hard to write the operations order for the next day's mission, and had neglected to feed myself. From their simple, caring gesture, I realized that my subordinates not only acknowledged me as their leader in title, they also accepted me in reality. I knew in that moment that I had to live up to their expectations.

And all my skills would be put to the test the next day. I was assigned to lead my men on a reconnaissance patrol in Karabilah, near the Syrian border. Not long after we arrived, we heard explosions off to the west. We figured that Lima Company was getting hit. So I got my squad running to the west, while my radio operator, Lance Corporal Sanders, called our vehicles to meet us on the main road and pick us up. Once we arrived at the place where the explosions had occurred, we realized our battalion commander's patrol had just been ambushed. So I pulled my marines off the vehicles, where they were easy targets, and got them ready to clear out the ambush site. I split my squad into its two fire teams, led by Hampton and Carbajal, and sent the vehicles to cordon off the village and cut off the insurgents. We soon came upon a line of cars on a street where there normally weren't any at all. Our platoon sergeant, Staff Sergeant Ferguson, said we needed to stop and search those vehicles, which were coming from the direction of the ambush.

The second in the line was a white Toyota Land Cruiser with four military-aged males. If there's ever a target indicator in Iraq of individuals up to no good, it's a Land Cruiser holding four young men. Private First Class Miller approached the passenger side and quickly determined that they had weapons hidden under their floor mats. I came around to the driver's side, and as soon as I opened the door, the driver sprang out and dived for my throat. I heaved my leg up and into his chest. We both plunged to the ground and began to wrestle.

Seeing the commotion, Private Miller hastily came to help. He whipped out his baton and began beating the insurgent, eventually getting into a position where he could put a chokehold on the man with his baton. I then noticed that Lance Corporal Hampton had also run to my defense and had his rifle trained on the insurgent. However, with Miller and me thrashing around, Hampton didn't have any chance to take the man down.

And it was a good thing he didn't, because I suddenly glanced at the man's hand and noticed he was holding a live grenade. The safety pin was already removed, and he had just released the grenade's spoon; we were all moments from being dead. As soon as I realized no one else had seen the grenade, I shouted, "No, no, no—watch his hands!"

As marines, we've all asked ourselves hundreds of times what we would do in such a case. I had discussed this very type of situation with members of my platoon just a couple of weeks ago. I believed that covering the grenade with your helmet would help smother the blast, so I had practiced removing my helmet quickly and slapping it on the ground. Of course, there's no time to think when you're actually confronted with the dilemma. You just go on instinct. And my instinct was to protect those men who thought enough of me to feed me when I was too busy to take care of myself. To protect those men who had embraced me as their leader. To protect those men who had put their trust in me to bring them home alive. When it comes down to moments like that, it's not about the war. It's not about politics. It's about each other. It's about the trust of your fellow marines and the bond of brotherhood we share. It's about putting someone else's life before your own. So without a moment to spare, I flung my Kevlar helmet and my body on top of the grenade to smother the blast.

At 10:45 p.m. on April 15, 2004, Corporal Dunham's parent, heard the phone ring. Since it never rang after 9:00 p.m., they immediately knew something was wrong. Debra and Daniel received word that Jason had suffered a critical head wound from the shards of shrapnel from a grenade explosion.

Eight days later he was gone

Two other marines from Second Squad, Fourth Platoon, Kilo Company, Third Battalion, Seventh Marines, suffered shrapnel wounds from that same grenade, but due to the courageous sacrifice of Corporal Dunham, both men survived. One of them was fire team leader Lance Corporal Hampton, who had brought Dunham dinner the night before.

Lieutenant Colonel Matthew Lopez, Dunham's battalion commander, submitted his nomination for the Medal of Honor, the nation's highest award for battlefield heroism, writing, "I deeply believe that given the facts and evidence presented, Corporal Dunham clearly understood the situation and attempted to block the blast of the grenade from his squad members. His personal action was far beyond the call of duty and saved the lives of his fellow marines." Two years after his passing, Jason's parents accepted the Medal of Honor on his behalf.

In the words of his company commander, Major Gibson, "As we remember Corporal Dunham, let us not be sad, but rather let us rejoice in our brotherhood and in the blessing of having fought alongside men of such nobility, honor and soldierly virtue. For it is our sacred honor to have served with men such as this.

"We have a very limited time on this earth—a limited time to live, a limited time to love and a limited time to make a difference. So let us keep Jason Dunham's memory in our thoughts as we move forward. Jason lived the life that he had to its fullest. He loved his family, he loved his brothers, and in the end, he has made a difference in all of our lives.

So he has put the challenge to us all. How will we live? How will we show our love? How will we make a difference?"

This story is told by Jason's parents, Debra and Daniel Dunham, and his company commander, Major Trent Gibson—as they are sure he would have told it.

To be successful, you need to...

Be willing to stick your neck out... **Take Some Risks**

Live your life

Nikki's Perspective: Like many Americans, I became very fearful of flying after 9/11. I actually found myself hyperventilating upon takeoff, and had visuals of everything that could potentially go wrong with the flight. I reached my low point during one trip where I came dangerously close to getting off the plane. I was taking an Olympic torch to a young girl, Ashley O'Rear, who was dying of cancer and was not going to live to carry the flame for the 2002 Olympics. Thinking of this little girl kept me on the plane that day, but the experience of visiting her kept me on the plane for every trip after that. The time I spent with Ashley was an enormous inspiration, and I would have really missed out on something special if I'd never met her.

This knowledge made me realize how many other life experiences I'd miss out on if I didn't go out there and grab every opportunity. Now when people ask me if I'm nervous about traveling overseas or skydiving or visiting disrupted areas in Africa, I simply tell them that I have a lot more to gain by going.

Your Tools for Success: Remember that "the brave do not live forever, but the cautious do not live at all." (Author unknown) Today, your challenge is to ask yourself if you want to lead a life with no change and no excitement, or do you want to take the chance to find some excitement and exhilaration and really *live*? Do you want to look back on your life and have regrets for not living to your full potential? Ask yourself if it's really better to live a safe, lackluster life or if you want to walk away with something to show for your time on this earth.

_____

_____

_____

_____

_____

Prince Albert

Ruler of Monaco

Photo provided by Palais Princier de Monaco

Prince Albert II Biography

H.S.H. Prince Albert Alexandre Louis Pierre, Hereditary Prince of Monaco, Marquis of Baux, was born on March 14,1958. His Serene Highness is the son of Prince Rainier III (May 31, 1923 - April 6, 2005) and Princess Grace born Kelly (Philadelphia, United States, November 12, 1929 - Monaco, September 14, 1982). The Princely couple also gave birth to the Princess of Hanovre and Princess Stéphanie of Monaco, who form with their brother the House of Grimaldi.

Prince Albert II succeeded his father on April 6, 2005. After the period of official mourning, he acceded to the throne, on July 12, 2005, to become the current ruler of the Principality of Monaco.

Ever since he was young, Prince Albert comported himself impressively in every sphere. He graduated with distinction from high school, before attending Amherst College in Massachusetts, where he studied political science, economics, psychology, philosophy and English literature. He practiced many sports and even competed in five straight Olympic Winter Games in bobsled, from 1988 to 2002. Prince Albert II of Monaco remains a dedicated academic and an enthusiastic sportsman.

During his time as hereditary prince, Albert assisted his father in conducting the affairs of state, becoming what many consider to be a brilliant statesman. Since May 28, 1993, the prince has led Monégasque delegations to the United Nations General Assembly. On October 5, 2004, he presided over their delegation at the official ceremony of the principality's accession to the Council of Europe. Monaco became the forty-sixth member state.

H.S.H. Prince Albert II of Monaco feels very much concerned about humanitarian and environmental issues, and supports various humanitarian projects in many countries around the world. In June 2006, he set up the Prince Albert II of Monaco Foundation dedicated to environmental protection, to encourage action and reflection about climate change, biodiversity and water.

Nikki's Intro to Prince Albert's Story

To this day, I get a queasy feeling at the very thought of doing fifty-foot-high triple back flips. When I was training for the Olympics, I would literarily be sick to my stomach each time I reached the hill to perform my triples. I think most people have that little internal voice that tells them getting sick is a significant sign to turn around and call it a day.

I heard that voice. But another voice told me how important that gold medal was. Luckily, that second voice was just a little louder. I would make my way to the top of the inrun, sneak off to the woods, proceed to get sick, then remind myself why I was doing this, so that I could calm my nerves just enough to get myself off the jump. After

I landed my jump, I would have an exhilarating rush that seemed to eclipse the memory of the fears I'd had just moments before, and I would ski away beaming.

I somehow always loved the ups and downs. I don't know if many people thrive on those incredible highs and lows, but there is one man I met at the 1994 Olympics who shares this roller-coaster ride, Prince Albert II…

Prince Albert II: My Story

Prince Albert II

Risk

"On deck, a bobsled team that is new to the Olympic track…Monaco! And surprisingly, holding the reins is Monaco's own Prince Albert II."

I think my bobsledding surprised many people—or "*troubled* many people" may be a more appropriate phrase. I know most everyone envisioned me sitting on a royal throne rather than in the driver's seat of an Olympic bobsled. Quite frankly, those closest to me were likely more comfortable with that "royal" picture as well.

As I visualized the undulating turns and dips that I would soon encounter, watched by a quarter of the world's population, my nerves began to dance and my pulse quickened. Soon I would be experiencing that tingly feeling I had before every bobsled run.

It was that same tingly sensation I would feel many years later, when confronted with the daunting task of speaking in front of over eight hundred dignitaries at the United Nations. But the years I spent testing my nerves at the top of various bobsled tracks around the world gave me the strength and bravado that I would need to conquer my fears.

I found myself hating my internal reactions to the danger, but somehow craving it at the same time. That danger always brought on a feeling of uncertainty, where I questioned if I was actually up to the challenge. There were even times when I wondered if I would survive the run. But deep down, I knew if I could get past my own fears and second thoughts and stick my neck out, I would grow physically and mentally at the same time. It's the greatest challenge, and subsequently, the greatest reward, to surmount our own fears.

As I stood at the top of the Olympic run, I thought back to the first Olympics I had the opportunity to attend—the 1980 games in Lake Placid, New York. After seeing the exhilaration of the bobsled event up close and personal, I knew I *had* to feel the sensation of whipping down the icy course at speeds of up to ninety miles an hour. I wasn't the reckless type, but I was always looking for new challenges in life, and bobsledding seemed the perfect outlet.

The very first time I clambered into a four-man bobsled as a passenger, in 1984, I was enveloped with the power and vibrations of the sled. My driver had just explained that we would be pulling four to five g's, and my stomach surged as the sled rocked around the sharp turns. After that first thrilling ride, I wanted to push the limits of my adrenaline level and feel what it was like to be in control of that 1,680 pound sled as it plummeted down the track. So in 1986, I convinced one of my daredevil friends to go through bobsledding school with me. I had been frustrated by the fact that I had not really gone anywhere in other sports growing up, and for a bobsledder, twenty-seven years old wasn't too late to start.

When I first signed up for the training, the thought of walking into the Olympic opening ceremonies carrying my country's flag hadn't even entered my mind. But when my coach eventually approached me about trying to qualify for the Olympics, it didn't take long for my look of shock to morph into a childish grin. It wasn't going to be an easy path, but I was more than eager to take it on.

Eleven months later I was standing at the top of the bobsled run of the 1988 Calgary Olympics, with a large "1" plastered on my sled. Not only was I actually competing in the Olympic Games, but my team was going to be the first to go. To calm my nerves, I tried to put everything in perspective, and realized that I had nothing to lose. I knew I had to rely on the instincts and feelings I had developed through facing endless other challenges. As soon as I pushed out of the start, I would officially become an Olympian—a title no one could ever take away from me. It wasn't something I was born into, but something I had taken a risk to do and developed myself.

This rush would invigorate me into steering my teammates through four more Olympic Games: Albertville, France, in 1992; Lillehammer, Norway, 1994; Nagano, Japan, 1998; and Salt Lake City, U.S.A., 2002. It created a high-voltage charge in my life that still pulses within me to this day.

My experiences in sport have continually helped me accept new and exciting adventures. Whether I was traveling across hundreds of hazardous miles of icecap to the North Pole, or making a terrifying speech in front of five hundred influential people, it always came back to those moments at the top of the track. Recalling my bobsled runs reminds me that I'm up for any challenge. The intent is still the same: conquer those fires in the pit of my stomach and get across the finish line. Those risks I took in sport have prepared me to reach all my goals throughout the rest of my life.

I certainly can't say there weren't fears involved. But I wasn't going to let my reservations hold me back from the feelings of elation that always flooded through me after I'd tackled those fears.

No, my life wouldn't have ended if I'd never climbed into that first bobsled…but I honestly don't believe I'd be the same person if I hadn't.

To be successful, you need to...

Be willing to stick your neck out… **Take Some Risks**

Fear is okay

Nikki's Perspective: Because I was afraid of injuries, doing triple flips fifty feet in the air was no easy feat for me. I'd be a fool not to have fears. I think that *most* people would be fearful of the prospect of injuries that could come from falling out of the sky with skis on. And it helped to know that this fear was normal.

I came to realize that the times I was actually getting hurt were when the fear was absent. Fear made me cognizant of all the hazards that could be lurking around the corner. I could rationally think through all the things that might go wrong, and make sure I was prepared for them. It was the times I was most fearful that I was actually the safest.

Your Tools for Success: Fear is a natural emotion and it is okay to admit that things scare us. Fears can actually help us to be alert; they keep us on our toes. Remind yourself that everyone has fears. By having them you are more aware of the consequences and more able to avoid them.

Today, write down the things you have been fearful of in the past, and how being cognizant of your fear has actually helped put you on your toes. Remember that the butterflies in your stomach are just readying you for the challenge. Interpret the added adrenaline that accompanies excitement—or fear—as a boost of energy to help you concentrate and perform better. What fear are you going to stand up to today?

_____

_____

_____

_____

_____

Lester Holt

Top Broadcast News Anchor

Photo provided by Lester Holt

Lester Holt Biography

Lester Holt is the weekend anchor for the flagship broadcast NBC Nightly News, *and is also the co-anchor of the weekend edition of* Today. *In addition, Holt serves as fill-in anchor and correspondent for NBC* Nightly News *with Brian Williams and the weekday* Today *program. He also contributes to MSNBC, NBC's twenty-four-hour cable news network.*

Holt has reported from many of the world's hot spots. In 2006, he reported from the front lines in Lebanon on the war between Israel and Hezbollah, and from London, England, he reported on the terror threat to U.S.-bound airliners. In 2005, Holt was on the ground for Hurricane Katrina, covering events both in Louisiana and Mississippi, and later that fall, covered Hurricane Rita in Texas.

Before becoming co-anchor of Weekend Today, *Holt anchored* Lester Holt Live, *a daily news show on MSNBC in which he covered breaking news and provided updates and analysis. Holt has also served as the lead anchor for daytime news and breaking news coverage on MSNBC. He has served as a primary anchor for MSNBC's coverage of the biggest news events of the last several years, including Operation Iraqi Freedom and the war in Afghanistan, and he was the lead daytime anchor for MSNBC's coverage of Decision 2000. Holt also served as anchor of* Countdown: Iraq, *a nightly news telecast concentrating on the latest developments surrounding the war with Iraq, from October 2002 through March 2003.*

Nikki's Intro to Lester Holt's Story

There is a saying by John Burroughs, "Leap and the net will appear." I put that concept to the test during my second World Cup competition overseas. The fog moved in and we could barely see thirty feet in front of us. No one wanted to disappoint the Japanese organizers, who were new to the circuit, so instead of saying, "Why don't we cancel the event?" the officials went to the next best "reasonable" response: "We'll just hold the *women's* contest." Being new to the circuit myself, I was hardly in a position to protest.

I made my way up to the inrun with the rest of the female skiers. As we prepared to take our first practice jumps, I turned to the other women and asked, "How do we do this if we can't even see the jump?"

Again, the response was not one I was too happy about. "Don't worry, you'll be able to see the jump just before you get to it," a Norwegian woman replied.

I nodded and smiled weakly. One by one, the athletes disappeared into the fog and we would hear someone yell to us, "Jump's clear!" Before I knew it, it was my turn to venture down into the sea of mist.

Sure enough, when I was within twenty-five feet of the jump, I made out its red spray-painted lines. I swung my arms and launched myself into a cloudy abyss. It was a terrifying experience, but a worthwhile one, for two hours later I had won my first World Cup competition.

"Leap and the net will appear." It's a saying Lester Holt is quite familiar with…

Lester Holt: My Story

Lester Holt

Risk

Firing or demotion. Not two choices anyone ever wants presented. But these were the two options open to me back in 1999.

I had worked my way up to the number two anchor spot of a Chicago news affiliate. Everything seemed to be going fairly well for ol' Lester Holt. I was in a very comfortable position, and life seemed easy. Or at least I thought so…until my contract ran out five years into the job. With the end of my contract, I learned that the station had no plans of keeping me as one of their main anchors. I was being offered a demotion or the door.

Life had been good as a local celebrity news anchor. Now I had no idea what I would do. Of course, the station's new position wasn't a bad offer. Sure, it meant less money and less prestige, but I had my family's security to think about. And there just weren't openings for a major network news anchor around every corner.

The answer seemed obvious—take the demotion. But there was one thing standing in the way: I just wasn't ready to give up on my dreams of finding my own personal success in the media world. And that demotion wasn't going to get me there. I decided that, instead of stepping down a few rungs on the ladder, I would take the risk of jumping on a new ladder altogether.

Problem was, new ladders aren't always swinging by within jumping distance. I had only a few months to find a new job before my six-month compensation package came to an end. This risk was affecting not only me, but also my wife and two boys.

The months quickly raced by. No jobs seemed to shake themselves loose, and fear finally set in during a preplanned ski vacation to Whistler, Canada. After tumbling in the snow for the fifth time that day, it dawned on me that I was shelling out all sorts of money I might not have. I retired to the hot tub and proceeded to fall into a mini-depression. I had no job, no prospects, and the six months were rapidly coming to a close

Again, my family was the predominant factor weighing on my mind. I wanted to be able to afford the better things in life for them, whether ski trips to Canada or vacations on the beach. But right now, I didn't know if I could afford a hot chocolate in.

the lodge! If I gave up a decent job, I'd be forced to dodge bullets. I started questioning if I might be setting my standards too high, and whether I should start settling for the status quo, regardless of whether it was the "best" job.

I somehow mustered the courage to hang tough, and with two weeks left until D-day, the phone finally rang. An affiliate in San Jose offered me a job, and a few days later, MSNBC also offered me a position. Back in 1999, working for a cable news station did not have the popularity or prestige of a major network, nor did it have the same paycheck. But what the job did give me was an open ceiling, an opportunity to grow. I was again presented with the dilemma of accepting a safe job or risk taking a job without all the perks, but where I knew I could truly discover Lester Holt's potential.

In the end, I was swayed by what I wanted to teach my kids...and ultimately myself. I needed to risk sticking my neck out and not cling to the easy life. My boys needed to see that the humiliation and setbacks didn't matter as much as striving to find my true potential. I wanted to make a decision that I knew my sons would someday be proud of, if they weren't already. I didn't make the safe choice and I didn't make the easy choice. I made the risky choice. I made the choice of hope.

And my time at MSNBC ended up changing my life. I wasn't the main anchor and I was only on air an hour a day, but I was now able to focus on the challenge I was looking for all along. I covered the Air France plane crash in 2000, the big presidential election recount and, of course, 9/11. Each event helped me find what I was ultimately made to do: relate important issues to the people who needed to hear them. My experience with these tough assignments helped me learn who I could truly be as a reporter.

And my gamble paid off. It helped elevate me to levels I had only dreamed of.

Several months after moving on to anchor the *Weekend Today* show, I ran into Hank Price, my old general manager at the Chicago news affiliate. Hank was the man who'd let me go from the station, and now, here he was, congratulating me for all my success.

I humbly accepted Hank's praise. But deep down, I knew that he, too, must have initially doubted the wisdom of my risky decision to leave the Chicago station. I couldn't help but smile to myself. "Doing well is the best revenge."

To be successful, you need to...

Be willing to stick your neck out... **Take Some Risks**

Get perspective

Nikki's Perspective: A few years ago, I had a friend approach me about having awful nerves before an upcoming speech. She had been asked to speak for a charitable cause she was closely connected with. My friend was dreadfully shy and the thought of speaking in front of more than a couple people terrified her.

I asked her, "If it goes poorly, then how will that ultimately affect you next week? You may feel embarrassed at first, but will it really matter seven days from now? Or next month?"

She agreed that it wouldn't do much harm in the future if the talk didn't go well. I then asked her to think of the benefits that could be gained if she did go through with the speech. To think of the impact she could have on people and how fulfilling this experience would be for her. My friend did decide to give the presentation, and her fears of speaking in front of a crowd have long since been forgotten.

Your Tools for Success: You are going to put your risks in perspective today. Ask yourself how accepting a challenge will impact you a week, month or year from now. If you take the risk and don't succeed, how will this setback affect your life in the future?

We are often focused on consequences right now. Thinking of how something will impact us beyond the present moment helps put the risk into perspective. Many times you will find that a setback won't matter a year from now...or even next week. So why not take a chance? You likely have much more to gain than you have to lose.

Vinod Khosla

Co-creator of Sun Microsystems & One of the World's Most Successful Venture Capitalist

Photo courtesy of Andy Freeberg

Vinod Khosla Biography

Vinod Khosla was a co-founder of Daisy Systems and founding chief executive officer of Sun Microsystems, where he pioneered open systems and commercial RISC processors. Sun was funded by the venture capital firm Kleiner Perkins, and in 1986, Vinod switched sides and joined Kleiner Perkins Caufield & Byers.

In 2004, driven by the need for flexibility and a desire to be more experimental, to fund sometimes imprudent "science experiments" and to take on both for-profit and for-social-impact ventures, he formed Khosla Ventures. Khosla Ventures focuses on both traditional venture capital technology investments and clean technology ventures. His social ventures include affordable housing and microfinance, among others.

Vinod holds a Bachelor of Technology in electrical engineering from the Indian Institute of Technology in New Delhi, a master's in biomedical engineering from Carnegie Mellon University, and an MBA from the Stanford Graduate School of Business.

Nikki's Intro to Vinod Khosla's Story

As an athlete ambassador for a charity called Right To Play, I was invited to visit one of their projects in Sierra Leone. Hearing about the disease and turmoil that has overwhelmed this disadvantaged country, many people asked me why I wasn't too scared to travel there.

I couldn't get my head around the question. Yes, of course there were risks, but there was also so much to gain from the trip. I'd be given the chance to make a difference in thousands of children's lives, and would discover more ways to help them. I would gain inspiration to return home and raise more funds for their benefit. I would learn more deeply why it was important to give to those less privileged. Though risk was involved, the trip was going to make me a better person.

Quite honestly, I would be more scared to think of how unfulfilled my life would be if I hadn't taken the risk. I can only imagine how unfortunate it would have been if Vinod Khosla, one of my closest friends, had not taken his risks...

Vinod Khosla: My Story

Vinod Khosla

Risk

With my skis teetering over the side of a steep, black diamond mogul run on this snowy mountain slope, I decided to take the leap, just as I have for every challenge I've encountered in my life. Pointing my skis straight down, I went for it.

As a teenager in India, my goals started like a dream that was unreachable. The one thing I knew for sure was that I wanted to wrap my life around meaningful things. I wanted to make an impact.

There were two tenets that always drove me: Try hard things and try new things. To this day, I challenge my children with these two tasks. I always knew you had to stick your neck out to make a difference.

I admit that I didn't always succeed at the many hard, new things I tried. But I realized that if you don't try, then you have failed already, by not taking the risk. I find that life isn't any fun in the comfort zone. If you're not pushing yourself, you're not growing. And if you aren't growing, life becomes boring.

My first hard, new task came in 1976, when I decided to move to the United States to go to graduate school. I first got my masters in biomedical engineering at Carnegie Mellon University, and then decided to continue on and get my MBA. I sent out applications to a number of schools, but my heart was set on going to the Stanford Business School, in the heart of the Silicon Valley. I felt that if I was going to make it in the technology world, this was where I wanted to be.

For whatever reason, Stanford didn't want me. Two years and two rejections later, I decided to take the Carnegie Mellon offer and return to the East Coast for my MBA. I packed my bags and leased a house in Pittsburg, Pennsylvania.

However, I never gave up on Stanford, and kept harassing people in the administration office, telling them I would be a great candidate for their business school. The week before classes started, I finally told them that I was coming whether they liked it or not. My attitude has always been that unless someone can definitively tell me something is not possible, then it *is* possible. And Stanford let me in.

Since I had thrown my last dollar into living arrangements in Pittsburg, I arrived at Stanford penniless and homeless. Yet I took the risk because I knew if there was a will, there was a way. The risk paid off. Not only did they let me enroll in the courses, but one of the women in the admin office let me crash on the couch in her living room until I could afford my own apartment.

The risks got greater as I moved forward. I would stretch myself to the brink, then push on.

In 1982, not long after moving out of my low-income-housing apartment, I took the leap to start Sun Microsystems with two friends and trusted fellow Stanford grads, Scott McNealy and Andy Bechtolsheim, and a U.C. Berkeley graduate, Bill Joy. We created the company name from the initials for Stanford University Network. While others suggested we build add-ons to the computers that established players like IBM and DEC made, we chose to go moon or bust and decided to try to replace them. The company became a quick success by bringing together the world's brightest technical minds to solve the world's biggest technical problems. Our innovation was not only admired by the competition, but companies like DEC fell in our wake.

Three years later Sun was in great shape and growing. Never being one to rest on my laurels, I made the jump once again, to join Kleiner, Perkins, Caufield & Byers. Working through more highs and lows, I began to flourish in a new career as a venture capitalist, with a whole new means of making a difference in the world.

I can't begin to fathom the opportunities I would have missed if I didn't continually push myself. Didn't continually try new things. Didn't continually try hard things. Didn't continually look to make things bigger and better than anyone could imagine. Some days I feel like an addict, needing bigger and bigger doses of whatever it is that drives me.

I've never cared how things *are*, but dream of "what they can be." For me, the goose that lays the golden egg is more important than the golden egg itself. Without this attitude, I wouldn't have been able to take on the hydrocarbon-driven economy via my new company, Khosla Ventures. Many people think it's crazy to imagine a world without oil. But I am willing to take a chance and challenge the conventional wisdom, because as a dreamer *and* a pragmatist, I can imagine what the energy situation could be with ethanol as a substitute for oil. I've set a similar vision for coal and, eventually, plastics. And until someone proves to me that it's not possible, I will continue to prove that it is. I may fail, but I certainly will try.

So this wintry, white ski slope is just one more leap I will venture to take. I don't know for sure what's on the other side of this snowy mound or what adventures I may find along the ski run that follows. But I do know that I will be living life to the fullest—wherever life takes me.

To be successful, you need to...

Be willing to stick your neck out... **Take Some Risks**

Weigh the pros and cons

Nikki's Perspective: I am terrified of heights, something few people would imagine of an aerial skier who launches herself high in the air at every competition. I would literally go in the woods and lose my lunch every time I had to do triple back flips. So why would I put myself through such agony? For an Olympic gold medal. I would never fling myself into space just for the fun of it; I needed an incentive. I knew that I'd have to risk doing one of the most difficult maneuvers in order to impress the Olympic judges and win gold. When I weighed the positives and negatives, I realized that the nausea, shaky legs and risk of injury were worth it.

Looking back, I believe I still would have made the same decision if my outcome had been a fourth place or even last place finish. I would have been more disappointed in myself for not trying.

Your Tools for Success: Weigh out the positives and negatives. If you saw a bridge collapsing, you wouldn't likely leap onto it. But if you knew you could save a bus of screaming children, you may consider taking the plunge, because saving lives would be worth the risk you were taking.

Today, decide on a risk that you have been contemplating taking. Make a list of the pros and cons so you can weigh the outcome and see if the threat is worth it. Be honest with yourself on how great the reward could be; don't downplay it because of your fears. Ultimately, only you can tell if the risk is worth it.

_____

_____

_____

_____

_____

Timothy Shriver

Chairman and CEO of the Special Olympics

Photo provided by Timothy Shriver

Timothy Shriver Biography

Timothy P. Shriver is a social leader, an educator, activist, film produce, and business entrepreneur. He is the chairman and CEO of Special Olympics, and in that capacity he serves more than three million Special Olympics athletes and their families in nearly180 countries. He has helped transform Special Olympics into a movement that focuses on acceptance, inclusion and respect for individuals with intellectual disabilities in all corners of the globe.

In his fourteen years at the helm of Special Olympics, Shriver launched the organization's most ambitious growth agenda, leading to the recruitment of over two million new athletes around the world. In addition, he has worked to garner more legislative attention and government support for issues of concern to the Special Olympics community.

As part of his passion for promoting the gifts of the forgotten, Shriver has harnessed the power of Hollywood to share the stories of inspiration and change, co-producing Amistad, *and* The Loretta Claiborne Story. *He is executive producer of* The Ringer *(a Farrelly Brothers film), and* Front of the Class *(a Hallmark Hall of Fame television movie). He has produced or co-produced shows for ABC, TNT and NBC networks, and appeared on* Today, CNN, MTV *and Nickelodeon's* A World of Difference.

Before joining Special Olympics, Shriver created the New Haven Public Schools' Social Development Project, now considered the leading school-based prevention effort in the U.S., and co-founded the Collaborative for Academic, Social, and Emotional Learning—which he now chairs—the leading research organization in the U.S. in the field of social and emotional learning.

Shriver earned his undergraduate degree from Yale University, a master's degree in religion and religious education from Catholic University, and a doctorate in education from the University of Connecticut. He is the recipient of numerous honors, degrees, medals and awards from prestigious schools, countries and organizations around the world. He has authored articles in many leading publications including the New York Times, the Washington Post and Commonweal.

Shriver serves on the boards of the WPP Group and Neogenix Oncology, Inc. He is a member of the Council on Foreign Relations.

He and his wife, Linda Potter, reside in the Washington, D.C. area with their five children.

Nikki's Intro to Timothy Shriver's Story

Through my volunteer work, I had an opportunity to speak at a United Nations Development Program meeting in Dakar, Senegal, several years ago. While there, I met a young woman from Mali who told me how she'd been shunned by all the boys in her community for participating in sports.

As a young girl she was told not to wear shorts to play sports or she would never get a boyfriend. It was, of course, okay for boys to wear them and participate in sports, but there continued to be a rigid bias against girls doing so. Barefoot and pregnant takes on a whole other significance in Africa. This young woman chose to buck the system, and eventually was given a chance to travel the world, make money and build her self-esteem through her track and field endeavors. She was no longer letting her circumstances limit her; she was creating her own advantages.

My short time with her energized and empowered my efforts to help women in sports. If this individual could gain so much through the risks she took, I couldn't wait to see how our efforts would impact many more newly empowered women.

But my contributions are a drop in a bucket—no probably 10,000 buckets—compared to the endless hard work of a true hero, Timothy Shriver...

Timothy Shriver: My Story

Timothy Shriver

Risk

Some of the greatest moments in sports are those defined by the supreme effort put forth by competitors who take every personal risk imaginable to advance the cause, who empty themselves of all energy and capacity, and then somehow find a reservoir of will that propels them beyond fatigue, pain, fear or exhaustion to achieve more than anyone ever thought possible.

Vince Lombardi captured the popular notion of this type of effort—of what it means to "leave everything on the field"—when he said, "I firmly believe that any man's finest hour, the greatest fulfillment of all that he holds dear, is that moment when he has worked his heart out in a good cause and lies exhausted on the field of battle—victorious."

The best known examples of this type of effort are held out as nearly superhuman feats. Michael Jordan, drained and dehydrated with severe flu, carrying his team to victory in a crucial game five of the '97 NBA Finals. Kerri Strug, unable to walk due to torn tendons in her ankle, sealing gold for Team U.S.A. in gymnastics with an unforgettably daring vault and landing at the Atlanta Olympics. Tiger Woods, playing with a bum knee and a broken leg, willing his way to win a sudden death playoff to take the 2008 U.S. Open.

Though not as well known as these feats, at Special Olympics, where athletes with intellectual disabilities compete for respect and acceptance off the field as much as victory on it, these types of heroic, risky, all-out-effort performances happen as well.

Think of Alexi Rogov, a Russian speed skater who competed in the 2009 Special Olympics World Winter Games. He was halfway through his race when he caught an edge and hit the ice, landing so hard and so awkwardly that he sliced through his Achilles tendon

Despite excruciating pain, he got up, and found within himself the will to continue the race and finish. Later, from his bed after surgery, Alexi said that stopping was not an option. "I didn't want to let my teammates down," he told me matter-of-factly.

What is it that propels this type of effort? What enables these athletes to summon this type of bravery—to give the performance of a lifetime when they seemingly have nothing left in the tank to give? What pushes them to say, "It's worth the risk"?

There is a range of characteristics that fuel such accomplishments, but the common denominator, I think, is desire. The desire to go out on the field despite realizing that the odds are against you. Knowing that you are in some way broken, vulnerable, less able than your competition, but nonetheless relentlessly willing to try. It is a desire that fuels the body in pain or the heart depleted that is unafraid of losing and unwilling to live with not having tried. It is the desire that comes from not caring how you look as you hobble along, struggling to complete a race on one skate, but caring deeply about how you'd feel if you didn't finish.

Over the years I've learned that some of these awe-inspiring performances come from the most unlikely competitors. And the most incredible one I ever witnessed, one that outdid Jordan and Tiger and all of them, came from a Special Olympics athlete in a wheelchair. His physical challenges were significant: he couldn't communicate verbally, couldn't feed himself, couldn't perform even basic manual tasks without Herculean effort. And yet he gave a performance that would have made even Lombardi redefine what it meant to be victorious.

The setting was the 2003 Special Olympics World Summer Games in Ireland. At these games, Special Olympics globally unveiled the Motor Activities Training Program (MATP), designed for people with significant limitations who don't yet possess the physical skills necessary to participate in traditional Olympic-type sports..

Examples of MATP activities include the beanbag lift, the ball kick and the log roll. As you might expect, the focus is less on competition and more on training, progress and participation. MATP is designed to give individuals with substantial challenges the opportunity to participate in Special Olympics, while reminding whole communities that no limitation is too great to suppress the desire of the human spirit.

Nonetheless, one might not expect MATP to be a compelling spectator sport. But how wrong! While the activities undertaken are, by themselves, fairly unremarkable, the displays of courage, grit, determination are anything but.

As chairman of Special Olympics, I confess that I was nervous about how the public would respond to an event showcasing the abilities of MATP athletes. However, at those World Games in Ireland, the public caught on quickly to the idea that there was something happening at the MATP venue that was worth seeing. Word spread and lines to get into the venue steadily increased. By the end of the second day there was a *two hour* wait to get inside. But by the time I went, on the third day of the games, the place was packed to the rafters with over fifteen hundred spectators, while hundreds more waited to get in.

In the crowd that day was President of Ireland Mary McAleese, and as she took her seat, out came the first participant, Irish himself, using a wheelchair and clearly of extremely limited mobility. His activity was the beanbag lift, where the goal is to move a bag across a tray attached to his motorized wheelchair. Grasp the beanbag, lift it, move it from one side to the other.

The crowd hushed as his name was announced and he was readied by his coach so that his hand was positioned on the tray within reaching distance of the beanbag. The coach whispered a word of encouragement in his ear, and then stepped aside as the clock started to time his performance.

The first minute passed in silence as he tried to get his fingers to grasp the beanbag. Fifteen hundred people emotionally pulled for this young mean as he struggled to accomplish something most of us take for granted thousands of times every day as we reach for a cup of coffee, or the phone, or a pen.

Halfway through the second minute, the silence was broken by a spectator who yelled out, like the golf fan who can't contain his excitement after a putt, "Come on now!" Other people began to murmur with encouragement.

By the third minute, he still hadn't managed it, but the crowd picked up its volume with every inch of progress made by his uncooperative fingers. And when he finally grasped the beanbag, after three full minutes of concentration and effort, the auditorium erupted.

For the next *fifteen minutes,* while he labored to move the object from one side of the tray to the other, the crowd didn't let up. As the spectators willed him on, he willed on his body, until finally, after eighteen minutes had expired on the clock, he had completed the exercise. As he dropped the beanbag on its target, the noise from the crowd was deafening, and the look on his face was one of total exhaustion, total exhilaration.

Never before had I seen a person risk more, expend more, or leave more of himself on the court than this young man that morning. The courage and confidence he displayed in showing up in front of a crowd that included the president of his country, to perform a task that any one of those watching could have done in three seconds, was hard to fathom.

He didn't know how the crowd would react. They could have pitied him, cringed at the time it took for him to complete his activity, felt embarrassed for him. But despite all the risks, he wanted his chance, he was ready to compete, he had a desire that could not be stopped.

All he could do was give it everything he had, and as a result, there was no pity, no averted eyes, no embarrassment. On the contrary, he had his moment and he claimed it. No one could doubt that he or she had been in the presence of a champion. We were inspired by him, uplifted by the fact that he possessed the courage and desire to risk everything to accomplish what he set out to do.

There is a saying that sports don't build character, they reveal it. For Special Olympics, the revelation can often be as much about the spectator as it is about the athlete. In this case, my experience that day in Ireland revealed something within me that I was often reluctant to admit, which was that even after a lifetime of involvement in Special Olympics, there was a part of me that was always apprehensive in telling the story of our movement. What would others think? Would they be silently dismissive of our athletes and our work? Would they judge us as (at worst) irrelevant or (at best) nice but unimportant? There was something in me that was always fearful of other people's opinions.

But in the eighteen minutes it took that athlete to complete his activity, I was changed. I arrived that day anxious and apprehensive about what others would think, but I left after that heroic performance worried no more. The power in the room wasn't in the shouts of the crowd; it wasn't in the long lines outside the venue; it wasn't even in the presence of the president of the country. It was in the athlete himself. He didn't worry. He wasn't deterred by a lifetime's worth of struggle. He didn't stay home because of fear of being judged.

He was brave, willing, real. He went within, found his strength, felt no limits, embraced all risk.

I try to take his energy to my family, to my colleagues, to those I meet. Sometimes I still wonder whether others are judging me and my message. But when I feel that, I remind myself of that performance in Ireland. I know if this courageous Irishman can stick his neck out to life's greatest risks, then I certainly can as well. It may take eighteen minutes or eighteen days or eighteen years—but somehow, I know the strength of the human spirit will win.

To be successful, you need to...

Be willing to stick your neck out... **Take Some Risks**

Don't build character, reveal it

Nikki's Perspective: *American Idol* is certainly not knocking down my door for my national singing debut. And no one is deprived if I miss karaoke night at the local club. In fact, aware as I am of my lack of singing skill, I always made a point of missing those nights. I wasn't going to embarrass myself by taking a turn at the mike! But one day I let a friend talk me into going and at least watching other people make fools of themselves. Seeing all sorts of people letting loose and having the time of their lives, I eventually threw caution to the wind and joined the ranks on stage.

I wish I could say that taking that risk opened a new avenue for me and melodious sounds came pouring out of my mouth. To be honest, it was more like cats screeching. But the night did help me shed my inhibitions and free myself of my insecurities. The experience was incredibly liberating.

Your Tools for Success: Learn to free your inhibitions and express who you really are. Take the risk of making yourself look foolish today by letting go of your hang-ups. You will likely find that if people do laugh, they are laughing with you and not at you. If they *are* laughing at you, it's the result of their own self-doubts. Only someone who accepts looking foolish is ever really free of their insecurities. You can accomplish much more in life when you aren't hamstrung by your inhibitions. So take time to reveal your true character.

Michael Bronner

Mastermind behind American Express Credit Card Rewards

Photo courtesy of Bob Perachio - RDPphotography.com

Michael Bronner Biography

Michael Bronner is the founder and chairman emeritus of Digitas and Upromise. Digitas, a global interactive marketing agency employing over three thousand people, was purchased by Publicis Groupe in 2006.

Upromise was founded by Michael to help make college more attainable for middle-class families. The company is now the largest private source of college funding in America, with ten million students enrolled in the free service. Upromise was purchased by Sallie Mae in 2006.

Michael serves on the boards of the Boys and Girls Club, Children's Hospital Boston and Boston University. He is a recipient of the Torch of Liberty Award from the Anti-Defamation League, and lives in Boston with his wife and their two sons.

Nikki's Intro to Michael Bronner's Story

As you can imagine, the first time you ski down a hill and into an eight-foot-tall snow jump is terrifying. I have yet to meet someone who didn't have his or her nerves pumping on that first aerial flight. We all have to muster the courage to push off and go for it.

I think the most impressive start I ever saw came from my teammate and fellow Olympic gold medalist, Eric "Bergy" Bergoust.

Whenever we arrive at a new site, athletes do what we call a "speed check," testing our velocity to make sure we'll be able to execute the proper rotation. We ski down the inrun, the radar gun checks our speed, and we stop just short of the jump.

In Bergy's first year jumping, our coach, Bruce Erikson, assumed he knew what a speed check meant. With little more than a shrug, Bergy headed to the top of the inrun. Bruce signaled for him to come down, and soon Bergy came zipping past the speed guns—without stopping. A second later he was flying off the jump and doing his first back flip on snow. His speed was a bit fast, and he went soaring past his landing and onto his back.

We all asked Bergy what he was thinking. He replied that he hadn't been thinking; he was just doing his job as the "speed checker." It made much more sense to him once he learned that a speed check didn't actually require someone going off the jump.

Whenever anything needed to be tested out after that day, we knew that Bergy would, literally, make a "leap of faith." Someone else who I've learned is also always willing to take that leap of faith is Michael Bronner...

Michael Bronner: My Story

Michael Bronner

Risk

I have always related my life as an entrepreneur to the story of the centipede and the grasshopper: "One day the grasshopper asked the centipede, 'How do you do it? You have one hundred legs…how do you know which foot to put down when you walk?' The centipede stopped to ponder the question, and never walked again."

When you want to achieve something great, you can't overanalyze the risks. If you do, you'll find good reason why you shouldn't even start the journey. So from day one, I decided that, to be successful, I had to stick my neck out. When I started my first company, I was twenty years old and had the good fortune of being naive. Sure, there were many reasons why my idea shouldn't have worked—the odds are *always* in favor of failure. Like the centipede, to make the journey requires taking one step at a time, and my first idea was a realistic, achievable step. Most important, my decisions, unlike the centipede's, were not made from a place of "thinking"—they came from a deeper place of knowing, the place of instinct.

As a college student, I went to the dean of housing with the simple idea of putting a free coupon book in all the student mailboxes, pages of which I would sell to local merchants. This was my first business plan and I gave everything I had to make it work. Four months later I had delivered books to nearly a hundred thousand student mailboxes in the Boston area. My next idea was a coupon book distributed to employees of Boston's biggest companies. Success here led me, at twenty years of age, to American Express. My idea was to mail a fancy coupon book to their best card members. So just by using their AmEx card, customers received valuable incentives at neighboring retailers and restaurants.

I knew that American Express would never buy into the idea of a twenty-year-old kid without any real resources developing the project. Creating the proposal and the coupon book was going to cost more money than an average college student has. So without a thought about which of my "one hundred feet" to put in front, I sold my car, borrowed money from my Nana and threw myself into creating the sales pitch. I somehow convinced American Express to let a kid take on this marketing project. My proposal was put to the test in Boston, and the results were astounding.

It wouldn't have been a big risk if the story ended there, but it also wouldn't have been a big reward. I found this was just the beginning of the journey—and risks—I would be taking.

With positive results from the Boston marketing test, American Express agreed to expand the plan to ten more cities. But what this Fortune 500 company told me next I really wasn't prepared for: "We'd like to come by your offices and meet your employees to discuss the details with you."

My offices? My employees? A small apartment and some college buddies didn't really count. I had to quickly locate some space for "offices" and find some "employees." I had two weeks to make sure those "offices" were up and functioning. Luckily, I had a bit of cash left over from my car and the Nana fund—and a contingent agreement for a ten-city program with AmEx.

Again, the centipede in me decided not to ponder the risks. Of course, at any point along the way, American Express could decide to drop my proposal, which meant I would have dumped my money into a lot of unnecessary office space. But two weeks later, when the representatives from American Express walked through our front door, we were a fully operational business. We sold them on the expanded proposal, and six months later the card incentive program was mailed to over a million card members.

The next year, I approached AT&T—then, the world's largest corporation—with my idea for a hundred million dollars annual marketing program that would reach their twenty-five million most valuable customers. It was a "coupon related" plan that would help them compete in the heated telecom market—and would be the largest marketing program ever created. When we launched the campaign it was immediately heralded a huge success, and it lasted for four years.

Because I made each of my smaller ideas come true—like the centipede successfully putting down each of its feet—I started dreaming a truly big idea: to create the country's leading marketing agency. To achieve this goal and sustain it would require that I build one of the most talented organizations ever in the agency and consulting businesses. Over the next ten years we grew to a thousand employees, and ultimately, to over three thousand today, around the globe, serving many of the world's top corporations. Our offices no longer fit in a college apartment!

It was one leg, one step—one dream—at a time.

If you have a dream, you have to be willing to give everything to it in order to be truly fulfilled. Having a dream is what makes life interesting. I did not overanalyze the process; I used my gut instinct to actively move toward each goal. I always knew that I might not succeed, but as long as I tried, I would never feel that I'd failed.

This centipede relied heavily on instinct. He never froze in his tracks to ponder the nearly daily risks...and he got a lot further than almost anyone thought a centipede could.

To be successful, you need to...

Be willing to stick your neck out... **Take Some Risks**

Don't be afraid of failure

Nikki's Perspective: When I was applying to colleges, I didn't have the grade point average or SAT scores of my scholarly sister, Laura. My high school guidance counselor asked me why I wasn't applying to more challenging schools, and my only response was that I didn't have the grades my sister did and I wouldn't get in. He asked me how I knew if I didn't apply. This time, I had no response.

What could I say? He was right. I certainly wasn't going to get in if I didn't apply, and there was no way I could be any worse off by sending in a submission. I took the chance, expanded my application pool and was accepted at six of the seven schools I applied to. The only downside was eating crow in front of my guidance counselor when the acceptance letters came in.

Your Tools for Success: We can't be afraid of failure. If we don't try, we have already failed.

Why not give yourself the chance to succeed? Pick something that scares you a bit, and decide you are going to take the risk to follow through with it today. The only real failure is not trying it at all. As Wayne Gretzky says, "We miss 100 percent of the shots we never take." Take the shot and take the chance.

_____

_____

_____

_____

John Di Lemme

Personal Growth Expert and Speaker

John Di Lemme Biography

In September 2001, John Di Lemme founded Di Lemme Development Group, Inc., a company known worldwide for its role in expanding the personal development industry. As president and CEO, John strives for excellence in every area of his business and believes you must surround yourself with a like-minded team in order to stay on top of your game.

In addition to building a successful company, John has changed the lives of many people around the globe as an international motivational speaker. Over the past eighteen years, he has shared the stage with the best of the best, including Dr. John Maxwell, Dennis Waitley, Jim Rohn, Les Brown, Mark Victor Hansen and Loral Langemeier, to name only a few. This is truly an amazing feat for someone who was clinically diagnosed as a stutterer at a very young age and told that he would never speak fluently.

John truly believes that everyone needs personal development to reach their full potential in life, and his determination to reach all forms of media with his motivational messages has catapulted his career. He is an accomplished author of several books, including his latest bestseller Champions Are Born, Losers Are Made! *John is also co-host of an international success show and has been featured on many television programs, including CNBC's* Power Lunch. *A multimillion-dollar entrepreneur, John is one of the most highly sought after strategic business coaches in the world.*

John's passion is to teach others how to live a champion life despite any labels society may have placed on them. Through his books, audio/video materials, sold-out live seminars, numerous television interviews, intensive training boot camps, live webinars, website (www. ChampionsAreBornLosersAreMade.com) and weekly tele-classes, John has made success a reality for thousands worldwide.

Nikki's Intro to John Di Lemme's Story

As Eleanor Roosevelt said, "No one can make you feel inferior without your consent." I know that as a young girl, I once gave someone my consent. We all know the reason for "smack talk"—to play with a competitor's head so you can beat her. As a young gymnast, I got on the wrong side of some serious smack talk.

A rival came up to me halfway through a competition and told me that I had been lucky in the first few events, but didn't have the talent to hold on to the lead and nail a floor routine with a more difficult tumbling pass. I broke down and let the girl get in my head. I went for the easier move and lost the All-Around...to *her*!

I think my teammates expected me to be mad at my rival. But I knew all too well that only I had the power to lose my nerve. I was so disappointed in myself. After that day, I promised I would never give anyone that consent again.

John Di Lemme certainly knows how I feel...

John Di Lemme: My Story

John Di Lemme

Interview

Donald Duck and Woody Woodpecker were my nemeses growing up. For most kids, these animated characters were a fun-filled source of entertainment. For me, they were a reminder of the taunts and teasing I received from my classmates. I still remember walking into my seventh grade class and hearing the other students tease, "Di-Di-Di-Di Lemme!" while holding up a drawing of Woody Woodpecker.

You see, I was a stutterer. We all remember going around the classroom in elementary school, each reading part of a story aloud. Maybe not everyone recalls it quite as vividly as I do. This participatory activity was something I dreaded more than going to the dentist for a major root canal. Kids can be cruel, and my stuttering was a source of great fun for some students in my class.

They were my dream stealers. They were trying to plant the seed in my mind that I'd always be a failure. What they didn't realize is that I could uproot that idea and plant my own seeds for success. Everyone is born a champion, but we have to learn the habits and strategies to succeed.

I remember being inspired to break from my anxieties of speaking aloud, while hearing a speech by John F. Kennedy. When asked if he'd consider running for vice president, he replied that when you choose second place, you develop a habit of coming in in an inferior position, or learn the option of not taking the ultimate risk. It hit me, when I heard that speech, that one day I would stick my neck out just as JFK did. I knew the whole world believed I would always be a stutterer. And I was shy at the time, full of anxiety and afraid of my own shadow. But I was determined that I was goig to speak in front of an audience someday. And when I spoke, I wasn't going to prove them right. I was going to succeed, and teach all my fellow cowering violets out there to overcome their fears.

After twenty-four long, painful years of ridicule, I realized that I had to finally put some action to my claims of conquering my fears.

Decision + Action = Results

I would never get to the results if this vision just lived in my head.

I attended a personal development seminar and decided it was about time I stopped listening to the dream stealers, and take ownership of my fears. I had to face down my doubts and take the chance to get my message out. I knew I'd never be the world's best orator, but I could be the world's best messenger. I believed there was a lot more John Di Lemme had to offer the world.

Every day for the next six years, I worked on my stuttering, one letter at a time. Sometimes I even had to scream and yell out loud to run through the hard ones. I worked on making myself a little more uncomfortable every day. I continually read about people like JFK and Martin Luther King, Jr. who set a precedence by stepping over that imaginary line of fear. My heroes taught me that nothing ever happens in the comfort zone. It was time to escape my comfort zone, venture into "enemy territory" and let them know I had arrived.

And after twenty-four years of vowing that I would someday speak to a crowd of people, I heard the MC at a large event announce my name. This time they weren't saying "Di-Di-Di-Di Lemme. They were saying my name with authority and respect. When I heard my name thundering through the speakers in the auditorium, I couldn't believe this moment was really happening. I was actually taking the risk and standing up to my biggest fears. Fears that a few years earlier would have likely made me faint.

Believe it or not, as I walked onto the stage, all my fears just fell away. I was actually excited to be there. I didn't see it as a chance of making a fool of myself, but as an opportunity to change someone else's life…not to mention my own.

Today, one of my biggest fears is that people won't think my story is true. Folks don't want to believe someone can go through such a momentous transformation, because they would then have to admit they aren't willing to take those same risks themselves. I just have to prove to my audiences that it's not as bad as they think.

I call it the cocoon process. I explain to people that if they have butterflies in their stomach, they've already gone through the hardest process. The transformation has already started. Those butterflies are created by excitement and belief that their dreams are possible. The next step is to allow those butterflies to break through their cocoons and spread their wings in the outside world. Yes, this means that the person is ready to take the risk to stick his or her neck out and refuse to be labeled by society.

Of course, I would like to believe that, when people think of John Di Lemme now, they imagine pictures of Superman, or Hercules, or even Mighty Mouse. But to be honest, I'd just be happy knowing that they were imagining a path to their future. A future that this stuttering woodpecker helped to guide.

To be successful, you need to...

Be willing to stick your neck out... **Take Some Risks**

Don't settle

Nikki's Perspective: Anyone who wanted to graduate from Union College with honors was required to complete a senior thesis. I had the grades, but writing a thesis was going to be quite a challenge because I was already working full force to come back from my spinal injury and prepare for the next Olympics. I was advised to give up my goal of earning honors, and just be happy that I was graduating with good grades.

I must admit I was tempted to take this route. But the fact that I'd be settling for an easier solution after so many years of hard work kept tugging at my conscience. I spoke with a professor who agreed to be my thesis advisor and push me through the challenges. I took the risk, and nine months later graduated from Union College...with an honors sash draped around my neck.

Your Tools for Success: Ask yourself if you are settling for second best. Are you telling yourself that's okay? That your efforts are "good enough"? Are you content with your relationship being "tolerable"?

You need to figure out what risks you could be taking to make sure you're not just aiming for what is comfortable. No great leader, CEO or Olympic champion ever settled for what was "satisfactory." Pick a new goal, one that makes you stretch, and don't settle for anything "easy." People rarely achieve a level of success higher than their ultimate goals, so aim high.

_____

_____

_____

_____

_____

Teamwork /
Support

Teamwork

As soon as the reality that I *had* actually just won an Olympic gold medal hit, I knew I had to find my soon-to-be-husband, Michael, and my parents. Most people wouldn't understand the sheer joy I was experiencing, but there were three people who I knew would feel the same way I did at that moment. I ran over to where the media had ushered my family. I spotted my parents by the American flags they were waving. I fell into their arms and we all broke down in tears.

The other medal winners and I were given a few hours to shower, dress in our podium uniforms and make our way from the ski resort to downtown Nagano, the site of the medal ceremony. Within forty-five minutes of arriving, the three women's and three men's aerial skiing medalists were escorted to a giant arena where a thousand screaming fans were waiting. Somewhere in the throngs of spectators were Michael and my parents.

We were told to wait for the music and then follow a beautiful little Japanese girl across a long platform to a stage at the front of the arena. I was amazed to hear hundreds of strangers calling out my name. Was this all really happening?

We were placed in front of an enormous podium in the center of the stage, Switzerland's Colette Brand to my left and China's Nannan Xu on my right. They announced the gold medalist first. Over the loudspeaker came the best words I had ever heard uttered: "Congratulations to *Olympic gold medalist Nikki Stone*." I had waited so long to hear those words!

I bounded onto the top step and threw my arms over my head to the sound of cheering spectators. I dropped my head back and closed my eyes to take it all in. When I opened them again, a woman was holding up a pillow with the most precious-looking medal resting in the center. I slowly bowed my head as a tall, gray-haired gentleman placed the medal around my neck. Chills ran up and down my spine as I wrapped my fingers around *my* Olympic gold medal. I leaned forward and pressed my lips against the cold metal. I wanted to take in every ounce of it.

Both Nannan and Colette were awarded their medals, and I recognized the same look of pride cross their faces. Just when I thought I couldn't handle any more emotion, I glanced across the stage and noticed three poles off in the distance. On the middle one, officials were raising a red-white-and-blue flag. Even folded, I could tell it was the

American flag, *my* flag. Almost simultaneously, the arena filled with the opening notes of the "Star Spangled Banner." This win was for me and for the United States.

A lot of people asked me if I would be happy finishing second or third. And I really would be happy just knowing that I had done my best. But when you win the silver or bronze, you don't get to hear your national anthem. As the U.S. anthem started to play, I couldn't hold back the tears that welled up in my eyes.

I thought back to that little pigtailed, freckle-faced girl who had made her own "Olympic podium" twenty-two years earlier. I realized that this moment represented the fruition of those dreams. This was what the hard work was for. This was what the pain was for. This was what the agony, the tears, the dedication and the sacrifice were all about. It was all for this moment, on the podium, listening to my country's anthem.

I kept shaking my head because I couldn't believe this was all happening to me.

I had recurring dreams about those Olympic finals for the next two weeks. Every night in my dream, someone would tell me, "You know what? It didn't really count. We need to do it all over again." And every night I would reply, "I knew it was too good to be true." Then I would wake up the next morning, shove my hand under my pillow and find my Olympic gold medal. And I knew it was mine, for life.

Well, I do still have that medal in my possession, and I'm the one who stood atop that Olympic podium. But it was listening to the American anthem that reminded me no one gets to the top alone. Our anthem represented all the people who worked to make our country strong, and my medal represented all the people who worked to make *me* strong. It was a team effort.

I needed the sponsors who made it possible for me to put my time into my training. I needed the medical staff who helped me recover from my injury. I needed the people who put banners around my hometown of Westborough, Massachusetts, to remind me there were folks rooting me on back home. I needed the letters from schoolkids around the U.S. to emphasize that I was a role model to others. I needed my friends, who promised they would be up watching me compete at 3:00 a.m., if need be, to cheer me on to victory. I needed my coaches, who learned who I was and what I required as an individual. I needed my competitors, who always pushed me to understand my true limits. I needed my teammates, who demonstrated loyalty by coming out on the day of finals to support me, even though they were depressed after just missing qualifying for finals themselves. And I needed the strangers that I met on planes, trains, shuttle buses and park benches, reminding me that I represented something much bigger than myself.

Possibly, more than anyone else, I needed my family. This wasn't just about my sacrifice, it was about theirs as well. I did a sport that was not only terrifying to watch in normal circumstances, it could have proved disastrous to someone with a spinal injury. But my sister, grandparents, aunts, uncles and cousins never let their concern dominate.

They all just encouraged me to pursue my dreams. I think they knew me well enough to understand that I really wouldn't have had it any other way.

No one understood my dedication as much as my future husband and my parents. I knew I would marry Michael someday—knew it the moment he told me he had just been fired from his job because he had left work to come to Japan to support me at the Olympic Games. I think he had more confidence in my abilities than I did. Even before we left he told me that he *had* to come or he would forever regret missing my winning performance.

Two other people who weren't going to miss that day were my mom and dad. I now have a daughter of my own, and understand how that moment at the games was likely more moving for them than it actually was for me. I later saw that the interview they did with TNT was more emotional than my own. My father became choked up talking about how he couldn't wait to see the American flag being raised…for *me*. And my mother barely got four words out before she dashed off to come find me.

I now find it funny that they call anything an "individual sport." Such an activity doesn't exist. It is unfortunate that it took me twenty-two years to realize that standing on a podium, or pulpit, or mountain, or stage, is not about that last exalted step, but about the journey to get there, and those who helped make it possible.

I often think that life is like that Olympic podium. We get caught up trying to clamber to the top, and forget to appreciate all those people giving us a boost up. It's all those individuals giving us a hand that inspire us to stick our necks out. I now know how important it is to make sure these people get a boost in return. When we work together, no podium is out of reach.

Erik Weihenmayer & Jeff Evans

First Blind Climber and his Climbing Guide to Summit Everest

Erik Weihenmayer. Photo courtesy of Michael O' Donnell

Erik Weihenmayer Biography

On May 25, 2001, Erik Weihenmayer became the only blind man in history to reach the summit of the world's highest peak, Mount Everest. On August 20, 2008, when he stood on top of Carstenz Pyramid, the tallest peak in Australasia, Weihenmayer completed his quest to climb the Seven Summits—the highest mountains on each of the seven continents. Erik is joined by fewer than a hundred mountaineers who have accomplished this feat. Additionally, he has scaled El Capitan, the sheer 3,300 foot overhanging granite monolith in Yosemite, Lhosar, a 3,000 foot ice waterfall in the Himalayas, and a difficult and rarely climbed rock face on 17,000 foot Mount Kenya.

A former middle school teacher and wrestling coach, Erik is now one of the most exciting and well-known athletes in the world. Despite losing his vision at the age of thirteen, he has become an accomplished mountain climber, paraglider and skier, and has never let his blindness interfere with his passion for leading an exhilarating and fulfilling life. Erik's feats have earned him an ESPY Award, recognition by Time Magazine for one of the greatest sporting achievements of 2001, induction into the National Wrestling Hall of Fame, an ARETE Award for the superlative athletic performance of the year, the Helen Keller Lifetime Achievement Award, Nike's Casey Martin Award, and the Freedom Forum's Free Spirit Award. He has also carried the Olympic Torch for both the summer and winter games.

Jeff Evans. Photo courtesy of Didrik Johnck

Jeff Evans Biography

Jeff Evans, founder of MountainVision Inc., grew up scampering around the Blue Ridge Mountains of Virginia and North Carolina, but soon found that the higher mountains of Colorado would be the ideal setting to challenge himself as a mountain guide. At the age of nineteen, Jeff packed up his truck and relocated to the Colorado Front Range, beginning his love affair with the Rocky Mountains.

The turning point in Jeff's guiding career came in the early 1990s, when he embraced the responsibilities to guide a then-unknown blind climber, Erik Weihenmayer. Together, they problem-solved methods of adventure, travel and communication to tackle the most challenging climbing and mountaineering endeavors ever attempted by a disabled athlete. Some of their more notable ascents include Mount McKinley, El Capitan, Leaning Tower and Aconcagua, culminating in 2001 with the challenge of Mount Everest that gained much international attention as the first successful summit of the highest mountain in the world by a blind person.

Somewhere in his years of mountain guiding, Jeff found time to squeeze in training as an emergency medicine physician assistant. He has focused his medical training even more with an emphasis on travel and altitude medicine, stressing safety and health on every one of his MountainVision trips.

However, Jeff's main passion is bringing the lessons he has learned from his experience as a world-class mountain guide to the presentations and training he provides to companies and organizations worldwide. MountainVision Presentations brings dynamic messages that resonate with corporate and civic groups.

Jeff is a graduate of the University of Colorado, Boulder, in cultural anthropology and religious studies, and Drexel Medical School in Pennsylvania. He also attended the University of Guadalajara in Mexico, where he spent a term studying Latin American culture and Spanish. He resides in Boulder, Colorado, with his wife, Merry Beth, and son, Jace.

Nikki's Intro to Erik Weihenmayer's and Jeff Evans's Story

Several years ago, I served as a board member of a program with the United States Olympic Committee, where eight Olympic medalists would help mentor future potential medalists. We would play different games and activities that would teach the current athletes important lessons in finding their own success. My fellow Olympians would go through training sessions ourselves to make sure we understood the important lessons to be learned.

One game we played, called Landmine, taught us about relying on a partner for teamwork and support. One team member was blindfolded and the other would act as a guide to direct him or her through a minefield of obstacles—chairs, balloons, buckets, puddles, etc. The goal was to make it to the other side of the room without touching any of the obstacles. The "guide" would call out when to step forward or sideways, take a big or small step, turn at an angle, duck down, and so on.

The game turned out to be much more challenging than I'd anticipated. I was amazed at how difficult it was to relinquish control and rely on my teammate's advice. When we switched positions and I became the "guide," I realized how crucial my input was for my partner's success.

A million analogies immediately flooded my mind, not the least of which was that sometimes someone else might have a better perspective on the route we should take. Do others trust my input? Am I finding the right people to guide me? Am I using other people's support when it's offered?

Luckily for Erik Weihenmayer and Jeff Evans, they figured all this out before they set foot on Mount Everest...

Erik Weihenmayer & Jeff Evans: Our Story

Erik Weihenmayer & Jeff Evans

Teamwork

<ERIK & JEFF> Sixty days in and, jointly, seventy-five pounds lighter, we found the peak of Everest finally within striking range. The last two months had taken their toll on our bodies, whether blind or sighted. Dysentery had set in and our bodies were cannibalizing themselves in order to get the proteins they needed for energy and survival. The extreme altitude would be enough to slow us down even if we'd been in peak condition. We were quickly running low on our oxygen supply and had to make sure we'd have enough to get back down the mountain. Neither of us had ever summited Everest, and it was a dream we were going to keep pushing each other to achieve.

The night before our final ascent on the summit of the tallest mountain on earth, 29,035 feet above sea level, we came upon two sets of ropes that led up the southeast ridge in different directions...

<JEFF> I realized I had an enormous weight on my shoulders and one of the biggest decisions of my life to make. The path to the left would be much easier for me, but much harder for Erik… But if I used the extra energy to pull the other ropes out of the snow, I knew that I would, in turn, be sacrificing my first and only summit.

After much contemplation, I kept coming back to the decision that, deep down, I knew I would make all along. This expedition wasn't about me. Our team was here for Erik. My summiting Everest wouldn't be the thing that inspired a group of young, blind Tibetan teenagers to climb a 23,000 foot peak. My summiting Everest would not cause jaws to drop. My summiting Everest would be a personal victory. I had to swallow my ego and get to work on those ropes.

Dig, chop, pull, dig, chop, pull. Two hours later, with every last ounce of my reserves spent, the ropes were finally freed.

<ERIK> I could feel Jeff's eyes on me as he declared, "This is going to have to be my summit. I left **everything** I had out there on those buried ropes."

I truly felt as if I'd been punched in the gut. The wind was immediately sucked out of me and I was completely deflated. How could I go on? We had always put ourselves out there together; we had done everything together. How could I continue without him? I just didn't want to summit without Jeff. He had sacrificed everything for me.

I suddenly felt his arms around me. And, in that embrace, I realized that it was my job to summit. Everyone had worked so hard for me, and if I didn't reach the summit, I would be letting our whole team down. If I succeeded, we all succeeded. That one embrace was so telling of the person Jeff was, and why I couldn't let him or the rest of our group down in this challenging pursuit. Louis, another teammate, was ready to take the reins and guide me toward team glory.

<JEFF> I watched Erik **push** forward and let go of his fears to attain a goal that no other blind man dared attempt. Being on so many adventures with Erik, I had long since stopped being inspired by his feats. The sight of him scrambling up a rocky ledge or standing on top of some snowy peak now seemed commonplace.

But as I looked up and saw Erik start along the ridge toward the highest peak on earth, those initial feelings of inspiration were suddenly rejuvenated. Erik was pushing out of his comfort level to show the team how grateful he was for everything we had done for him. He was surpassing limits, smashing preconceptions about what a sightless person can accomplish. He was sticking his neck out…for me.

That tank that appeared to be on Empty unexpectedly had fuel to burn. Through sheer inspiration, Erik was giving me the energy I needed. I saw him pushing himself those last few steps toward the summit and I reached deeper within myself to summon the strength and will to push toward the top. I slowly pressed on, focusing on putting one foot in front of the other.

<ERIK> With forty feet left, my breathing slowed. Six breaths between each step. Only half an hour to go… One of my teammates, Chris Morris, gripped my shoulder and said, "Big E, you are about to stand on top of the world." A smile spread across my face.

The exhilaration of my last step was only eclipsed by the sound of a voice that shortly followed. It was the best thing I had heard throughout the entire journey: "I wasn't going to let you stand up here, and have to hear about it the rest of my life." Jeff was right there by my side.

<ERIK & JEFF> One by one, our teammates took that final step. We ended up having nineteen people from our group summit that day, the most people from one team to ever reach the top of Everest in one day. It was a mutual effort and there is no way any of us could have done it alone. Time Magazine even listed us as one of the best teams ever to climb Everest.

After a long embrace, we knew that everyone was thinking about that same unspoken fact: it only counts if we get down. The majority of those who die on Everest do so on the descent.

<ERIK> I had purchased a **roundtrip** ticket and intended to stick to that itinerary. I readied myself for the grueling trip back down. The snow squeaked behind me as I sensed Jeff edge up alongside me. "Hey Erik, I know you're anxious to start down, but take a minute to look around. You're likely only going to be here once. And it would be a shame if you didn't take it all in."

I'm so glad that Jeff encouraged me to take the time to appreciate that moment. I reached down and touched the snow through my gloves, and stopped and listened. Even in silence, I could always hear sounds of the world around me bouncing off the peaks of other mountaintops. But at the top of Everest, all I heard were sounds of space. I felt as if I was being swallowed up by the sky. Though I lost the use of my eyes long ago, on that day I saw a glorious vision.

<JEFF> Spiritually, **emotionally** and professionally, it was the most powerful experience I ever endured, and the view from the top took my breath away. Erik's depiction made us all perceive that mountaintop experience much differently. Who would have thought that a blind man would be the one to truly help me see?

To be successful, you need to...

Be willing to stick your neck out... **Use Teamwork**

No one gets to the top alone

Nikki's Perspective: Many people think that because I took part in an individual—versus team—sport, there wasn't a teamwork element. I absolutely guarantee that I wouldn't have my Olympic medal if I didn't know how to find, rely on and get help from many people around me. Take my coach, for instance. If you want to understand trust, try spinning at a hundred revolutions per minute five stories in the air, and counting on someone to tell you when to land right side up. Aerialists flip and twist through space so quickly that we have a hard time deciphering how high we are off the ground. So my coach would call out instructions—to stretch my body and slow down my rotation, if I was flipping too quickly, or to pull my knees in to increase my revolutions if I was somersaulting too slowly. If I didn't rely on his directions, and follow them implicitly, I likely would have found myself in a hospital bed rather than on an Olympic podium. Trust me, *no one* gets to the top alone.

Your Tools for Success: It doesn't take a genius to find the support you need. The real genius lies in recognizing that you need it! Take the time to see if you are letting others in to help you.

Are you one of those people who insist on controlling a situation? How uncomfortable are you in releasing some of that control? Ask yourself why you need to maintain this power. Try to see if you can let go of even part of that stubborn side by asking someone for help or delegating responsibility today for some small task you would normally do yourself.

Notice that someone else's support and perspective can actually enhance the finished product. And may even allow you time to turn your attention toward more important issues.

_____

_____

_____

_____

_____

Thomas Sullivan

World Trade Center Survivor and Citizen Soldier

Photo provided by Thomas Sullivan

Thomas Sullivan Biography

Thomas P. Sullivan is a native of Brooklyn, New York. Born September 20, 1971, he is one of seven sons of John and Ursula Sullivan. Thomas and his wife, Deborah Ruane of Levittown, NY, have three children, Sean, Jack and Grace. They reside in Breezy Point, NY. In his civilian career Thomas is a financial advisor for AXA Advisors, LLC, in Lake Success, NY.

Thomas received a Bachelor of Science degree in business and finance from Mount Saint Mary's University in Emmitsburg, Maryland, in May 1993. In conjunction with his undergraduate studies, Thomas completed the Reserve Officers Training Program, ROTC, and was commissioned a second lieutenant in the Army Reserve on May 22, 1993. He received his master's in business administration from Mount Saint Mary's in May 1996. During his graduate studies Thomas served as an assistant professor of military science to first-year and second-year cadets.

As a citizen soldier, Major Sullivan has served in various leadership and operational positions, including: transportation movement officer, detachment commander, aide-de-camp, company commander, and currently as a brigade plans & operations officer. He mobilized on January 16, 2003, as the company commander of the 623rd Transportation Company in Support of Operation Enduring Freedom. On February 23, 2006, he commanded and deployed with the 773rd Transportation Company in support of Operation Iraqi Freedom.

His formal military education includes the Transportation Officer Basic and Advanced Courses, the Pre-Command Course, and Combined Arms Exercise Course.

Major Sullivan's awards include the Bronze Star Medal, Meritorious Service Medal 1-OLC, Army Commendation Medal 4-OLC, Army Achievement Medal 4-OLC, National Defense Service Medal, Armed Forces Reserve Medal w/ "H" & "M" Device, the Global War on Terrorism Service Medal, and the Army Service Ribbon.

Nikki's Intro to Thomas Sullivan's Story

As a freshman in high school, I had the surprise of being elected captain of our school's gymnastics team. I knew it was a crucial role and I would have to lead my teammates through a number of heated meets, including the event against Westborough's biggest rival, Algonquin High School. Even freshmen knew about the ongoing competition between the two schools. The tension at the competition was evident before we hit the floor exercise.

I was having my best high school meet to date. Going into the final event, I was in first place, and all I needed was a simple vault to wrap up the all-around medal for myself. But by doing a quick calculation, I realized the team needed for me to bring in a high score, in order to win the meet, and the simple vault I had planned just wouldn't cut it. I was thrown into the dilemma of whether to go for the easier vault, to win the all-around, or risk a more difficult maneuver, and possibly win the team competition. After weighing my options, I decided that, as the captain, I had the obligation to take the risk, for our team and for the school's honor. I nailed the more difficult vault and Westborough High won its first team competition in five years.

It's one thing to sacrifice for a high school competition, but a whole different realm for someone to consider sacrificing his or her life. There are few people I've met who have completely blown me away with their actions. Major Thomas Sullivan is one of them…

Thomas Sullivan: My Story

Thomas Sullivan

Teamwork

As usual, I arrived at work at 7:30 a.m. that day and made my way up to the Fiduciary Trust International offices. I couldn't wait to tell my coworkers that my wife and I were expecting twins. I ate breakfast at my desk and waited for my boss, Anthony, to arrive.

I marched into Anthony's office at 8:40 a.m. and eagerly sat down to tell him the news. He shared in my obvious joy and we went on chitchatting for another five minutes. His office window looked north over Manhattan, so my gaze wandered to the view as I listened to him speak. My jaw dropped and my eyes must have popped out of my head when, in my peripheral vision, I saw a large airplane career into the north tower next to ours.

The date, as all the world now knows, was September 11, 2001. At the time, I didn't know why it happened or what more was in store for the World Trade Center. There was nothing signifying that our tower was next and I never for the life of me thought another jet would be coming. But seeing with my own eyes the plane strike the adjacent highrise, I was fearful that our building could also catch on fire. I just knew we had to get out.

Our offices were on the ninety-fifth floor, and being the deputy warden for the floor, I made the decision to tell everyone we should evacuate. Anthony quickly rushed out the door. I later found out that he had run up the stairs to our other offices, on the ninety-seventh floor, to warn the others. He was one of many friends I never saw again.

I warned everyone on the floor, did everything I could to convince them of the urgency of evacuating fast, and then made my way to the stairs. With the chaos I had just seen, I expected the stairwell to be clamoring with frantic people. Eerily, everything was very quiet.

I quickly made my way down to the seventy-eighth floor and the main elevator banks. The frantic mobs I had been anticipating were all stacked up and pressing against the elevator doors. Since using the elevators was hopeless, I jumped back into the stairwell and continued down the staircase, several steps at a time.

At around the sixty-fifth floor or so, we heard a loud crash and the floor beneath us shook. The wall beside me split open and I would have found myself upside down on the staircase had I not been holding on to the railing. Within seconds, the stairwell doors flew open and people started yelling about a second plane. I took a deep breath and calmly made my way down the stairs with hundreds, if not thousands, of other World Trade Center employees. I knew there were still many people in the tower's top ten floors, so my heart sank when I looked up and found that I was one of the last individuals descending the staircase. People were terrified, but I don't think everyone experienced the fear I felt, having witnessed the impact firsthand. I was just fortunate enough to have seen the plane explode, and to have had that fear thrown into me. It was like a force pulling us down the stairs as we made our way to the tower's lobby. Along the way, many of us assisted those who were in more obvious immediate distress. It was a group effort, and no one wanted to leave anyone behind.

When we reached the main lobby we were ushered back into the stairwells, through the basement and out onto Church Street, because of the falling debris. I followed the mob of people hurrying away from the towers. One after another, we would turn and look over our shoulder at the horror behind us. Both towers were now engulfed in flames and people were leaping from the blazing windows to a terrifying death. Uncontrollable sickness pooled in my gut. It was like a scene from hell, and one that will live with me until I die.

While I was getting my bearings, I heard a horrifying noise that seemed to start far below my feet. I immediately thought that another plane must have slammed into the buildings. I never imagined the towers would come crashing down. But as we looked up, a flood of debris came rolling off the south tower as each floor sank through the ones below it. Everyone around me must have had the same fear of the buildings toppling over sideways, for on cue, we all set off, running away from the destruction as fast as our legs could carry us. The full weight of the situation came crashing down on me. I'd been in that building just minutes earlier.

When the dust and debris started to settle and the cloud hanging over Manhattan lightened, we all looked around to survey the damage. Shops were vacated. The ferries were closed. And everyone was covered in a layer of dust. People were handing out water, brushing each other off and trying to come to terms with what just happened. Then the second tower came crashing down. Once again, the collapse shook me to my soul.

I felt that if I didn't try to get out of the city right away, I never would. Along with tens of thousands of other New Yorkers, I made my way on foot over the Brooklyn Bridge. I was headed for home, now eleven miles away. About two miles into the walk, I realized that I had torn my pants and was missing a shoe. I was at the end of my rope, and had to find a phone to let my family know that I had made it out.

I joined an ever-growing lineup at the phone booth, and when I finally dialed, I couldn't wait to hear the voice on the other end of the line. My lifeline. Before the second syllable was out of my mouth, a cry shot through the phone, "He's alive!" Though I knew I meant a lot to my family, the cheers I heard were unbelievable in that moment.

I walked another couple of miles before my brother finally picked me up and brought me home to my family. I don't think I have ever been happier to see them. As I walked in the front door, my father looked as if he'd seen a ghost, and grabbed me to make sure I was real. My wife gave me one of the biggest hugs I had ever felt. And I realized how lucky I was.

The phone rang off the hook every day for the next couple of weeks. So many people wanted to ask me about family members who didn't make it out. Had I seen them? What were they wearing? What were they like the last time I saw them? Were they in a good mood that morning?

I went to a great many funerals over that time. Occasionally, I would hear someone say he or she was so happy I had gotten out alive, and one man even gave me credit for saving his life, because I'd convinced him to evacuate when he didn't think it was necessary. But on several occasions there were questions, and even harder, accusations. Why couldn't I help them? How come I couldn't save more people? My wife decided she wasn't going to any more funerals, and wanted to know how I tolerated the insults. I told her that I *had* to go. I told her those people were just struggling with their loss. We were all struggling.

It was for a time just like this that I had remained active with the Army Reserve—even when my obligation of service finally ended, one year before. I had stayed on in case of a national emergency. In case my country needed me. Then, in January 2003, I was called up to go to Iraq. I understood that they needed me. And to be honest, I also needed them. I needed to feel a mutual support system.

To my disappointment, that deployment didn't go through. After nearly being deployed several times after that, I was finally given my chance to go overseas to serve my country in January 2006, and I joined the Iraq war unconditionally. Whether or not I agree with the war was irrelevant to my service. It wasn't a question; I was in. I just wanted to be a part of helping my country, and I'm proud of my service. I felt I could finally give all the 9-11 mourners answers to what I did for my country. Especially after my country had done so much for me.

I often look back and hope that everyone finds peace somehow…myself included. I still struggle to find it. Sometimes I get quite angry. There is no closure yet. There are those moments when I think *what if?* I see the way my mother looks at my children, and I know she's thinking the same. *What if?*

I always wonder what tomorrow will bring. But life has to go on, and we need each other to make the best of every day. I hope I've done so.

September 11 affected us all in ways we never imagined possible. I became a part of history that day…whether I wanted to or not. There were horrific things that came out of that experience. But it really helped me realize that we won't get anywhere in this world without sticking our necks out for each other. We have to supply support for others if we're ever going to expect it in return.

My life as a citizen soldier let me find the support I could give other people. I'm not a doctor, so I can't save lives on a daily basis. I'm not a teacher, so I can't bring up the citizens of the future. But if I can work to preserve their freedom, then I've found my way to give back.

My thoughts and prayers for the hundred and four friends and colleagues who perished on September 11, 2001. You will never be forgotten.

To be successful, you need to...

Be willing to stick your neck out... **Use Teamwork**

Find a better you

Nikki's Perspective: I had a friend who was so negative that I would often be in a worse mood after visiting with her than I had been before. I was becoming so negative myself that I was bringing people around *me* down. I didn't like who I was becoming.

I found that I was much happier and more productive when I started hanging out with people who were positive, and I even confronted my friend and worked with her to improve her outlook, resulting in her becoming a happier person, too. I want to make sure that I'm the type of individual people will turn to when they need some positivity in their lives.

Your Tools for Success: Find people who will support you and make you a better, more productive person. Today, stop and ask yourself if your support system is actually helping you to become that way. Do you like who you are when you are around your friends and colleagues? Consider whether members of your social network are supporting you or draining you.

If certain people are draining you or bringing you down, do you really want them in your life? If you truly need these individuals, suggest ways you might improve your situation together. And always be sure that you are doing your part to help bolster your supporters. Ask yourself if you are finding ways to make those around you better people.

_____

_____

_____

_____

_____

Branford Marsalis

Top Jazz Musician

Photo courtesy of Palma Kolansky

Branford Marsalis Biography

World-renowned saxophonist Branford Marsalis has always been a man of numerous musical interests, including jazz, blues, funk and classical music. The New Orleans native was born in 1960 into one of the city's most distinguished musical families, and gained initial acclaim through his work with Art Blakey's Jazz Messengers, and his brother Wynton's quintet, in the early 1980s, before forming his own ensemble. Branford has also performed and recorded with a who's who of jazz giants, including Miles Davis, Dizzy Gillespie, Herbie Hancock and Sonny Rollins.

Known for his innovative spirit and broad musical scope, Branford is equally at home on the stages of the world's greatest clubs and concert halls, where he has performed jazz with his quartet, his own unique musical approach to contemporary popular music with his band Buckshot LeFonque, and as a featured soloist with acclaimed symphony orchestras in the United States and Europe.

The three-time Grammy winner founded the Marsalis Music record label in 2002, through which he has produced both his own projects and those of the jazz world's most promising new and established artists.

Marsalis is also dedicated to changing the future of jazz in the classroom. He has shared his knowledge at such universities as Michigan State, San Francisco State, Stanford and North Carolina Central, with his full quartet participating in an innovative extended residency at the NCCU campus. Beyond these efforts, he is also bringing a new approach to jazz education to student musicians and listeners in colleges and high schools through Marsalis Jams, an interactive program designed by Marsalis, in which leading jazz ensembles present concert/ jam sessions in mini-residencies.

Among the most socially conscious voices in the arts, Marsalis quickly immersed himself in relief efforts following the devastation of Hurricane Katrina. He is the honorary chair of the New Orleans Habitat for Humanity effort to rebuild the city, and together with his friend, Harry Connick, Jr., conceived the Habitat Musicians' Village currently under construction in the city's historic Ninth Ward.

Nikki's Intro to Bradford Marsalis's Story

My impressions of the Olympic spirit were forever changed on August 5, 1984, at the very first women's Olympic marathon. I had long ago become an Olympic junkie, and my admiration of world-class athletes was firmly established, but not until that day did I truly understood what sportsmanship was all about.

It wasn't the winner or other medalists who impressed me most that day. It was two women who entered the Olympic stadium fifteen minutes after the winner crossed the finish line. Swiss competitor Gabriele Andersen-Scheiss was staggering from heat exhaustion. It took her more than five minutes to hobble around the track, occasionally stopping to hold her head. Her tenacity was inspiring, but what touched me even more was the athlete who entered the stadium after her. This runner—I don't even know her name—stopped by Andersen-Scheiss to see if she was okay, and to ask if she wanted to cross the finish line in front of her. How noble of the young woman to acknowledge that Gabriele had led her for twenty-six miles, and only by unfortunate circumstances would she lose that lead in the last fraction of a mile!

Just as noble, Andersen-Scheiss waved the gracious runner on, to surpass her at the end. It was so moving to see two people so appreciative and supportive of each other's efforts.

Another individual who I know would always support others in need is Branford Marsalis...

Branford Marsalis: My Story

Branford Marsalis

Teamwork

I can still remember sitting on my front stoop when I was young, listening to the local musicians of New Orleans. They were part of a real community, and supported each other like no group of artists I've ever encountered elsewhere.

So I was shocked when I moved to New York City and saw firsthand the competitive nature of the "real world." The Big Apple made me realized how unique New Orleans truly was. Growing up, you would hear one musician finish his gig and then encourage the crowd, "You have to go across the street to take in this other guy's set because he's even better than me."

The New Orleans I knew changed forever on August 29 2005, as the world witnessed. The music stopped; there were no more musicians in the streets, and no crowds tapping their feet to the rhythms. A destructive presence changed it all, and her name was Hurricane Katrina.

I remember getting the call from my parents that fateful day. They were safely on their way to Baton Rouge, but they warned me of the devastation that was left behind. Despite these warnings, nothing prepared me for what I saw unfold on the following morning's news. Katrina had swallowed up our New Orleans and nearly half the population in her wake. She was merciless to the people who had worked so hard for generations to establish their families, homes, businesses and communities.

The devastation revealed to me how people can initially shut down in response to horrific acts. I myself felt utterly helpless, and could not figure out how to react. My manager called to tell me there were tons of press requests for comments, but I turned them all down. I did not wish to be a cheerleader or a finger-pointer, and I wanted—needed—to do something more than run off at the mouth.

My friend and fellow New Orleans native, Harry Connick, Jr., was heading home to see if there was anything he could do to help, and asked if I would like to join him. After talking our way into the city past various checkpoints, and going by our families' houses, we rowed/drove around, trying to help anyone we could find. Viewing the implausible destruction, I was even more determined to help.

After our New Orleans visit, Harry and I drove to Houston, to try to comfort the large number of Katrina evacuees stuck in the Astrodome there. On our journey, we started talking about what we could do to make a difference. We decided to try to help the musicians. Harry's work with Habitat for Humanity, plus my concern about relying on the local bureaucracy, led us to agree that we should focus on rebuilding wards that the government would treat as low priorities.

With New Orleans area Habitat for Humanity on board, we put plans in motion to build a Musicians' Village in the Upper Ninth Ward. For many New Orleans musicians, their lifestyle and immediate earning potential did not allow them to even consider home ownership. We wanted to make sure they were given the opportunity to return to New Orleans and take advantage of the musicians' network, just as we had in our years as aspiring musicians. Our project began in March 2006 on a large, empty, desolate lot, and rapidly gained momentum. On that spot we now have a thriving community of musicians and other families.

In the summer of 2009, ground was broken for the Ellis Marsalis Center for Music. Thanks to tens of thousands of volunteers from all over the world, and thousands of donations large and small, Musicians' Village is a reality. (Check us out at www.nolamusiciansvillage.org.) If we have played some small part in helping a handful of musicians find a home, then we have done our part to redress a huge wrong.

People thank me every day for the village, but I really just helped to start the ball rolling. So many folks responded to our pleas with kindness and concern, people with no caveats or hidden agendas. Throughout the process, the true inspiration for me has been the multitudes who donated time and money to help people they'd never met. Universities and corporate entities sent students and workers to put in time. Individuals gave up vacations to come build homes. Countless others donated lumber, building materials and other essential items that helped make the Musicians' Village a reality. In an era of cynicism, I am delighted to be associated with groups and individuals who have stuck their necks out for those in need.

Every time I return to New Orleans, I am moved by the vast undertaking that has made our dream a reality. I am often left speechless by what Americans can do when we pull together, and I draw inspiration from the great example of humanity that is out there. In many ways these efforts make me feel quite small. They also make me feel connected to a community that, working together, can move mountains...or rebuild a legacy. The musical legacy that has made me who I am.

To be successful, you need to...

Be willing to stick your neck out... **Use Teamwork**

Our real success

Nikki's Perspective: When someone introduces me, I always hope they'll say something about my character or personality, not my accomplishments. I figure if someone wants to know me just because of what I've done, they may not be worth getting to know. I once used my Olympic gold medal to win people's respect, but quickly realized I would hate to feel someone wanted to be my friend just because I won a gold medal. So I worked on putting more of my personality out there. I now hope that my character is strong enough that it doesn't matter what titles I hold.

Your Tools for Success: Detach yourself from your victories and titles. They don't define who you are. Some say our greatest achievements are the people we surround ourselves with: our family, friends and colleagues.

Go out today and ask a few close friends how they would describe you. If they define you only in terms of your accomplishments, take the time to show them who you are in terms of your relationships. Think about the things you may be doing to project a title rather than a personality, and correct that. What you are inside is much more important than the shield you hold up.

_____

_____

_____

_____

_____

Shaun White

Olympic and X-Games Gold Medalist in Snowboarding and Skateboarding

Photo courtesy of Adam Moran

Shaun White Biography

Rolling Stone *calls him "the coolest kid in America" and* Outside *magazine flat out declares, "It's Shaun White's world." A double threat with X Games medals in snowboarding and skateboarding, as well as shiny gold hardware from the 2006 Winter Olympics, Shaun possesses insane skills and instantly recognizable looks. That serendipitous combination has made the freckled-face redhead a worldwide superstar, earning him three ESPY awards.*

Shaun entered his first amateur snowboard contest at age seven, and went on to take his first Winter X Games medal in 2002. Between slopestyle and superpipe, he hasn't failed to stand on the Winter X podium since. Shaun now holds fourteen X Games medals, a record eight of them gold.

While Shaun was being lauded as a snowboard prodigy, he was simultaneously snapping heads on the skateboard scene. Shaun started skating seriously at age nine and went pro in skate in 2003. Two years later, Shaun won a silver medal for his vert performance at the Summer X Games. He was the first athlete to compete—let alone reach the podium—in both Summer and Winter X Games, in different sports.

Shaun came into the games somewhat under the radar, and finished on top of both the podium and the popularity polls. His come-from-behind gold medal win in halfpipe was compelling enough, but his unscripted wit and casual charisma in interviews sealed the deal. Shaun continues his competitive career by training for the 2010 Winter Olympics, and the possible addition of skateboarding to the 2012 Summer Olympics.

In additional to his athletic endeavors, Shaun is taking on the film, gaming and apparel industries with streetwear and outerwear collections. Admirers are buying up Shaun's personal White Collection outerwear line for Burton, and signature streetwear line in Target. In a follow-up to the 2006 hit The Shaun White Album, *the 2008 release of* The Ultimate Ride: Shaun White *reflects on the wonders—and drag—of being one of the world's most famous athletes at age twenty-one. And fans can do more than watch Shaun, they can now play him on UbiSoft's* Shaun White Snowboarding, *a video game launched late in 2008.*

Shaun's blogs, videos, news and products can be seen on his Red Bull-designed website: www.ShaunWhite.com

Nikki's Intro to Shaun White's Story

For some reason, I would often have an awful performance whenever my parents came to a competition. I think it must have been nerves. I never wanted to let them down after they had put so much into my aerial career.

But when they suggested they stay home from the Olympics so they wouldn't put any extra pressure on me, I laughed. I explained to them that I wouldn't be going to the

Olympics if it weren't for them. They deserved to be there just as much as I did. Plus, if I couldn't handle the pressure of having my parents watching, how was I going to handle all the added pressure associated with the Olympics? In a foreign country, with forty thousand strangers at the bottom of the hill, I would find it reassuring to know that there were at least a couple people rooting specifically for me.

Additionally, I could be sure that I wouldn't be the only one moved when my country's flag was raised during the podium ceremony. This would be the same red-white-and-blue banner that would be raised eight years later for a proud Shaun White and *his* family…

Shaun White: My Story

Shaun White

Teamwork / Support

The start of my career was probably the craziest part. The X Games had just been created. Snowboarding wasn't yet an Olympic sport, and the public saw it more as a party than a serious athletic discipline. I was six years old at the time, just five years after overcoming a heart condition. I know people were telling my parents that they were nuts for allowing me to pursue such a dangerous sport, particularly one that had no future and no financial incentive.

My parents never saw my childhood heart condition as a disability, and they certainly wouldn't let me consider it a setback. They recognized early on that I had to be a kid, regardless of any previous health situations. It may have been that early condition as a baby that helped the family see what was most important. They realized that life was short and precious. My family never let me take anything for granted. And that included allowing me to pursue my athletic aspirations.

My parents' staunch support of my athletic aspirations came from their understanding what the sport of snowboarding could give me. They knew I needed real skill to excel, and the sport was teaching me how to be successful in athletics and in life. Not everyone saw it this way. While I was growing up, my folks struggled with teachers' ridicule, as well as with financial difficulties. Despite all this, they would still hop in the family van each weekend and drive me three hours to the "local" California slopes of Snow Summit and Bear Mountain, or seven hours up to Mammoth Ski Resort.

It wasn't just about me. It became a family experience. All of us would hit the runs together, and we camped out in the van at the snowboard events I attended. My mom recognized my potential early on and gave up her job to travel with me. When I became older, my brother took over as my team manager and traveling companion.

Like any kid, I wanted to be set free, but quickly realized how nice it was having family on the road with me. They gave me the support I needed, so I could focus on my riding.

With the freedom just to ride, I excelled quickly. I competed in my first National Championships at age thirteen, and six years later in my first X Games. Two years after that I was competing for a spot on the U.S. Olympic team. I narrowly missed placing, and vowed to come back with a vengeance.

I was given that opportunity at the very next Olympics, in Torino, Italy, and I prepared for it like it would be my last. My sights were set on that Olympic medal. I went into every contest with a new strength. The venues were always changing, but the one constant was my family among the throngs of spectators at the bottom of the pipe.

I didn't fully understood how much my parents had done for me until I stood on that podium at the 2006 Olympic Games in Torino and saw how proud and overwhelmed they were.

We all felt the weight of the experience at the medal ceremony. I looked out and saw my parents in the front row, and it completely changed the scope of what this milestone was all about. This was far greater than me, Shaun White, winning a medal. It was something that had been accomplished by everyone who'd believed in me and supported me along the way. Who'd helped make sure I stuck my neck out to reach that place that changed my life.

Someday I hope I'm as understanding and supportive as my parents were when my own kids are trying to accomplish their goals.

To be successful, you need to...

Be willing to stick your neck out... **Use Teamwork**

Acknowledge your front row

Nikki's Perspective: I've often thought it sad that people receive the best bouquets of flowers after they pass on. I long ago decided not to wait to express my appreciation. Whenever someone takes initiative to help me, I send flowers or a gift basket in gratitude. Gestures like that have always moved me when someone does it for me. I still recall the first thank-you flowers I ever received. They were from a good friend, one I'm still close to today. And the flowers hang dried on my wall as a reminder of that gratitude. As you can imagine, it's not the last effort I've made for this friend.

Your Tools for Success: If you were given an award for reaching your ultimate goal, who would you want in the front row of the audience? Most authors include an acknowledgment section in their books, to thank all the people who helped make it possible. I can't tell you how uplifting it was to share my own acknowledgment section with the people who truly supported me.

Take ten minutes to write the acknowledgment section for your greatest accomplishment. If you're brave enough, share it with those you mention. We all assume that our family, friends and supporters know how much their assistance means to us, but surprisingly, they often don't. You will find that people are much more likely to offer future help—to you and to many others—when they are appreciated for their support.

_____

_____

_____

_____

_____

George Jones

Former President and CEO of Borders Group Inc.

Photo provided by George Jones

George Jones Biography

George Jones served from July 2006 to January 2009 as president and chief executive officer of Borders Group Inc., a $3.8 billion retailer of books, music and movies with more than 1,100 stores worldwide. During his tenure, the company established its Borders Rewards loyalty program and built membership to over 30 million, giving the company access to a valuable database of customer information. He also began to move the company into the digital world by developing highly successful and widely praised new concept stores, which uniquely mesh the Internet with bricks and mortar, as well as by reclaiming its e-commerce business and launching Borders.com.

Prior to joining Borders, Jones was president and chief executive officer of the Saks Department Store Group, a post he took on in 2001. At the time, the group had sales of $3.8 billion and included 240 department stores in 24 states, under various brand names including Carson Pirie Scott and Parisian. There he implemented a turnaround plan that focused on differentiating the company's stores and merchandise assortments from competitors.

From 1994 through 2001, Jones served as president, worldwide licensing and retail, for Warner Bros., where he was responsible for a global business with operations in 23 countries and annual sales of over $7 billion. In addition to the company's core licensing, retail and promotion activities, Jones also led a variety of other businesses including Warner Bros. Worldwide Publishing, Kids WB Music, Warner Bros. Interactive Entertainment, WB Sports and Warner Bros. Studio Stores.

Jones faced one of his career's biggest challenges when he led Rose's Stores as president and chief executive officer. At the time, Rose's had 257 mass merchandise stores, but was on the verge of liquidation, overwhelmed by competition from Wal-Mart, which had entered the majority of the retailer's markets. Jones developed a strategic plan that improved operations and merchandising, ultimately facilitating the sale of the business and securing its future.

A significant part of Jones's retail career was at Target, where he served as executive vice president of store operations, responsible for all the company's stores, and previously as senior vice president of merchandising. Throughout his tenure, Jones played a key role in the development of Target's innovative merchandising, store operations and customer service strategies, which effectively differentiated Target from its competitors and ultimately helped lead the brand to icon status.

Nikki's Intro to George Jones's Story

I happened to be in San Francisco on June 8, 2000, the day Steve Young announced his retirement from the 49ers. It was the big story on all the local news channels. Having retired myself just a year before, I found the event really captured my attention. Many people got up to speak, congratulating Steve, but there was one comment that really stood out to me.

Steve had mentioned that his only regret in retiring was that his kids would not be able to see him play, because they were so young. A short time after, his assistant coach came to the mike and told Steve that having his kids see him play would be nothing compared to supporting his kids and watching *them* play.

A motivational speaker, media training coach and a mom now, I realize that being a support for others can be much more rewarding than accomplishing things ourselves. And in the long run, our support of others actually makes us better at what we do. No one needs to explain that to George Jones. He figured it out a long time ago...

George Jones: My Story

George Jones

Teamwork

I don't think most Fortune 500 CEOs got their start in a rock band. But that is exactly where I got *my* start.

I started playing the guitar at age thirteen, and by my freshman year in high school I was getting paid to do something I really loved—play music. I was a member of several bands while attending high school and college in Arkansas, including one named Jamestown Flood, which became very popular throughout the region. Losing my father in a car crash at age three and struggling with my mother to make ends meet, I was ecstatic to have a job that not only paid well, but moved me deeply.

Being one of the few band members at the time that club owners and agents could always count on staying lucid, I quickly took on the responsibilities of band manager. I made sure we got booked, that we arrived on time and that we had the best talent around. We created one of the most popular bands in the mid-South area.

One thing I innately brought to the job was a desire to succeed. But I realized that, even as a leader, I needed everyone else to be successful as well. I couldn't worry about being the star. Quite simply, if the band did better, then I would do better.

Though I loved to play, my skills with the guitar never really developed to the level I hoped they would. I was realistic enough to admit that to myself, and proceeded to surround myself with musicians more talented than me to ensure that we had an excellent, successful band.

In the grand scheme of things, my musical ambitions had way exceeded my skills, and by the time I graduated from college, I knew it was time to put my business degree to good use. I began knocking on that big business world door to see if I could handle what lay on the other side. I began to climb the ladder, making my mark in unlikely positions. I was prone to take a job that my gut told me I would enjoy—and maybe more importantly, with people I thought I would enjoy working with—often over higher paying or more prestigious opportunities. With each new job and promotion, my biggest fear was that I wouldn't be as eager to get up and start each day as I had been in my last job. And I can still say that, to this day, I have never dreaded getting up to tackle another day on the job.

No matter how much you enjoy what you do, you can't love a job without also enjoying the people you work with. My guitar was long since put aside, but the valuable things I learned from the band came with me into the business world. Playing with those musicians was such a positive experience that the lessons never left me. The more we'd improve quality of personnel, the better the band got, and the more gigs we landed. So, when hiring people for management positions, I was never reluctant to surround myself with very talented people—even if they were as good as or better than me. I actually wanted people like that. Forgetting my ego, I developed the ability to recruit people who have the talent and drive to make their own success.

My responsibility as a leader was not just to dole out commands, but to make those I worked with perform better. I found I got the best results out of colleagues, whether members of my band or VPs at Saks or Warner Bros., when I took the time to communicate my decisions, so that they understood the overall objective.

And sticking my neck out to my "team" not only paid off for me, it paid off for them as well. I am proud of what my résumé lists as my career accomplishments, but even more so about what it doesn't list. I can proudly say that I worked with one band member who went on to play with Paul McCartney, another who played with Ray Charles, and thirteen business prodigies who have gone on to become presidents or CEOs of major national and international corporations.

Back in college, I think my band would have had a hard time picturing me dressed in a coat and tie every day. I don't, however, think they would be surprised to know that I have been the CEO of a Fortune 500 company. If I could consistently get a bunch of free-spirited musicians of the early '70s to a gig on time, *anything* is possible.

To be successful, you need to...

Be willing to stick your neck out... **Use Teamwork**

Networking

Nikki's Perspective: The greatest support I've received in my speaking career has been through the Olympians I've known and met. My career was jump-started by my Olympic friends' suggestions, encouragement and mentoring. I found that they *wanted* to help... and I found I wanted to help them.

I still meet new Olympians all the time. Our common bond compels us to help one another. I don't know if I would be half as far up my career ladder without the support of those Olympic friends I reached out to. But then again, I don't know if they would be where they are without me, either.

Your Tools for Success: Extend your support system by doing some networking. First, go through your directory, address book, business cards, Rolodex, pile of past letters or e-mails, and come up with the names of five people you haven't been in contact with for a long time—individuals who could be influential to you or you to them. Write these people a letter or e-mail to reconnect with them, and establish some possibilities for helping each other move forward.

Next, go out and introduce yourself to five new people who could potentially help you in the future, or vice versa. Again, try to suggest how you might be a support to each other, moving forward. If you can find ways to help these people out, you will likely find that the favor is returned sometime down the road.

_____

_____

_____

_____

Stephen Bollenbach

Former CEO and Co-chair of Hilton Hotels

Photo courtesy of Hilton Hotels Corporation

Stephen Bollenbach Biography

Stephen F. Bollenbach recently retired as co-chairman and chief executive officer of Hilton Hotels Corporation, positions he held from May 2004 and February 1996, respectively.

After joining Hilton, Bollenbach oversaw a complete transformation of the company, including the acquisition of Bally Entertainment, which made Hilton the world's largest gaming company. He also spun off Hilton's gaming operations in a tax-free transaction to shareholders, to form Park Place Entertainment—formerly Caesars Entertainment, Inc., now Harrah's Entertainment, Inc.—and acquired Promus Hotel Corporation. The Promus acquisition added 1,400 hotels and several well-known hospitality brands including Doubletree, Embassy Suites Hotels, Hampton and Homewood Suites by Hilton, to their portfolio of outstanding properties. In 2006, the company acquired the lodging assets of Hilton Group, PLC, reuniting the Hilton brand for the first time in over forty years and making Hilton Hotels Corporation the world's largest hotel company. The Hilton Family of Hotels now includes 2,800 hotels with 485,000 rooms and 150,000 team members in 80 countries.

Prior to joining Hilton Hotels Corporation, Bollenbach was senior executive vice president and chief financial officer for The Walt Disney Company, where he was instrumental in the execution of that company's $19 billion acquisition of Capital Cities/ABC—at the time, the second-largest acquisition in U.S. business history. Before Disney, Bollenbach was president and chief executive officer of Host Marriott Corporation, an organization he helped create in 1993. From 1990 to 1992, Bollenbach was chief financial officer of the Trump Organization.

Bollenbach serves as chairman of the board of KB Home, and as director of Time Warner Inc., Macy's, Inc., and American International Group. He is also a member of the board of directors of the Los Angeles World Affairs Council. He is recognized as one of the world's leading authorities on the hospitality industry, financial affairs and transactions, Bollenbach has been a featured speaker and panelist at business and industry conferences and events around the world, and is the recipient of numerous industry leadership awards.

A native of Southern California, Bollenbach lives with his wife in Los Angeles. They have two grown sons.

Nikki's Intro to Stephen Bollenbach's Story

We all have that one teacher who makes us realize education professionals don't get paid nearly enough. For me, that teacher was a man named Nelson. At our high school tutorial ski academy, we called our teachers by their first name, so I couldn't even tell you his last name. But I can tell you that Nelson changed my outlook on writing and on school in general.

Whether he was blowing smoke or not, he got me to believe that I could write. And once I had started, I found I couldn't stop. I devoured my class assignments and started writing on my own. For the first time, I couldn't wait for the school day to start. I never disliked school before, but never really looked forward to it, either. All it took to change that was someone who believed in me.

I now realize that, without his support, this book likely wouldn't have been written. That's why I begin the acknowledgments thanking the man with one name…Nelson.

For Stephen Bollenbach, the acknowledgement goes to a man of two names, but the recognition and gratitude is the same…

Stephen Bollenbach: My Story

Stephen Bollenbach

Teamwork Story

To most people, a paperweight doesn't have much significance. But it does to me, for a paperweight helped shape my life. Before I got it, I wasn't quite sure of the path my life would take.

Like many young adults in southern California in the '60s, I didn't know what college was and why anyone would really want to go. College was basically something you did because your friends were doing it and it seemed a better option than working all day. So I enrolled in a junior college.

Several classes into my degree at Long State City College, I came across a man who would end up changing my outlook, George Rienholter. Professor Rienholter saw much greater potential in me than I ever saw in myself. He recognized that all I needed was a bit of support and encouragement. He decided to send my name to the *Wall Street Journal* for a national award. Somehow, the *Journal* agreed with Professor Rienholter's recommendation, and I received what was basically a certificate in a Plexiglass paperweight with a coin in it.

Now, this paperweight was obviously no Nobel Prize. I don't even remember what the award was for. But realizing that someone had that kind of faith in me, I greatly valued it. That Plexiglass object couldn't have meant more if it were made of gold. Besides family members, no one had ever gone out of the way like that for me, and I couldn't take it for granted. So I put my nose to the grindstone to prove my appreciation to Professor Rienholter, and went on to get an A in his class.

Professor Rienholter amazed me once again with his incredible support by taking the time to enroll me in UCLA. Looking back, I can easily say that this encouragement was the most important factor in shaping my professional life. He was helping me to stick my neck out at a time when I likely wouldn't have done so myself. It was the greatest influence I could have received at that crucial age. Because of his encouragement, my undergraduate degree in business had so much more meaning.

From there, I continued along my academic path and received a master's from California State University, Northridge. And that led to great changes in my life. Who would have thought a former junior college student would be leading a Fortune 500 company someday? I learned that one person can profoundly influence another's destiny.

This one person helped me discover the tremendous value in having an education. I see how critical and rewarding it can be. And it's not just the individual who profits; whole countries can prosper from the power of academics. Several years ago, Ireland affirmed its commitment to education and became the fastest growing economy in Europe. The gift of opening someone's mind to learning is invaluable.

I knew that I wanted to have this same persuasive effect on others, so in 2003, I set up the Bollenbach Scholarship Foundation to sponsor individuals. I also became personally involved with Teach for America, a nonprofit organization that helps children from different socioeconomic backgrounds attain an excellent education. Teach for America's goal, like Professor Rienholter's so many years before, is to use educational resources to make a fundamental impact on students' lives. Both have taught me the significance of going out of your way to make a positive change in someone else's life.

Every now and then I get a letter from one of my scholarship recipients, thanking me and letting me know how he or she is doing. With each letter, I think back to Professor Rienholter and how different my life might have been without him. I know that someday I will hear how these young individuals have gone on to reach—and surpass—their dreams, and for that reason, I save their letters in a safe spot...under my Plexiglass paperweight.

To be successful, you need to...

Be willing to stick your neck out... **Use Teamwork**

Really listen to what people are saying

Nikki's Perspective: My husband once pointed out to me that I wasn't really listening to his point of view when we were having an argument. I realized he was right when he asked me what he'd said, and I couldn't recall his last statement. I was busy thinking up my counterargument rather than really hearing him. I started watching myself in a number of other situations and found that I was often more concerned with how I would present my standpoint rather than truly listening to other people's views. I realized that I was missing the opportunity to learn more...and, if nothing else, improve my argument.

Your Tools for Success: We often think we know what is best for ourselves, and ignore other people's opinions. It is important to involve others as often as possible, because listening is more valuable than speaking. We never learn anything new when we're talking or are preoccupied by our own thoughts.

Whenever you are invested in a debate this week, ask yourself if you are really stopping to listen to everything the other person is saying, or if you are using much of the time to devise your response. Also, ask yourself if you are always open to listening to others, or do you just seek out individuals who you know will support your opinions? You may be missing out on valuable information.

_____

_____

_____

_____

_____

Ben Goldhirsch

Major World Philanthropist and Benefactor

Photo courtesy of Timothy Greenfield

Ben Goldhirsch Biography

Benjamin Goldhirsh is the founder and chairman of GOOD, an editorially led, member-driven community of people, NGOs and corporations committed to pushing our world forward. GOOD's mission is to provide content that coalesces this community, experiences that deepen the relationships within this community, and utilities that empower this community.

Active in both regional and international philanthropic endeavors, Goldhirsh is one of the directors of the Goldhirsh Foundation, which supports dynamic social programs, environmental initiatives, innovative medical research and leading cultural institutions.

Goldhirsh serves on the board of Millennium Promise, an organization guided by the UN's Millennium Development goals to end extreme global poverty by 2025, as well as the Los Angeles boards of the National Foundation for Teaching Entrepreneurship, and of City Year Los Angeles.

A graduate of Brown University and Phillips Academy, Goldhirsh currently resides in Los Angeles.

Nikki's Intro to Ben Goldhirsch's Story

I have always been very close to my grandparents. So I was devastated in 2001 when my grandfather suffered a sudden heart attack, and died a few days later. The timing of that shattering event couldn't have been worse for me. I was doing a ski industry tour at the time and had to present a speech about an hour after hearing the distressing news that my grandfather had passed away. I didn't know how I was going to hold myself together.

Coincidentally, someone had recently told me that birds often show up to let you know everything is going to be okay after someone close to you passes on. As I listened to the MC introducing me, I recalled the comment and thought how absurd it was. Besides, I was in a convention center, so could at least count the bird out for the afternoon.

I made my way onto the stage and started my talk. I was fumbling over my words and couldn't concentrate. Suddenly, out of nowhere, a bird swooped down and landed on the screen right behind me. I smiled as I shared the inside joke with myself, and continued on with the rest of my speech...flawlessly. I knew I was going to be okay.

Whether or not that bird had any significance, I was reminded that my grandfather's spirit would live on with and in me forever, and that he had taught me everything I needed to know about staying strong in challenging times. I would be okay.

Sometimes support can come in the most unexpected places. Just ask Ben Goldhirsh...

Ben Goldhirsh: My Story

Ben Goldhirsh

Teamwork / Support

Half-empty or half-full? It's the dilemma we are all challenged with when we're presented with a tragic circumstance. Do we see the glass as half-full, through a lens of optimism, or half-empty, through a lens of pessimism?

I can admit that, when I encountered *my* first tragic circumstance, I decidedly saw my glass as half-empty. I believe it's the instinctual response anyone would feel when faced with the same misfortune. I was a junior in high school when I received the call. My father informed me that my mom had passed out and the doctors had discovered blood in her stomach. The tests would show that she had stomach cancer, and less than fifteen months later, she passed away.

Fifteen months after that, I received a second call. My dad had brain cancer. As prepared as you think you might be after having one parent afflicted with a life-threatening disease, it never gets easier. In many ways, it was much more difficult. I was thrown the one-two punch and felt I was going down for the count. The walls were crashing in around me.

Surgery and chemotherapy seemed to work for my father initially, but despite a determined fight, he lost his battle to cancer a few years later. It was hard enough to deal with the death of my mother, and now my father was gone as well. The tally was cancer: 2, Ben: 0. I was selfish. I wanted to grow into being their friend rather than just their son. I envied others who had eventually developed this relationship with their parents.

It became obvious to everyone that I was struggling to get a handle on my overwhelming loss. However, I'm sure there were people murmuring behind my back, "What's Ben worried about? His father left him a boatful of money from his creation of *Sail* and *Inc.* magazines." Really, the money was just a superficial support. I yearned for the emotional and psychological support that my parents had always given me. I questioned whether I was really qualified to pursue any avenues without them.

I even questioned how the world would go on without my parents. It saddened me to think of how much life they had left to live, and what they still could have achieved. It was a shame that the world would be missing out on all the contributions they could have offered. I thought of how they would have responded to the challenges of today and the valuable role they could have played. They had been truly invested in moving humanity forward. How was I going to carry the burden of what the world had lost?

With time, I slowly began to release the landscape of anguish I was holding on to, and open my eyes to the fact that my parents had left me much more than just a pile of cash. What I had to comprehend was that my glass actually could be seen as half-full. I couldn't dwell on the fact that my parents were no longer with me. I learned to appreciate that I'd had them in my life for as long as I did. They had taught me to learn from everything I did, and I realized they were still doing so after their passing. I envisioned my stout, five-foot-five-inch father lecturing me, "Well, this has brought an intriguing perspective to the value of the day. You have an opportunity born from your circumstances. How are you going to pursue it?"

That was the challenge. How was I going to actively pursue the potential born from my circumstances? Utilize the financial benefits left to me, without being hamstrung by the anxiety and pressure to do so wisely? Wealth itself didn't take the psychological challenge away. I had to find a way of meeting that challenge. What else was I going to do? Just stop living? It was time to follow my parents' lead.

Before my father passed away, he'd instilled in me the same desire that he had to give back to society and move the world forward. He demonstrated how rewarding it was to do so through your work. I knew that if my parents were alive, they would be trying to find a way to do that. I had a responsibility here—to the opportunity they'd provided me, the life they'd set up for me, the lessons they had taught me, the potential they'd defined for me. It would be an insult to everything they meant to me if I didn't go after this potential with everything I had. But how best to accomplish that was yet to be defined.

I thought about how my father had reasoned out his pursuits, and the answer finally came to me—there was a great void in media coverage of meaningful events. My college friends and I felt we represented an audience that was hungry for valuable, relevant information with an aesthetic frame that catered to important global issues such as race, poverty, religion, gender, violence and celebrity. We would listen to relevant stories and decide what media vehicle would be the most powerful and effective way to deliver that message. We wanted the dexterity to bring valuable content to many audiences.

Through our film projects, we found the microperspective of the geopolitical dynamic of the day. Through the Internet, we took the opportunity to celebrate the universe of humanity. And through *GOOD Magazine*, we celebrated the ideas, relations, businesses and people bringing change to our world. Not only would the magazine present a hip look at energy, organic food, sweatshop-free fashion, politics, indie culture, philanthropic business, and green living, we also decided that all subscription fees would go to one of twelve GOOD-approved nonprofits.

In essence, we decided we wanted to create a platform for cool people doing cool things for the benefit of society. We wanted to expose audiences to a broader media jet stream than they were previously experiencing. With broad-minded content. Like my father before me, I was throwing myself into meaningful work that was hopefully improving the world.

My parents' deaths highlighted the nature of life for me. Every day, we have one less day on this earth. The potential my parents left me with is the driving force that gets me out of bed on days I might want to just huddle under the covers. And I'm often kept late at the office because I don't want to blow the chance they gave me to make a difference. It's crazy to think that the people who continue to help me stick my neck out every day are the two who are no longer with me.

So I often ask myself, "What would my parents think if they were still alive today?" I can honestly say that I think they'd be proud.

To be successful, you need to...

Be willing to stick your neck out... **Use Teamwork**

Drawing Inspiration from Others

Nikki's Perspective: Growing up, I often heard pearls of wisdom that had been passed down from my great-grandmother. One saying of hers I remember was that women can do anything men can do, but often have to work a bit harder to get there. I took her words to heart.

I sometimes wonder how Great-grandma Mary would view how I'm handling her advice. Just thinking of her compels me to never give up regardless of how challenging the task.

Your Tools for Success: Think back to some important lesson or piece of wisdom that someone you respected gave you. Are you living up to this advice? Now pick someone to pass it along to. Ask this friend, colleague or family member to share some insight they were given that was meaningful to them.

Passing on wisdom is a powerful and inspirational practice. It helps so much to be reminded every day how we can better shape our lives. Would your "advisor" be proud of what you have accomplished?

_____

_____

_____

_____

_____

Conclusion

Conclusion

I always wondered how I would ever repay my parents for teaching me the Turtle Effect and encouraging me to embody its invaluable lessons. Several years ago, I was given my answer in a way I had never hoped for.

In 2004, my mother found out she had breast cancer. Two years later, my father learned he had prostate cancer. I've always considered myself a very healthy person. I was even awarded an Olympic medal to prove it! And now I found that my family's gene pool was no better off than anyone else's.

For my mom, the recovery process started with surgery, the prognosis to be determined from there. We all hoped that the cancer had not spread from her breast into her lymph nodes. My father and I were there when my mother woke up from surgery, and had to tell her the terrible news. It *had* spread—which meant tacking chemo and radiation onto the recovery process.

As with my Olympic experience, if one family member was going through this, we all were. My sister, Laura, was halfway around the world in China, with two small children, so couldn't travel back for the surgery. But she was always on the phone, offering encouragement. For my part, I realized that I could use all the valuable lessons I had learned through my years in aerials to help my mom on her challenging path to recovery. And I know that support made a difference.

Two years after my mother's diagnosis, my father was diagnosed with prostate cancer. Despite a horrific storm sweeping up the East Coast, I made my way across the country again to be by a parent's hospital bedside. What with flight cancellations and lost bags, my parents told me more than once to scrap the trip. But I knew that *nothing* would have kept them from being with me at the Olympic Games, and nothing was going to keep me from being with them at the hospital. Fortunately, surgery was all it took to rid my father's body of cancer, and he was back to tennis and skiing within a few weeks.

My mom and dad are both in remission now and will continue to use their Turtle Effect attitude to make sure they stay that way. No matter if it's cancer, jobs, academics, sports or even child rearing, we are always going to remind each other what it takes to swing the odds in our favor. Our genetic blueprint may not be any better than any other family's, but our soft inside, our hard shell and our ability to stick our neck out is.

I'm not arrogant enough to believe that I was the prime factor in my parents' recovery. As with the Turtle Effect, it takes a whole team to reach success. I am so thankful for our support groups, family and friends, doctors and nurses, and the advances in modern medicine.

I always knew I would find a way to contribute to those advances someday. This book gave me that opportunity. It's the reason I decided to give twenty-five percent of my net proceeds from *When Turtles Fly* to the American Cancer Society to help fund cancer diagnosis and research.

Many people have asked me how I persuaded so many incredible individuals to contribute their inspirational stories to the book. I know that they, too, share this desire to give back. It's just one more way that, by sticking their necks out, they are successful.

An Invitation

I wrote this book to share how everyone can incorporate the Turtle Effect into their own lives, no matter what field or endeavor they pursue. I wanted to breathe inspiration into people at a time when we all could use some motivation. What I found was that I became more inspired myself. Gathering the stirring tales of all these impressive individuals was not an easy undertaking, but each story uplifted me and convinced me not to give up. I am continually revitalized by the many passionate and caring people I encounter.

Now I want to hear from you! I'd like to invite *you* to share *your* Turtle Effect stories on the blog http://www.WhenTurtlesFly.com. We all have our own successes, and I want to hear how you discovered your soft inside, developed your hard shell, or found a way to stick your neck out. So post your story and let others breathe inspiration from *you*!

Nikki Stone
Olympic Gold Medalist

At the Olympic Winter Games in Nagano, Japan, Nikki Stone became America's first-ever Olympic champion in the sport of aerial skiing. What made this performance so unbelievable was the fact that, less than two years earlier, a chronic spinal injury prevented her from standing, much less walking or skiing off a twelve-foot-tall snow jump that launches aerialists fifty feet into the air. She overcame the injury and went on to earn 35 World Cup medals, 11 World Cup titles, 4 national titles, 3 World Cup titles, a World Championship title, and membership in the Ski Hall of Fame. Nikki is also a magna cum laude graduate of Union College and a summa cum laude masters graduate of the University of Utah. Her aerial retirement is less than restful as she trains Olympic athletes and business professionals in speaking/media skills, coaches personal and professional development courses, hosts group skiing adventures, sits on five different charitable committees, and writes articles and colums for many magazines, newspapers, and websites. Nikki's career focus is now on traveling around the world working as a sought-after motivational speaker, sharing her secrets to success by inspiring her business audiences to "Stick their necks out." Every spare moment is spent with husband, Michael Spencer, and daughter, Zali, in Park City, Utah.

**Photo courtesy of
John Strand**

Photo provided by Nikki Stone

BUY A SHARE OF THE FUTURE IN YOUR COMMUNITY

These certificates make great holiday, graduation and birthday gifts that can be personalized with the recipient's name. The cost of one S.H.A.R.E. or one square foot is $54.17. The personalized certificate is suitable for framing and will state the number of shares purchased and the amount of each share, as well as the recipient's name. The home that you participate in "building" will last for many years and will continue to grow in value.

Here is a sample SHARE certificate:

THIS CERTIFIES THAT
YOUR NAME HERE
HAS INVESTED IN A HOME FOR A DESERVING FAMILY

1985-2005
TWENTY YEARS OF BUILDING FUTURES IN OUR COMMUNITY ONE HOME AT A TIME

1200 SQUARE FOOT HOUSE @ $65,000 = $54.17 PER SQUARE FOOT
This certificate represents a tax deductible donation. It has no cash value.

YES, I WOULD LIKE TO HELP!

*I support the work that Habitat for Humanity does and I want to be part of the excitement! As a donor, I will receive periodic updates on your construction activities but, more importantly, I know my gift will help a family in our community realize the dream of homeownership. **I would like to SHARE in your efforts against substandard housing in my community!** (Please print below)*

PLEASE SEND ME _____ SHARES at $54.17 EACH = $ $_____

In Honor Of: _____

Occasion: (Circle One)   HOLIDAY   BIRTHDAY   ANNIVERSARY

        OTHER: _____

Address of Recipient: _____

Gift From: _____   *Donor Address:* _____

Donor Email: _____

I AM ENCLOSING A CHECK FOR $ $_____ PAYABLE TO HABITAT FOR HUMANITY OR PLEASE CHARGE MY VISA OR MASTERCARD *(CIRCLE ONE)*

Card Number _____ Expiration Date: _____

Name as it appears on Credit Card _____ Charge Amount $ _____

Signature _____

Billing Address _____

Telephone # Day _____ Eve _____

PLEASE NOTE: Your contribution is tax-deductible to the fullest extent allowed by law.
Habitat for Humanity • P.O. Box 1443 • Newport News, VA 23601 • 757-596-5553
www.HelpHabitatforHumanity.org